FERMANAGH

From Plantation to Peace Process

First published by Eastwood Books, 2020
Dublin, Ireland
www.eastwoodbooks.com
@eastwoodbooks
First Edition

Eastwood Books is an imprint of The Wordwell Group

Eastwood Books
The Wordwell Group
Unit 9, 78 Furze Road
Sandyford
Dublin, Ireland

ISBN: 978-1-8380416-3-2 (Paperback)
ISBN: 978-1-913934-06-4 (mobi)
ISBN 978-1-913934-07-1 (epub)

British Library Cataloguing in Publication Data.
A catalogue record for this book is available from the British Library.

FERMANAGH

From Plantation to Peace Process

Margaret Urwin

Eastwood

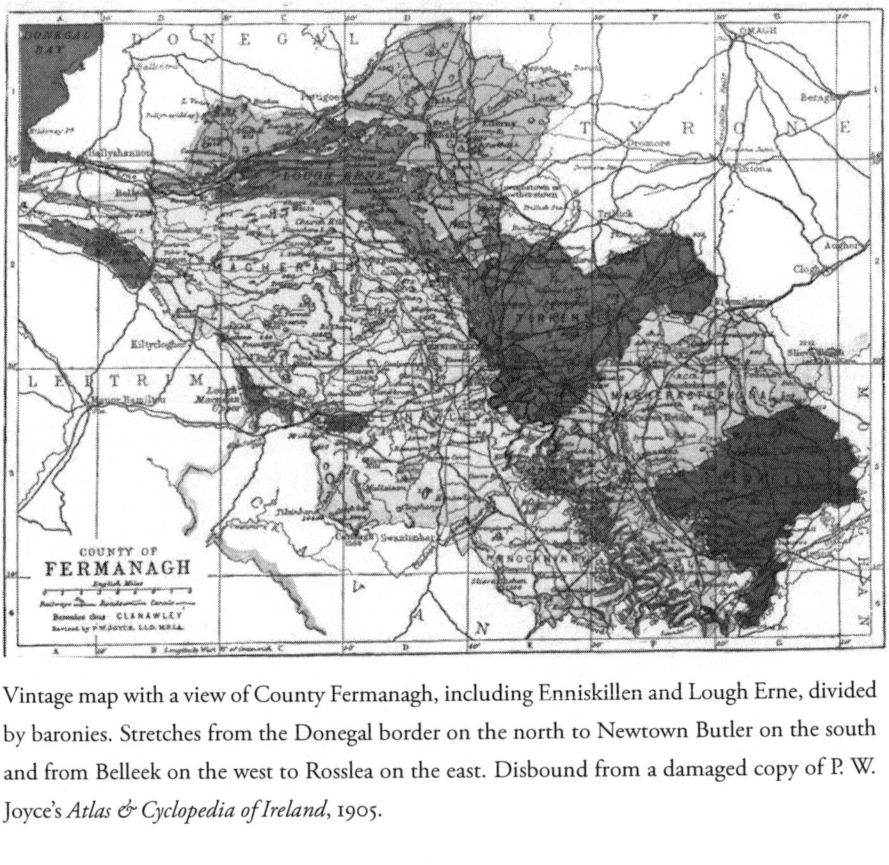

Vintage map with a view of County Fermanagh, including Enniskillen and Lough Erne, divided by baronies. Stretches from the Donegal border on the north to Newtown Butler on the south and from Belleek on the west to Rosslea on the east. Disbound from a damaged copy of P. W. Joyce's *Atlas & Cyclopedia of Ireland*, 1905.

CONTENTS

ACKNOWLEDGEMENTS

There are many people who have assisted with this publication. I would like to thank my colleagues in the Pat Finucane Centre (PFC) for their encouragement and support – our Project Manager, Paul O'Connor, whose idea it was that I should write this book; Alan Brecknell; Anne Cadwallader; Sara Duddy; Adrienne Reilly; and Micheál Smith.

I am grateful to PFC Board members, especially Dr Paddy Hillyard, for his guidance throughout the project and for his valuable insights and advice; also Tony Brown, Joe McGleenan and Dr Stuart Ross for their editorial input. I am also greatly indebted to Dr Edward Burke, University of Nottingham and Dr Thomas Leahy, University of Cardiff, who both took the time to read the manuscript and provide expert comment. Thanks also to Brian MacDonald for sharing his knowledge of the famine in Fermanagh with me.

I appreciate the assistance and patience of London-based freelance journalist and researcher Dr Tom Griffin for accessing the many relevant files in the UK National Archives, Kew, and Raymond Walker for his IT support.

I wish to thank sincerely those families who kindly agreed to allow details from their case files and Historical Enquiry Team (HET) reports to be included in the book and also those who agreed to be interviewed.

A special thanks to Denzil McDaniel, journalist and former editor of the *Impartial Reporter*, for agreeing to write the foreword to this book and for his valuable suggestions.

Last but not least, thanks to my husband, Mark, for his unfailing support throughout the project.

FOREWORD

Fermanagh is one of the most beautiful counties in Ireland, with the backdrop of Lough Erne providing a spectacularly scenic setting in a tranquil place. The friendly people are equally calm and laid back.

It does seem, therefore, incongruous that the area suffered so grievously in the conflict of Northern Ireland in the final quarter of the twentieth century. For all Fermanagh's remoteness, some of the most iconic and bloody events of what became euphemistically called 'the Troubles' happened there, including the election of Irish Republican Army (IRA) hunger striker Bobby Sands in 1981 and the Remembrance Sunday bombing at Enniskillen in 1987. Both events were to have far-reaching consequences as catalysts for change in Northern Ireland as it moved from decades of war to a political peace process.

A study of the conflict in Fermanagh, and its historical context, is in some important ways a microcosm of the overall conflict; the social and political divisions in the county are a significant example of the conditions that created the circumstances whereby the battle between differing communities resulted in bloodshed.

The county is nestled in south-west Ulster, just inside Northern Ireland, almost equidistant from Belfast and Dublin, which are the capitals of the two jurisdictions to which Fermanagh people feel separate allegiance. Along its border with the Republic of Ireland, it touches Donegal, Cavan, Monaghan and Leitrim. Indeed, the Boundary Commission report of 1925 recommended that parts of Donegal and Monaghan should be in Northern Ireland and parts of Fermanagh should be in the fledgling Free State. But while the report was kept secret and never implemented, this gives some idea of how the geographical position of the county becomes an additional factor in the conflicting identities of its people.

The county town is Enniskillen, which sits on an island between Upper and Lower Lough Erne. Visitors driving through it at various times of the year may notice some streets bearing Union Jack flags on lampposts; in other areas, it is the Irish tricolour. In some measure this shows the complex nature of identity crisis; but in large measure the people of Enniskillen lived well with difference, and community relations were better than in most areas of the north. It was the same in the rest of the largely rural and sparsely populated county, where Protestant and Catholic farmers would help each other out.

But political and cultural difference had been there for centuries. Enniskillen's historic and beautiful castle, which still stands today, was originally built to strategically protect the town in the fourteenth century by Hugh 'the Hospitable', one of the Maguire chieftains who ruled in those days. But in the early 1600s, after various battles, it became an English garrison under Captain William Cole, who was appointed by King James I. The Plantation of Ulster saw Fermanagh inhabited mostly by Anglican Protestants, rather than the Scottish Presbyterians more common in the east.

In more recent times, the parliamentary seat of Fermanagh and South Tyrone has become symbolic of the battle for control of the different identities. In the 1950s, the Westminster seat was held by Lieutenant-Colonel Robert Grosvenor, later to become Duke of Westminster and Britain's richest man; though he lost an election to a Sinn Féiner, Phillip Clarke.

Grosvenor was succeeded in the 1960s by his cousin, the Marquis of Hamilton, and the seat has switched hands on occasion, from IRA hunger striker Bobby Sands and then his election agent, Owen Carron, to the former Ulster Defence Regiment major Ken Maginnis.

Fermanagh is a county of contrasts: beautiful and calm, yet scarred by awful violence. Genuinely friendly people who, for the most part, got on with their neighbours of a different religion, but who were deeply committed to fighting for what they believed in.

So, from the arrival of the English planter Captain Cole and other families through to the 'Big House' occupants of the twentieth century, unionism has been dominated by the British ruling class, and in an area like Fermanagh, and other places, this led to clashes over social issues such as the allocation of housing and jobs. And Irish nationalists, resentful at what they saw as unfairness, have opposed them – and this has periodically involved physical force. It's what one republican described as 'We didn't bring the war to them, they brought it to us.' So, the Troubles didn't just happen in a vacuum, and this book walks us through the salient points over centuries, contextualising the most recent outbreak of violence.

The analysis of Troubles deaths in Fermanagh is meticulously researched from impeccable sources and detailed factually. While the statistics show that the vast majority of killings were carried out by republicans, the catalogue of incidents shows that combatants included republicans, loyalists, the State and security forces.

As a journalist covering many of these deaths, and indeed as a Fermanagh man born and bred who has an emotional stake in the community, recollection of the cost in human lives makes tough reading, especially when one recalls the sadness of many of the bereaved homes. Every death is a stain on the community; the pain of loss is no respecter of difference, and as the conflict went on, the violence became ever more shocking. While the peace process saw an end to the conflict and gave the warring sides space to come to some accommodation, the process remains vulnerable due to the deep-rooted mistrust that centuries-long division has ingrained into our psyche – even to the point of debate over the narrative of the legacy of violence.

Behind each of the statistics and each account of an incident lies a loved one, taken too soon; family and friends whose pain is the same regardless of which side; and a community trying to pick up the pieces. This telling of each story respectfully serves to remind us how far we sank into the abyss and performs a service in ensuring that people should not be forgotten, and that the best way to honour each and every victim is to ensure that the people of the beautiful county of Fermanagh, and indeed the beautiful country of Ireland, must learn to share a space. That despite centuries of difference, being one community of many strands is the way to ensure these particular decades of death and destruction mustn't happen again. We must remember, but remember and change.

Denzil McDaniel

INTRODUCTION

Every war is fought twice: once for supremacy on the battlefield, then for control of its memory

– Ruadhán MacCormaic (*Irish Times*, 22 September 2018)

For many years the Pat Finucane Centre for Human Rights/Justice for the Forgotten has provided advocacy support to a number of families in County Fermanagh who were bereaved as a result of the Northern Ireland conflict. In addition, Justice for the Forgotten had researched cross-border attacks carried out in the early 1970s by loyalists based in and around Fermanagh. As a result, it was decided to produce a publication focusing on the families we support whose relatives were killed by loyalist paramilitaries and members of the security forces. As our research advanced, however, it became clear that there was a wider and more challenging story to be told. Of the 115 conflict-related deaths between 1971 and 1994 in the county, the IRA was responsible for 100 of them (87 per cent). Loyalist killings in the county ceased in 1975 and did not follow the pattern in other counties of resuming in the late 1980s. Fermanagh was, therefore, a place apart, and it became clear that our publication needed to reflect that reality.

As a result of our work with a number of bereaved families, we have been granted access to Historical Enquiry Team (HET) reports[1] and various sources; for this reason, a significant amount of information on these cases has been made available to the author. Extensive research, accessing newspaper reports and other sources as far as possible, has also been undertaken on the other victims' deaths to try and include all salient facts. Many bereaved Fermanagh families receive advocacy support from other organisations that have documented their loss, and we have drawn on the publicly accessible sources they have made available. This publication does not purport to tell the full story of loss, hurt and trauma that resulted from the political conflict in the county, but in providing even limited details on each death, we hope it will provide some context to the terrible loss of the 115 men and women who lost their lives.

In order to provide background and context, the book begins with the Ulster plantation and explores how, from the early seventeenth century to the signing of the Good Friday Agreement in 1998, central and local government policies and decisions have impacted on the two principal communities of County Fermanagh. It is primarily a detailed analysis of all conflict-related deaths that occurred in the county in this period, and investigates why the impact of the IRA campaign there continues to be felt so acutely.

Focusing on the period from the 1920s onwards, a number of key themes have emerged from this research: the alienation of the Catholic community from the new Northern Ireland state after partition; their disillusionment with, and feeling of being utterly abandoned by, the Free State government after the Boundary Commission debacle; the institutionalised discrimination against Catholics in Northern Ireland and the outworking of the Special Powers Act; the Protestant community's distrust of their Catholic neighbours as a result of the IRA campaign of 1956–62; the contrasting effects of the civil rights movement on both communities; the beginning of the IRA campaign in the county after the introduction of internment; the very low level of loyalist paramilitary activity compared to the neighbouring counties of Armagh and Tyrone; the permanent halting of fatal attacks by loyalists in the mid-1970s; the role of the border in the IRA campaign in the county and, for a short while, in the loyalist campaign; the apparent loyalist focus on members of the Northern Ireland Civil Rights Association (NICRA); the strong suspicions of collusion in loyalist killings; the suspected use of excessive force in killings by the security forces; the disposition of the Irish government towards cross-border co-operation with the British authorities; and the negative impact of specific events on both communities.

This research sheds new light on the victims of the conflict in the county. Due to the IRA's responsibility for 87 per cent of this death toll, there is a perception, particularly among Fermanagh unionists, that the IRA campaign in the county was conducted with a greater ferocity than in any other area of Northern Ireland. Reflection on those stark figures gives rise to often-repeated claims of 'ethnic cleansing along the border'. The book considers this claim in detail.

In percentage terms, killings carried out by republicans in counties Armagh and Tyrone is appreciably lower because of the much higher death toll exacted by loyalists in these counties. In Armagh, of 519 deaths, republicans carried out 376 (72.4 per cent), while in Tyrone, of 357 deaths, they were responsible for 261 (73.1 per cent).

Between 1972 and 1975, loyalists killed four people in Fermanagh – three Catholic civilians and an IRA member. After 1975 they were not culpable for any more deaths. By contrast, in Tyrone, while loyalist killings dropped off in 1977, they resumed in the late 1980s, after the signing of the Anglo-Irish Agreement, and increased exponentially in the early 1990s before ceasing in 1997. In Armagh, loyalist killings followed a similar pattern, dropping considerably in the late 1970s and early 1980s, and increasing again in the 1990s, ceasing only in 2001.

Analysis of the 115 conflict-related deaths in Fermanagh shows that thirty-three of those killed (29 per cent) were not residents of the county: twenty-one British soldiers, seven IRA members, one Garda and four Catholic civilians. Of the 100 killed by the IRA, seventy-five were residents of Fermanagh. At least six of the Royal Ulster Constabulary (RUC) officers killed, although resident there, were not natives of the county. A number of security force members were killed in road traffic and other accidents during these decades, but they have not been included in this book. An exception is made for one Ulster Defence Regiment (UDR) soldier who was accidentally killed by a member of the regular army.

When we examine the circumstances of the deaths of the four people killed by loyalists, there is evidence that outside assistance was brought in from Belfast in 1972 for their first victim, that of IRA member Louis Leonard. It is possible that this *modus operandi* was repeated in the killing of their second victim, James Murphy, in April 1974. There is information indicating that Patrick Kelly, an independent councillor, may have been killed by local UDR members in July 1974, although his death is still blamed officially on loyalist paramilitaries. In 1975, a local member of both the UDR and Ulster Volunteer Force (UVF), Robert Bridge, was convicted of the murder of the final victim of loyalists, Catholic civilian Patrick O'Reilly.

The Fermanagh-based gang, of which Bridge was a member, was also active in counties Cavan, Monaghan and Donegal in the early 1970s. It was responsible for a bomb attack in Belturbet, Cavan in December 1972, which resulted in the deaths of two teenagers, and at least ten non-fatal bombings in the three border counties, which caused property damage and numerous injuries.

Protestants, particularly in south Fermanagh, felt surrounded by threats from outside the county, with IRA active service units operating from Monaghan to Donegal. The sheer length of the Fermanagh border created a sense of unique Protestant vulnerability. An interesting correlation with loyalism is that many of the killings on the republican side were also carried out by outsiders, not Fermanagh natives.

The strongly held belief of the unionist and Protestant population of Fermanagh that they were singled out for special treatment was reinforced by specific events. One such instance was the election of hunger striker Bobby Sands as MP for Fermanagh and South Tyrone in April 1981, which they regarded as a betrayal by their Catholic neighbours. This belief was compounded in November 1987 when the IRA exploded a no-warning bomb in Enniskillen on Remembrance Day – probably the most hallowed day of their year, when the war dead are commemorated.

The often-repeated claim that the Irish government and its security forces failed to co-operate with the British side on the border has been tested by detailed analysis of relevant official British government documents over the decades of the conflict.

A range of archival material has been gathered from the UK National Archives. The primary source material used in the study includes numerous official declassified British and Irish government documents - these provide very useful insights into the governments' policies and mindset, but do not provide a complete picture, as many relevant files are closed and will remain so for many years. Other primary sources include contemporary articles from Irish national and provincial newspapers; online sources, such as digital transcripts of the 1641 Depositions (Trinity College Dublin) and twentieth century Dáil debates; the Historical Enquiry Team (HET) reports; the Barron reports (Independent Commissions of Inquiry into various conflict-related deaths in the Republic of Ireland in the 1970s); and interviews with relevant individuals.

Chapter 1

THE SEVENTEENTH CENTURY

THE ULSTER PLANTATION

The unexpected flight of leading Ulster chieftains to Europe in 1607, after their defeat in the Nine Years' War,[2] gave England the opportunity it had been waiting for; it facilitated the confiscation of vast tracts of land encompassing present day counties Armagh, Tyrone, Derry, Cavan, Donegal and Fermanagh. Sir Arthur Chichester, who was appointed Lord Deputy of Ireland in 1605, wrote joyfully to the King that 'all will now be His Majesty's' and made the proposal of 'driving out all the inhabitants of Tyrone, Tirconnell and Fermanagh with their goods and cattle to inhabit waste lands across the Bann, the Blackwater and Lough Erne'.[3] Fermanagh was a stronghold of the Maguire clan. The Ulster lands for disposal included not only districts under Hugh O'Neill and Rory O'Donnell but also the large portions of Fermanagh vacated by Cuconnacht Maguire, who accompanied the chieftains in their flight.[4] Two million acres in total were confiscated by the English Crown.[5]

More than 5,000 acres of Fermanagh land were to be allocated to bishoprics and parsons. Nearly 28,000 acres[6] were to be divided between twenty 'undertakers' (wealthy landowners who came from England and Scotland) in parcels of 1,000, 1,500 and 2,000 acres. Each proportion was to be made into a parish and a parish church 'erected therein'. They were to plant their properties with English or Scottish tenants. Nearly a thousand acres (937 acres) were allotted to the building of three corporate towns: one at Lisgoole, near Enniskillen; another at Castle Skeagh; and a third mid-way between Lisgoole and Ballyshannon. Over 600 acres were allocated towards a free school at Lisgoole.[7] (The school was actually built at Portora, later the *alma mater* of Oscar Wilde and Samuel Beckett). Land around Lisgoole

Abbey, amounting to 1,500 acres, was allocated to Sir John Davies, the Attorney General and chief architect of the plantation.[8] In this way, a new Protestant community composed entirely of loyal British subjects was to be created.

The baronies of Magherastephany and Clankelly, as well as the half baronies of Tirkennedy and Knockninny – over 12,000 acres – were allocated to Conor Roe Maguire (who had taken the side of the Crown in the Nine Years' War), but he was to be allowed to keep only one proportion of 2,000 acres and to 'make sales of freeholds in the rest', as would be prescribed by the commissioners.[9] His Majesty's Commissioners, who were responsible for land distribution, were: the Bishop of Derry, Sir James Ley, Sir Anthony St Leger, Sir Henry Docwra, Sir Oliver St John, Sir James Fullerton and Sir John Davies. Of the remaining eleven proportions, servitors (those who had served as soldiers of the Crown in the Nine Years' War) were to receive four, and natives seven.

The commissioners were to transplant natives who were not to be freeholders – some upon the bishops' lands and the glebes of parsons; others upon the lands of 'such Irish as shall be thought fit to have any freeholds there'; some with servitors who were unable to get Scottish tenants and who 'know best how to rule the Irish'. The native 'swordsmen' were to be transplanted to 'other parts of the kingdom' – waste lands – namely into Connaught and some parts of Munster, where they were 'to be dispersed and not planted together in one place'; and those without followers or cattle were 'to be disposed of in the king's service'.[10]

This plan, however, was less than successful because of political uncertainty in Ireland. The undertakers had difficulty in attracting settlers because of the risk of attack by the dispossessed Irish. This meant that they were forced to keep some Irish tenants, destroying the original plan of complete segregation between settlers and natives. In an attempt to rescue the plantation, the twelve great guilds from the City of London were coerced into investing in the project. Thus, the city of Derry and the county (previously County Coleraine) became Londonderry. The Attorney General, Sir John Davies, after a visit to Fermanagh, described the land on either side of Lough Erne as 'the fattest and richest soil in all Ulster'.[11]

Most of the English planters who arrived in Fermanagh came from East Anglia (Norfolk and Suffolk) as undertakers. Most of the servitors who got land in Fermanagh were also English. Some of the planters came from south-west Scotland, but many of their tenants came from the unstable regions along the border with England. It was thought that by moving the Borderers (Border Reivers)[12] to Ireland, particularly to Fermanagh, that it would both solve the English border problem and tie down Ulster.[13] Border Reiver family names were found in concentrated numbers in Fermanagh – Armstrong, Irving, Murray, Kerr, Maxwell, Johnston, Elliot, Carruthers, Potts, Burns, Douglas, Bell, Crozier, Scott and Graham.[14]

Fermanagh is the only Ulster county in present-day Northern Ireland that is not dominated by Presbyterianism. Its Protestant population was, and is, solidly Church of Ireland (Anglican). The tenacity of the Borderers to ride out the 1641 rebellion is borne out by the surname statistics of the plantation counties in the present day. In Cavan, Donegal and Tyrone, the top five most numerous names are Irish; in Armagh and Derry, there is only one planter name in the first five. In Fermanagh, by contrast, three of the five most numerous names stem from the Scottish Borders – Johnston, Armstrong and Elliot. The other two are Irish – Maguire and MacManus.[15]

By 1609, Enniskillen Castle, built by the Maguires, was in an English garrison in the charge of servitor Captain William Cole. He rebuilt the castle and was granted land to establish the new town of Enniskillen. He also built his family home beside the castle. The Coles later moved to a new country residence at Florencecourt.[16] Lisnaskea, Newtownbutler and Ballinamallard owe their origins to the small plantation villages that grew up alongside the planters' castles. The powerful Earls of Enniskillen were very influential in the following centuries.

A common thread found in many of the sources demonstrates the enormous influence of Fermanagh's aristocracy on the political, economic and social affairs of the county throughout the whole period. The most important influencers were awarded land during the Ulster plantation or later in the seventeenth century. Most prominent among them are the Cole family (Earls of Enniskillen), the Brooke family (Baronets and later Viscounts Brookeborough), the Crichton family (Earls of Erne), the Archdale/Archdall family (Baronets) and the Lowry-Corry family (Earls of Belmore).

The first Basil Brooke (1567–1633) was a soldier-adventurer who distinguished himself as a servitor in the Nine Years' War and was one of those selected for a proportion of the plantation. He was, initially, granted land in Donegal, but having fought on the Cromwellian side in the English Civil War, he was rewarded with further grants of lands in Monaghan and Fermanagh. Basil's son, Henry, acquired some of the lands of Hugh McMahon in Monaghan, while in Fermanagh he acquired most of the confiscated estates of Lord Conor Maguire in Magherastephany; Maguire was hanged, drawn and quartered in Tyburn in 1645 for treason. This property, which until then had survived as 'a little bit of Gaelic Ireland left untouched', now became the basis for the Colebrooke estate.[17]

The Archdale family was the most prominent of the original undertakers to survive down through the centuries. John Archdale of Norfolk was granted 1,000 acres of land in Fermanagh in 1612. He erected a castle that was burned down at the beginning of the 1641 Rebellion.

One of the new industries established by the planters was the smelting of iron ore, which was carried out at a terrible price to the Irish landscape. This wholesale deforestation began the process that has resulted in Ireland being one of the least forested countries of Europe, with only about 9 per cent covered in trees compared with, for example, France's 40 per cent.[18] On the other hand, the removal of trees resulted in more good land being available for farming.

The people of Fermanagh were accustomed to invasions, but the plantation was an invasion with a difference. Peadar Livingstone describes it as having established 'a new race in Fermanagh, to live side by side with the old and to abolish the old if possible.'[19] This ambition was, however, moderated by the fact that there was a swift recognition that the native Irish were useful and necessary for labour. Ulster, traditionally a bastion of Gaelic society and culture, was transformed in a relatively short time. The native elite saw their glory fade as they were progressively displaced by a new colonial ruling class; this shift had cultural, linguistic, religious, economic, demographic, psychological and social consequences. The collapse of this last stronghold of power was a colossal blow to Gaelic Ireland.[20]

Some contemporary poems in the Book of O'Conor Don[21] reflect the effect of this transformation on the native people. An anonymous poem reflects 'the powerful and pervasive sense of trauma, alienation and communal dispossession' of the native intellectual elite.[22] Another poem in the Book of O'Conor Don, by Lochlainn Ó Dálaigh, laments a dramatic reversal of fortune for aristocratic Gaelic society. He claims that churches were occupied by intruders so that Catholic religious services had to be conducted in the open and priests' vestments were used as bedding for cattle.[23] The cultural norms of Gaelic society had also been supplanted – poetry, harp and organ music, dynastic tales and genealogical scholarship.[24] This change has reverberated down through the centuries, even to our own day.

REBELLION OF 1641

Three decades later, in October 1641, fears for the position of the remaining Catholic elite in Ireland, combined with simmering resentments caused by the colonisation of Ulster, prompted the outbreak of a rebellion.

The ruthless and despotic actions of the then Lord Deputy, Thomas Wentworth, had further reduced living conditions for Catholics. Moreover, the breakdown in relations between King Charles l and the English parliament led any remaining property-owning Catholics to fear their seizure should the King's power be further limited. The rebellion was spearheaded by the Catholic gentry of Ulster, who feared the consequences of Puritan rule and who pledged allegiance to the embattled English monarch. Paradoxically, the Catholic families of many of the rebels of 1641 had previously been the most pro-English. They had 'played the game of life by British rules and they had lost badly'.[25]The bad harvest of 1641, and rising rents that were hitting the Irish peasantry hard, aggravated their desire to remove the planters. This contributed to the widespread attacks at the start of the rebellion. The sense of grievance among Ulster Catholics remained very raw thirty years after the plantation.[26]

Early English Parliamentarian pamphlets claimed that over 200,000 Protestants had lost their lives;[27] however, recent research suggests that the number is far more modest – in the region of 4,000 are estimated to have been killed, though many thousands were expelled from their homes. It is estimated that up to 12,000 Protestants may have died in total, the majority from exposure and disease. Livingstone quotes an earlier historian, Dunlop, who suggested – with a very precise figure – that 4,901 people were killed. He also claims that most of the Protestants were killed by acts of war, and of those English who died off the battlefield, most perished from hunger and exposure; he accepts that the rebels engaged in some 'acts of savagery'.[28]

Though co-operation between settlers and the native Irish, on the surface at least, was relatively peaceful in the early seventeenth century, the rebellion aggravated 'quietly simmering animosities' between the two communities into explosive violence.[29] On the night of 22–23 October 1641, several Gaelic chiefs rose in rebellion against the English and Scottish planters. Fires were lit on Ulster hillsides as a signal for the disinherited Irish to rise. They were led by Sir Phelim O'Neill and Conor and Rory Maguire, who claimed they were fighting for full civil and religious rights.[30] Rory Maguire was the leader in Fermanagh – the burning of Lisnarick, near Irvinestown, on 23 October was the signal for the rebellion to begin. He orchestrated the capture of planter houses throughout Fermanagh.[31]

Castle Archdale was destroyed in the fire. Edward Archdale, son of the original John, was now the landowner. All of the Archdale children are said to have been killed except for a daughter who didn't live in the castle and her infant brother, William, who was saved by his Catholic nurse. William's son, Edward, married the eldest daughter of John Cole of Florencecourt at some point in the 1720s.[32]

The 1641 depositions[33] are the main evidence for the sharply contested allegation that the rebellion began with a general massacre of Protestant settlers. David Gerder claims that they were highly controversial sources because they were quickly edited in strategic ways so as to garner financial and military support against the Catholic rebels and to emphasise Protestant unity and blamelessness.[34]

One hundred and sixty-four depositions were taken from Fermanagh landholders by a group of eight clergymen, who were acting on the authority of the Commission for the Despoiled Subject issued by the Dublin government.[35] They were sworn statements taken from Protestant refugees – planters, their tenants and others in Fermanagh and elsewhere. Also included are the examinations of suspects, and of those believed to have information on suspects, taken by the Cromwellian courts in the 1650s. These examinations sought to clarify the extent of Catholic violence in Ireland; they are trial records rather than depositions, representing the only direct Catholic voices in the depositions collection.[36] Gerder claims that the depositions were largely characterised by Protestant anti-Catholic bias, describing the rebels negatively as ethnically and religiously 'other'.[37]

From Ulster, it is the southern counties that are most numerously represented in the depositions – Cavan, Fermanagh, Monaghan and Armagh, in that order. The commission's formal function was to register claims and issue certificates of loss to the deponents; its informal function was to act as an information-gathering system. Many of the Fermanagh deponents declared that the rebels claimed to have the approval of King Charles l for their actions.

Some of the depositions make gruesome reading. One Laurence Knowles of Newtownbutler deposed that he, his wife and five children fled, with many other Protestants (he estimated nine-score), to his local church, where they remained for two days. He said that when Rory Maguire burned the town, they were forced out of the church and stripped naked. He also claimed he was credibly told that when the rebels took over the church, they caught an English child, whose parents lay sick in the church, and boiled it in a cauldron of water over a fire in the same church. He said his own five children died because they were so famished.[38] The depositions of Margaret Parkin and Elizabeth Bairsee also describe this incident during which 'the rebels boiled a young child to death'. None of the three deponents claimed to have witnessed the incident – they were hearsay accounts told to them by allegedly 'credible persons'.[39]

There are widespread claims of the rebels stripping the clothes from evicted Protestants, which allegedly led to many deaths from exposure on the road to safety in Dublin. The ritualistic stripping was regarded by many commentators as a socio-economic levelling – literally stripping signs of English or Scottish wealth and prosperity.[40] Gerder cites Nicholas Canny's opinion that stripping was 'even more of a degrading crime than sexual violence', as it carried metaphorical significance as a social 'equaliser'; it was a symbolic dispossession, reducing the settler to the status of the 'mere Irish'.[41]

Carlo Gebler, in his book on the siege of Derry, also refers to the custom of stripping. He describes how, on 2 July 1689, 'the first 200 Protestants who had been taken into custody were herded towards the city. They were mostly naked, cold and hungry.'[42]

With regard to the claim of the child being boiled in 'a cauldron of hot water', Gerder observes that such imagery was used in Europe during the Thirty Years' War, where murders 'were embellished with descriptions of the cooking or other preparation of children for eating'.[43]

Ann Bond, one of the deponents, claimed that all the half barony of Knockninny was involved in the rebellion – all followers of Rory Maguire.[44] Another deponent, John Morton, claimed that his captors remarked, 'Are you not worthy to be killed for holding our lands from us?'[45] Morris Midlebrook claimed that he had been told that 'the English Protestants had kept their lands from them and hanged their priests and friars in England.'[46]

John Cox reported that he was taunted with the words, 'We have been your slaves all this time, now you shall be ours.'[47] Several of the deponents claimed that about forty settlers had been murdered in the parish of Newtownbutler.

William Baxter of Rathmoran swore that Rory Maguire seized his lands, around 1,000 acres, on the grounds that 'they belonged to his father before the said plantation.' Baxter also listed his other losses, which illustrate his prosperity: 200 horses and mares worth £210; household 'stuffe' worth £40; corn in the field and barn worth £110.[48]

One of the notable aspects of the depositions is the apparent wealth of the deponents, in terms of land, cattle, horses, sheep, farm produce, household goods, money and occasionally jewels. Avis Braishawe claimed to have lost £240 worth of goods, which would be worth at least £28,000 in today's value.[49] It is possible, however, that the claims may have been exaggerated so as to obtain enhanced compensation.

A number of deponents claimed that some of their people, whom they named, had converted to Catholicism and joined with the rebels. Elizabeth Taylor claimed that four men of her acquaintance, including Lt William Grimes, 'were with the rebels and went with them to Mass'.[50]

Alice Champion (Champyn) is a deponent who is mentioned by a number of authors. Her husband, Arthur, was murdered, as described by Gerder, on the morning of 23 October 1641 'in an act of apparent symbolic and personal political vengeance'.[51] Livingstone notes Champion's claim that she had heard the rebels boast about murdering ninety people at the Castle of Lisgoole during the attack on her husband and his friends. However, Lisgoole was not attacked until 23 December.[52] Her deposition does appear to confirm Livingstone's view, who he suggests that, in their state of panic, the planters 'sought consolation in their vivid imaginations'.[53] While there may be some truth in that claim, Alice Champion also describes in detail the murder of her husband and six other men at her home, the Castle of Shanoge (Shannock).[54] Raymond Gillespie notes that Arthur Champion was a justice of the peace and sheriff of Fermanagh, and he had also been elected as MP for Enniskillen in 1640.[55] He also owned Castlecoole estate.

Champion liked to entertain, and several of his friends were gathered in his home on the evening of 22 October. When the entertaining was over, both family and guests retired to bed. Very early the next morning, a number of Champion's tenants, led by Donn Carrough Maguire and Edmund Carrough Maguire, arrived at the gates of Shannock alongside between forty and sixty others. They brought with them a prisoner accused of stealing cattle, and requested Champion, as justice of the peace, to make a judgement on the matter. When Champion opened the gates, they stabbed him with their long knives and also killed Thomas Ironmonger, Humphrey Littlebury and Christopher Lynas.[56] Gillespie suggests that Champion may have been singled out as a recent arrival in the neighbourhood because such newcomers were often less tolerant of the native Irish than older settlers.[57]

This assassination in the opening hours of the rebellion was a catalyst for panic throughout the region. Champion's widow recounted many stories in her deposition that fed propagandists with sensational accounts of 'Irish barbarism'. As the widow of an early victim, her corroboration of well-known atrocity stories lent the alleged accounts increased credibility.[58] She later married Henry Gilbert and retained ownership of the lands of Castlecoole; in 1656 they sold the estate to John Corry, whose successors became the Earls of Belmore.

Out of a total of 164 deponents, sixty-eight of them claimed to have either witnessed or heard about multiple killings, but many of these referred to the same victims.

Hugh O'Reilly, a Catholic bishop, arranged a synod of bishops at Kells, County Meath in March 1642 to discuss the ongoing rebellion. The synod called for an end to robberies and the killing of unarmed civilians, but most considered that the aims of the conflict in support of Catholic rights and King Charles amounted to a just war.[59]

The aims of the 1641 Depositions Project at Trinity College Dublin were to conserve, digitise and transcribe the depositions, making them available online. The project ran from 2007 to 2010. The Depositions Project comments:

> Thus the depositions do not prove the authenticity of the general massacre that was thought to have accompanied the outbreak of rebellion; they do provide evidence that Protestant settlers were killed in considerable numbers in the north of Ireland and a few other places throughout its first year.[60]

The Old English of the Pale and beyond joined with the Gaelic Irish cause. It was an insurgency of all Catholic Ireland.[61]

While it looked likely for a time that the rebellion would succeed, the Irish were eventually defeated at the battle of Glenmaquin, near Letterkenny, County Donegal, on 16 June 1642.[62] According to James Godkin, however, the rebellion in Ulster had almost collapsed before the end of 1641.[63] He claims that the thousands who had rushed to join the rebel forces were by then reduced to weak and disorganised collections of armed men taking shelter in the woods. The English garrisons scoured the Ulster counties, including Fermanagh, with little opposition, and where they met any, they showed no mercy. According to Godkin, Sir William Cole proudly boasted of his achievement in having 7,000 rebels 'famished to death' within a few miles of his garrison.[64]

Oliver Cromwell arrived in Ireland in 1649 on 'a mission of religious right and regaining political control.'[65] He also saw it as a 'reckoning' for the 1641 massacre of Ulster Protestants, justifying the slaughter at Drogheda and Wexford. He set about consolidating the plantation, declaring all lands of the Irish rebels forfeit. Maguire land at Magherastephany was given to the Brooke family.[66] Some small portions were given to William Montgomery, John Leonard, Dr Thomas Wyatt and Sir William Balfour.[67] The influential Earls of Erne acquired the Crom estate in 1655. The family had been building up their Fermanagh estate since 1613 by a piecemeal acquisition of land.[68] By the late 1650s, the Irish Protestant elite had collectively become the wealthiest and most powerful grouping in Ireland.

A day of commemoration was established after the Restoration of Charles ll to the throne of England in 1660; it was held annually, on 23 October, for more than 200 years, serving as a yearly reminder of 'Catholic treachery and savagery'.[69] According to Patrick Corish, however, some settlers also massacred Catholics, particularly in 1642–3 when a Scottish Covenanter Army landed in Ulster. Corish quotes the nineteenth century historian William Lecky, 'It is far from clear on which side the balance of cruelty lies.'[70] The bitterness created by the plantations and the 1641 rebellion proved extremely long-lasting. Livingstone claims that, in Fermanagh, by 1641, the Irish and planters were beginning to coalesce. If that had continued, he opines, the plantation, like earlier ones, would have been a failure. He asserts that the rebellion put a stop to all that, and the planters felt that they could never again trust the Irish.[71]

It seems inconceivable, however, that the settlers did not appear to expect any reprisals from those who had their homes and lands seized in the plantation. Some depositions, as noted, clearly indicate Irish resentment. Perhaps the planters had grown complacent after thirty years in relatively peaceful possession of their new estates. It must be borne in mind that the Dublin government did not establish a commission to take sworn statements from the dispossessed Irish after the plantation, so there are no written accounts of their losses and hardships. As elsewhere, the documentary record is weighted heavily towards the state and away from those who opposed its power.

THE WILLIAMITE WARS

When James II ascended the throne of England in 1685, succeeding his brother, Charles II, he set about restoring the Catholic religion. His Catholicism increasingly alarmed British Protestants. In 1688, seven Protestant noblemen invited William, Prince of Orange, the husband of James's daughter Mary, to intervene and end the attack on 'their religion, liberties and properties'. William landed in England from Holland on 5 November.[72] James fled to France, arriving in Paris on Christmas Day 1688 and receiving a less than enthusiastic welcome from his ally Louis XIV. James then travelled to Ireland, landing at Kinsale with French troops in March 1689,[73] and when he lost his throne, Ireland remained loyal to him. Only two centres stood out against him – Derry and Enniskillen.[74] Many battles took place in Fermanagh in 1689, with William's forces emerging victorious, although William himself did not arrive in Ireland until June 1690.

The greatest assault by Irish Catholics in Fermanagh took place at Crom Castle, the residence of the Earl of Erne, on 28 July 1689.[75] General Justin McCarthy, Lord Mountcashel, reached Crom with over 3,000 men and besieged the castle. The Earl (Lord Crichton) sent word to Enniskillen for help, but before help could arrive, Mountcashel's men charged the castle and the besieged fought back bravely. When seventy of their men were killed, the Irish withdrew to Newtownbutler. The Enniskilleners, in response to Crichton's appeal, engaged the Irish near Lisnaskea, where they were victorious. The next battle was fought at Newtownbutler, where the Irish lost over 3,000 men, and this defeat finished the hopes of James ll in Ulster.[76] The Inniskilling Dragoons emerged from this struggle,[77] and when William landed at Carrickfergus on 14 June 1690, they joined his army.[78] The Royal Inniskilling Fusiliers also came into being at this time.[79] The Williamite forces won the day at the Boyne and at Aughrim, where the Inniskilling Dragoons suffered heavy losses. In this last great battle to preserve the Irish way of life, Cúchonnacht Maguire led the Irish of Fermanagh. They, too, suffered heavy losses – Cúchonnacht and Alexander Maguire were killed. [80] William's forces, which came from all over Protestant Europe, were highly professional and exceptionally well trained.

With the last significant stronghold of Limerick under siege, the Jacobite leader, Patrick Sarsfield, opened talks with the Williamite Baron de Ginkel. The war ended with the Treaty of Limerick in October 1691.[81] After William was victorious, the planters were determined to replace the native Irish and so began a new plantation.[82] These planters were ordinary working people brought in from England and Scotland. In this way, large tracts of Fermanagh were cleared of Irish Catholics.[83]

In 1600, Fermanagh had been one hundred per cent Gaelic and Catholic. By 1700, the Gaels were completely dispossessed by the Ulster plantation, the Cromwellian Settlement and the victory of William, and the Catholic Church was forced underground. When it appeared that things couldn't get any worse for the native Irish, the Penal Laws were imposed at the beginning of the eighteenth century.[84] The tensions that were provoked during the seventeenth century have, arguably, lasted to the present day.

Chapter 2

FROM THE PENAL LAWS TO THE FAMINE

THE PENAL LAWS

Before the turn of the eighteenth century, by the Act of Supremacy[85] and the Act of Uniformity,[86] all Catholic bishops and priests of religious orders were commanded to leave Ireland and not to return. The parochial (or secular) clergy were allowed to remain but only one priest was permitted to each parish. By this method, it was assumed that the priesthood would die out, as no new priests could be ordained or enter the country.[87] Priests had to register in order to practise their ministry. In Fermanagh, only thirteen priests registered, and their average age was 54.[88]

The purely religious anti-Catholic laws were not the main difficulty that faced the church. Because of the wars, the plantations and the other laws of the Penal Code, the Catholic people were in dire poverty and thus unable to support many priests. The priests who did serve, lived heroic lives, very often having no fixed abode, as their churches had been confiscated.[89]

Hugh McMahon, who was consecrated as Catholic Bishop of Clogher[90] in March 1707, entered Ireland surreptitiously and eventually, in 1710, made his way to his diocese in disguise and under various assumed names. He wrote in 1714:

> Although all Ireland is suffering, this province [Ulster] is worse off than the rest of the country, because of the fact that from the neighbouring country of Scotland Presbyterians are coming over here daily in large groups of families, occupying the towns and villages, seizing the farms in the richer parts of the country and expelling the natives [...] The result is that the Catholic natives are forced to build their huts in mountainous or marshy country.[91]

According to Henry Jefferies, the fact that only 1 per cent of the 892 'Mass houses' recorded for the whole of Ireland in 1731 were in Clogher diocese reflected the persistent poverty of the Catholic community, where there had been a considerable influx of British planters. It also reflected something of the persisting sectarianism among the Protestant community there. This sectarianism was fuelled by what Protestants saw as a mission to spread Protestantism and to please the English Crown, but it was also due to paranoia about their Catholic neighbours. The experience of dispossession and of religious persecution affected the Irish Catholic community very profoundly, and not only in Ulster.[92]

The Penal Laws, however, failed to destroy Catholicism in Fermanagh, although those who remained were very much second-class citizens. They were excluded from parliament, from voting, from corporations, from the magistracy, from the bar, from the bench, from grand juries, from the army and from being sheriffs, constables and game-keepers.[93]

Because Catholics were excluded from education, so-called hedge schools sprung up all over the country in order that Catholic children would not be left in ignorance. The ownership of land in Fermanagh was not relevant to Catholics, as the whole county was owned by Protestants.[94] Fermanagh, however, although officially Protestant, remained Catholic numerically. The reason for this, as has been noted, was due to the necessity of retaining a certain number of Catholics as tenants; also, they were required to carry out what were regarded by the settlers as menial tasks. It was Lord Drogheda who, fearing the loss of Catholics, said, 'I shall be very glad to see the Protestant religion strengthened; but what shall we do for hewers of wood and drawers of water, for labouring men to plough our lands, thresh our corn.'[95]

THE UNITED IRISHMEN AND THE ORANGE ORDER

While the Penal Laws were aimed primarily at Catholics, Presbyterians also suffered. They were barred from public office in 1707, their marriages were not legally recognised by the state and their children were regarded as illegitimate.[96] For many members of the establishment, Presbyterians were regarded as more of a threat than Catholics, especially because of their numerical superiority in much of Ulster. The founders of the United

Irishmen were middle-class Presbyterian radicals frustrated by the lack of civil rights available to them. They were influenced by the revolutions in America and France, as well as by the philosophy of the European and Scottish enlightenments.[97] Their aim was to unify all the people of Ireland, but they made little impact in Fermanagh. As noted, the leaders were mainly non-conformist (Presbyterian), while the majority of Protestants in Fermanagh were Church of Ireland and part of the establishment. Nevertheless, pockets of United Irishmen were to be found around Enniskillen, Roslea and in the Belleek-Garrison districts.[98]

In Fermanagh, as elsewhere, the leaders and organisers of the United Irishmen were Protestants, whereas the majority of the members were Catholics. In the Roslea district, the leader, Captain Thompson, was a native of the district but had been brought up in Belfast.[99] It is not known whether he was Church of Ireland or Presbyterian, but he may have been radicalised in Belfast. He was the man who laid and executed the plans in that area. Under his direction, pikes were forged and raids were made on Protestant houses. In one of these raids, over eighty guns and 1,200 cartridges were stolen. The Belleek group was linked with the United Irishmen in Ballyshannon.[100]

Ironically, while the United Irishmen were doing all in their power to heal religious differences, another powerful organisation came into being that accentuated these differences. The first Orange Lodge was founded in Loughgall, County Armagh, in 1795. The purpose of the new society was to maintain a Protestant kingdom for a Protestant people, to maintain the constitution, to preserve Protestants from the dangers of Rome and to promote devotion to William of Orange.[101] It is also ironic that, in Fermanagh, the same area, Roslea, was the first to welcome both of these societies.[102]

The founder of Orangeism in the county was John Emerson from Roslea. The Order flourished in Fermanagh, and one of the earliest lodges in the county was at Lisbellaw. The founder and first master was Samuel Johnston, a wealthy farmer from Kilsallagh. Unlike many other counties, where, in its early days, the Orange Order was often regarded as not being respectable, the landlord class of Fermanagh was associated with the Order from the beginning and guided its activities. The names of those involved include the Hon. Arthur Cole of Florencecourt, Gerald Irvine of Necarn, Captain Edward Archdale of Castle Archdale, Lt Henry Irvine of Irvinestown and

James Armstrong of Enniskillen.[103] The landlords' policies determined its political policies. Livingstone argues that they saw the Order as a very useful weapon 'to keep their tenants' minds off their own grievances.'[104]

The Insurrection Act was passed in 1796; it enabled the Lord Lieutenant to place any district under martial law. It directed that all arms be surrendered, imposed the death penalty for administering an unlawful oath and gave magistrates power to seize any suspect and send him to serve on the fleet. Francis Brooke described a raid for arms and suspects under the Colebrooke Cavalry that took seven United Irishmen on Slebagh Mountain. They were examined for taking and administering unlawful oaths and were placed in Enniskillen gaol. Three of the seven men were tenants of Brooke and the remainder were Lord Belmore's.[105]

In October 1797, three young Roslea men were hanged in Enniskillen – Patrick Smith of Mullaghbrady, John Connolly of Potyiagh and James MacMahon of Knocknagross. Crowds of people journeyed from Roslea to attend their trials and executions. When their bodies were cut down from the gallows, the local people received them and formed a procession to carry their coffins across Carnmore to Roslea. Before the procession reached Carnmore, it was a mile long.[106] The executions were the result of a raid by United Irishmen in April of that year. The Roslea men raided the house of Samuel Mayne of Tattygormican, who was called upon to surrender. As he was slow to do so, a shot was fired through the window which resulted in Mayne rushing out and handing over his gun. As the rebels cheered, a group of Yeomen in the vicinity heard them and rushed to the scene, but the rebels had escaped. Some time later, a group of United Irishmen were boasting about the incident in a public house; they were overheard by an informer, who relayed the story to a Clones magistrate. Archie Carey, one of the rebels involved, was arrested and confessed all, informing on several of the participants.[107]

The 1798 Rebellion, led by the United Irishmen, took place the following year. While the rebellion failed in Dublin, it spread to other counties in Leinster, most notably Wexford. In the north-east, rebels led by Henry Joy McCracken, most of them Presbyterian, rose in Antrim. The rebellions in Leinster and Antrim had some successes, but the northern rebels were ultimately defeated at the Battle of Ballynahinch on 12 June 1798 while the Wexford Rising was defeated at the Battle of Vinegar Hill on 21 June.

Sir Galbraith Lowry-Cole from Florencecourt was wounded fighting against the rebels at Vinegar Hill above the town of Enniscorthy, County Wexford. He was a professional soldier and a son of William Willoughby, 1st Earl of Enniskillen. Captain Thompson, the Roslea rebel leader, fought alongside Henry Joy McCracken at the Battle of Antrim.[108]

After the defeat of the United Irishmen, fears were growing in London that Catholic emancipation[109] could not be too far off. England's Prime Minister, William Pitt, decided that Ireland should no longer have a separate parliament because he feared that this would ultimately lead to Catholic control of Ireland. The ruling class in Ireland, the Protestant Ascendancy, had also been alarmed at the swift growth of the United Irishmen, and many of them were of the belief that their interests would be better protected through a closer union. The bill to legislate for the Act of Union, however, was opposed by the Fermanagh MPs Archdale and Cole, General Galbraith Lowry-Cole and Arthur Cole-Hamilton. In the House of Lords, Lord Belmore opposed it, while Lord Erne and the Protestant Bishop of Clogher supported it.

In Fermanagh, the greatest opposition came from the Orange Order in Magheraveely, Newtownbutler and Wattlebridge.[110] Many members of both the gentry and the Orange Order believed they were being rewarded for standing up against insurgency with a loss of political power. The Act of Union would sweep away the old establishment parliament in Dublin. In order to be a member of that parliament, one had to belong to the Church of Ireland – Catholics and Presbyterians were excluded. The Orange Order at that time was also dominated by Anglican figures. Nonetheless, despite objections, the Act of Union of Great Britain and Ireland was passed and took effect from January 1801.

CATHOLIC EMANCIPATION

According to the author and historian Kevin Whelan, one of the most successful British strategies in this period was to encourage the growth of sectarianism 'in order to divide the workers and peasants of Ireland'. Key to this process, he believes, was encouraging the growth of the Orange Order and sectarian warfare in Armagh.[111] He describes General John Knox as the architect of this policy; Knox described the Orange Order as 'the only barrier we have against the United Irishmen.'[112]

By the 1820s, religious conflict in Ireland had intensified. On the one hand, Protestants, especially Church of Ireland members, had embraced a campaign known as the 'New Reformation' or 'Second Reformation', which aimed to achieve what the sixteenth century Reformation had failed to accomplish in Ireland – the conversion of its Catholic majority to Protestantism.[113] With the support of prominent landowners, missionary, Bible and educational societies and clergy of the established church, the New Reformation Movement, which was bitterly anti-Catholic, aimed to consolidate the union of Britain and Ireland around a common Protestantism. The campaign had some success in Cavan, having over 1,000 converts by 1827.[114] Its patron was Lord Farnham. The movement spread to Fermanagh, where the Earl of Enniskillen (Cole) was one of its leading proponents.[115] In 1828, he is said to have ordered his Catholic tenants to attend Church of Ireland services or be evicted. Three families were in fact evicted, and they settled in the hilly country at Ruscaw.[116]

On the other hand, largely in response, the Irish Catholic majority, under the leadership of the lawyer and landowner Daniel O'Connell, organised a national and democratic movement for Catholic emancipation. O'Connell adopted a much more robust and aggressive approach in contrast to the deferential tone of the Catholic peers. The Orange Order had, inadvertently, fallen victim to the Unlawful Societies Act in 1825. The act was designed essentially to curb O'Connell's campaign for Catholic emancipation, but the Orange Order was unintentionally caught in its net. The Order, however, continued at an unofficial level until the act expired in 1828, when large Orange parades returned. It reacted with fury to the granting of Catholic emancipation the following year; this manifested itself in violent clashes with Catholics throughout the summer of 1829.[117]

During the Twelfth celebrations that year, eight people were killed in Enniskillen; seven in Clones, County Monaghan; and one in Stewartstown, County Tyrone. In Maghera, County Derry, several Catholic homes were burnt down, prompting the intervention of the military. Trouble also broke out at marches in Armagh; Portadown, County Armagh; Bellaghy, County Derry; Comber and Greyabbey, County Down; Glenoe, County Antrim; and Strabane, County Tyrone.[118]

In Fermanagh, a skirmish took place at Macken on the evening of Monday, 13 July (the Twelfth was being celebrated on a Monday because the actual day fell on a Sunday), between Catholics and Protestants in which a Protestant man, Robert Mealey, was stabbed to death with a pitchfork by Ignatius McManus.[119] Three other Protestants, George Price, John Robinson and Edward Scarlett, were injured and died later of their wounds. Nineteen Catholics, including McManus, from Cornacrea, Kinawley, were charged and convicted. McManus was hanged, while the others were transported for life to Botany Bay.[120] There are conflicting accounts of the skirmish – the Protestant one being that the Catholics involved were fired up by the granting of Catholic emancipation. The Catholic version of events claims it was caused by the anger of the Orange Order at its granting.

Catholic emancipation finally put an end to the Penal Laws, which had been relaxing gradually, after more than a century.

THE EFFECTS OF THE GREAT HUNGER (AN GORTA MÓR) IN COUNTY FERMANAGH

In 1841, Fermanagh's population was 156,481, but ten years later, in 1851 – after the famine – it stood at 116,047, a loss of a quarter of its population. An examination of the pre- and post-famine population of Ulster's nine counties shows that, comparatively, Fermanagh fared badly during the famine years. Between 1841 and 1851, Monaghan's population decreased by 29.2 per cent, Cavan's by 28.4 per cent and Fermanagh's by 25.8 per cent. These three counties suffered Ulster's greatest population loss. Tyrone's decreased by 18.3 per cent, Armagh's by 15.6 per cent, Donegal's by 13.9 per cent, Derry's by 13.6 per cent, Down's by 11.2 per cent and Antrim's by 9 per cent, whereas the population of Belfast rose by 23.6 per cent.[121] Clearly, this indicates that many individuals left rural Ulster and crowded into Belfast.

There are no means of knowing how many of these missing thousands died of hunger or disease, or whether they emigrated to America or migrated to Belfast or Dublin. John Cunningham argues that emigration was an unlikely option for the majority. He believes it is more probable that many died in their homes because of dire poverty.[122]

The potato blight appeared early in Fermanagh, in September 1845. Although in the early days it was one of the least affected counties, by the end of 1846, it was clear it was not going to escape the worst rigours of the famine.[123] It was necessary to open three workhouses in the county shortly before and during the famine years. In Lisnaskea, one was constructed on a site that was purchased from Lord Erne in 1841 for £336.[124] A third of the population of Lisnaskea workhouse was Protestant throughout the famine years. During 1846, the number of inmates rose from 263 in January to 817 in December.[125] Lowtherstown (now Irvinestown) workhouse opened in October 1845 and Enniskillen workhouse two months later.

Enniskillen workhouse admitted its first inmates on 1 December 1845. Between that date and 4 July 1847, 3,764 persons were admitted. Of these, 2,370 were Catholics (63 per cent), whereas 1,238 (33 per cent) were Protestants. Religion was not stated for 156 (4 per cent) of the admissions.[126] Since Enniskillen Union's population was almost equally divided in religious terms, this implies that Catholics were significantly over-represented among the workhouse inmates during the famine. Moreover, the Catholic share grew as the crisis intensified.[127]

According to Guinnane, McCabe and Ó Gráda, between 1 December 1845 and the spring of 1851, a total of 2,040 people died in Enniskillen workhouse.[128] They note that the number admitted between these two dates was about 10,500, implying a ratio of deaths to admissions of one in five, but in the period up to mid-1847, about one in four of those admitted died. In May 1847 alone, 156 inmates died. These authors claim that the cost of the construction of Enniskillen workhouse was increased by 33 per cent due to sharp practice by the Earl of Enniskillen.[129] The Earl sold a site on the lake shore near the town to the Board of Guardians. The land was sold at a fixed price per acre, giving the impression that the Irish acre was the intended measure, but shortly after the transfer of the land, the Earl demanded the price per acre in statute acres (the statute acre was two-thirds of an Irish acre).[130]

A report of an inquest from the *Enniskillen Chronicle* of 21 January 1847 throws into sharp relief the dreadful suffering caused by the famine:

> The third [inquest] was on the body of a man named Patrick [Mc]Mullen, aged about 60 years, which was held at Kesh in the parish of Magheracoolmoney, barony of Lurg, on the 18th instant. Anne Mullen, his wife, deposed that deceased left home about 9am on Saturday, 16th instant, to go to his duty to the Rev. Mr. Tinollen, at Ederney. He had not got any food that morning, and only a little water gruel the night before. He had 9d a day at the public works,

> which was not sufficient to support seven of a family. They had been short of food for a long time before, but she had done the best she could for him. She followed him a distance of three miles, the reason she did so was that he was weak, and had fallen on Friday at the public works and she feared that something would happen him. She conceived it was cold, and want of sufficient nourishment that caused his death. She met her husband in Mr. Tinollen's; he gave deceased six pence. She had not asked food from Mr. Tinollen. He got weak a quarter of a mile from Kesh and sat down on the road – he was not able to go further. She went to Kesh and got assistance to bring him home. Dr. Johnston attended him immediately but he died about 3 o'clock a.m. on Sunday 17th inst […] William Johnston, Surgeon, Kesh Dispensary, deposed to having examined the body […] he conceived his death was caused by want of sufficient nourishment, nature having become exhausted […] VERDICT: 'That Pat McMullen died at Kesh from want of sufficient nourishment, on Sunday 17th instant; and we conceive that the rate of wages he received from the public works was insufficient to support him and his family.'[131]

Below are two examples of deaths as reported by Livingstone:

> We have it on good authority that two children, by the name of Philips, died in Enniskillen from starvation. They were unable to buy soup from the public soup kitchen. […]
>
> Another woman, on the same land [at Currin] was found dead and the infant on her cold breast in the act of sucking her. The wretch who rented her the cabin seized her dead body until 1/6 was subscribed by the neighbours and paid.[132]

Brian MacDonald writes that, on 29 December 1846, George Graham (a member of the Church of Ireland) dropped dead at the public works near Wattlebridge, the cause of death being 'privation and want'. The inquest into his death provides detailed evidence of conditions at the works in the bitter winter weather:

> Ellen Graham of Clonkee, wife of deceased, deposed that her husband, George, left his house for the purpose of going to seek employment at the public works at Annaghmullen, a distance of two miles from his residence,

about nine o'clock on the morning of 29 December. He had been employed at the works for about six weeks. His health becoming delicate, he was unable to perform heavy work, and was then ordered to break stones. He had not been accustomed to work of this kind, and from the small wages he could earn at this employment he would not be able to provide food for himself. The family consisted of seven, five children, her husband and herself. For the week prior to his death, the food for the entire family was two lb of meal made into stirabout without any milk. On Christmas day she killed a hen and purchased a hock of beef;[133] the money she had got from her sister. The hock was very bare. She conceived that on Christmas day he had enough. On Monday her store got less, and Tuesday took her entire stock. She conceived if she had had more food he would have lived longer.

William Marshall Thompson, surgeon, examined. He had made a post mortem examination of deceased. The viscera seemed healthy. There were about 4 ozs of a fluid like thick cabbage water in the stomach. From the stomach to the rectum was perfectly empty; not even a particle of matter in them. He conceived that the deceased had died from want of food.

John McCabe of Drummully, a labourer at the works at Annaghmullen, deposed that he had seen deceased pass about 10 minutes before his death. He asked deceased if he had commenced to break the stones. He replied that he had not, and walked on. He seemed quite feeble and staggering on his limbs [...]

Thomas Elliot, of Annaghmullen, labourer at the public works deposed – On the men quitting for the night on Tuesday, 29 December 1846, he found deceased lying in a field in the townland of Annaghmullen, a few perches from where he was seen by John McCabe; he had not seen him that day before [...] he conceived had he been employed at the daily works and not ordered to stone-breaking, he might be still alive [...]

James Little, of Cleenagh, barony of Coole, a labourer at the work at Annaghmullen, deposed [...] he heard Robert Ford, the Baronial Inspector, tell James Foy, the overseer, to set the old men and boys to break stones; James Foy told him the weather was cold and frosty, and that it would kill them to break stones; his reply was, 'he did not care if there would die seven men an hour – that they might as well die there as in their houses, but the stones must be broken.'

James McGilly of Drummully examined – he was working with deceased the day he was told off to break stones; deceased said he never had broken any, and observed, 'I suppose I may die when I am put to the breaking of stones, for I cannot break any.' I saw him coming along the line two or three times. I asked him what he was about. He said he was striving to get into the daily labour. Deceased had had seven of a family and so have I [...]

James Foy examined – is overseer of works at Drummully and Annaghmullen; deceased worked under him for some weeks; he began to fail and was unable to work; he frequently complained of want of food, and one time witness took him from the pit and gave him his breakfast [...] Mr Ford came to visit the works; he said witness had more men than were necessary and as the stones should be broken, he desired witness to select six or seven and twenty men and put them to break stones; witness reasoned with him and told him as the weather was hard and snowy, they would die on the road; witness said he would wait for a day or two till the weather became more moderate – he told witness to do so; cannot remember that he ever heard him say he did not care whether the men would die or not.

Verdict – Died of starvation.[134]

A report in the 3 July 1845 edition of the *Enniskillen Chronicle* demonstrates the severe penalties handed down to starving people for theft of potatoes. At Enniskillen Division Court, Mary Killday, Mary Mihan, Mary McEntire and Ellen McEntire were sentenced to six months' hard labour for having stolen potatoes at Domard, the property of William Dane, on 15 April. George Henderson and Michael Gallagher were also sentenced to six months' hard labour for the same crime, against William Frith. In their case, they were also to be whipped in the gaol before being discharged.[135]

Many people died of fever, which was no respecter of age, gender, religion or social class. Paupers, priests, policemen, magistrates, relief workers and doctors were particularly exposed. Among those who died of the fever were: the school mistress of Lisnaskea workhouse, who died in April 1847; the Rev. Simon Nelson of Pettigo, at the age of 36; Rev. Charles Porter, the curate of Hollymount Glebe; Mark Hall, a Poor Law guardian; David Vaughan, a newly elected wardmaster of Lisnaskea Union; Stewart Betty, a guardian of Enniskillen Union and the seneschal;[136] and Richard Jackson of Roslea. Mortality from fever peaked in Fermanagh in 1847.[137]

It is possible to extrapolate from the comparative census figures for 1841 and 1851 that the following parishes were the most severely affected: the small part of Currin parish located in Fermanagh (most of the parish is located in Monaghan) lost 57 per cent of its population, declining from 231 persons to 99; Drummully parish lost 44 per cent, declining from 2,947 to 1,655; Trory lost 42 per cent, declining from 2,028 to 1,186; Aghavea lost 40 per cent, declining from 6,730 to 4,034; and Galoon lost 35 per cent, declining from 11,135 to 7,195. By contrast, Enniskillen parish lost only 7 per cent of its population, declining from 14,678 to 13,683,[138] while Belleek lost 15 per cent, declining from 2,875 to 2,446.[139] Three of those parishes that suffered the greatest loss – Currin,[140] Drummully and Galoon – are very close to the Monaghan border.

A number of memorials have been erected to those who died in Fermanagh during the famine years, most strikingly the Famine Pit in Ardess graveyard, in which over 200 local people lie.[141] The pit, which had been abandoned for many years, was restored, and a memorial was unveiled in 2000.

POPULATION CHANGES POST-FAMINE

In each subsequent census, the population of Fermanagh continued to fall so that by 1911 it had been reduced to 61,836, a further incredible 46.7 per cent drop in sixty years. This drastic loss of population, however, was sadly the norm in that period – Monaghan's declined by 49.6 per cent, Cavan's by 47.7 per cent, Tyrone's by 44.2 per cent, Armagh's by 38.6 per cent, Down's by 36.3 per cent, Donegal's by 34 per cent and Antrim's by 25.4 per cent.

The other provinces tell a similar story, with some counties faring even worse in this sixty-year period. In Munster, Tipperary lost 54 per cent of its population and Clare 50.9 per cent. In Leinster, Westmeath lost 46.2 per cent, Wexford 43.2 per cent and Wicklow 38.7 per cent. In Connaught, Galway lost 43.4 per cent and Mayo 30 per cent.

By contrast, Belfast increased its population by a massive 344 per cent – from 87,062 in 1851 to 386,947 in 1911 – while Dublin had a very modest increase of 18 per cent, from 258,369 to 304,802. Belfast's huge increase was partly due to the extension of the city boundaries at the expense of Antrim and Down by an act from 1896.[142]

In 1911, the religious composition of Fermanagh was 56.2 per cent Catholic and 43.8 per cent Protestant.[143]

Chapter 3

THE LAND WAR IN FERMANAGH (1879–1883)

When the Irish National Land League[144] was founded in 1879, with the aim of abolishing landlordism and enabling tenant farmers to own the land they worked on, it attracted support from both Catholic and Protestant farmers in the poorer western counties of Ulster, including Fermanagh.

Ulster support for the Land League continued to spread despite the existence of the so-called 'Ulster Tenant-Right Custom' – the settlers who came from England and Scotland had come over under the premise of obtaining security of tenure from the undertakers that was equal to that of English tenants.[145] In 1894, a barrister, W.F. Bailey, wrote that this custom likely originated in the early seventeenth century and was the direct outcome of the Ulster plantation, when 500,000 acres of land were forfeited to the Crown. The settlers built their own houses and made improvements at their own expense. They were granted fixity of tenure at a fair rent with the right of free sale of their interest in a farm. The 1870 Land Act legalised the 'Ulster Custom', but paradoxically, because of its wording, it weakened the position of Ulster farmers.[146]

Frank Thompson argues that in no other county in Ulster did the Irish National Land League have a greater impact on landlord-tenant relations than in Fermanagh. [147] This was despite the fact that Fermanagh had played no part in the tenant-right agitation in the late 1840s.[148] He observes that there was little evidence during the 1870s to suggest that tenants in the county would 'throw themselves wholeheartedly' into the land war.[149]

This situation changed with the agricultural depression in the late 1870s. In 1879, the worst harvest since the famine was experienced throughout Ireland. It was the coldest, wettest year since records began in 1766. Small farmers suffered greatly, and many of them were evicted for owing two or three years' rent. The collapse of agricultural prices had the effect of universalising demands for rent reduction, including in Fermanagh.

A meeting of 'pretty large dimensions' was held at Belcoo on St Stephen's Day, 26 December 1879.[150] This early meeting did not have Protestant support, and many priests were in attendance. Such meetings in Fermanagh at this time were greatly facilitated by the expansion of the railway network. A new line had recently been opened from Enniskillen to Sligo.[151] The first railway line in Fermanagh ran from Derry to Enniskillen and had been opened in August 1854.[152]

In March 1880, James Maguire of Ederney organised a second meeting, and on 26 August, the first public demonstration was held near Arney. A huge 'Céad Míle Fáilte' banner hung over a lane into the field where the meeting was being held and green flags hung all around. It looked like a typical nationalist meeting, but in fact, a quarter of the attendance was Protestant.[153]

It was reported that 'one of the signs of the times is the union of the Orangemen, Protestants and Catholics, in accepting the League in Derrygonnelly.' Two Orange lodges in Fermanagh had their warrants cancelled because of the Land League activity of their members. Tyrone landlord Hugh Montgomery wrote to the Prime Minister, Gladstone, to warn him that some Fermanagh farmers, Protestant as well as Catholic, were joining the Land League, believing it to be the best way to lend support to Gladstone's proposed land legislation.[154]

Also, in March 1880, in a visible effort to prevent such unity of purpose between Protestants and Catholics, Viscount Crichton and Captain Mervyn Archdale arranged meetings around the county at Letterbreen, Derrygonnelly, Roslea, Tempo, Newtownbutler and Lisnaskea to discuss tenant rights, drainage of Lough Erne and the general welfare of tenant farmers.[155] At these meetings they tried to exploit Protestant fears.[156]

In anticipation of a mass meeting due to be held in Belleek in November 1880, a number of local magistrates met in Enniskillen courthouse following a special summons from the Earl of Erne, Lord Lieutenant of Fermanagh. About forty were present, including the Earl of Enniskillen. The object of the meeting was kept private, but it was believed that those attending discussed the action to be taken with regard to the planned Land League meeting at which two Irish Parliamentary Party MPs, Charles Stewart

Parnell and John Dillon, had been announced as speakers. Senior police were also in attendance.[157]

Two days later, it was reported that 'the Orange landlords of Ulster' were anxious to have the land question settled because they feared the Land League would spread to that province. It was reported that 'the movement would go into Ulster and on next Tuesday' a meeting would be held where the Orangemen of Fermanagh 'would take their stand beside their Catholic brethren'.[158] On the same day, a placard was posted throughout the county by John Porter (Archdale) of Bellisle, the unsuccessful Liberal candidate at two previous elections. The poster stated, 'The Land League is about to invade this county with plans which would raise civil war.' He requested local men to help him at Belleek to protest quietly 'against mad and greedy schemes of plunder against private property, against political union'.[159]

However, the protest failed to materialise and the Belleek meeting went ahead successfully with a Protestant chairman, Jeremiah Jordan.[160] The claim was that they were not trying to settle a sectarian question but rather one that affected 'every man who tilled an acre of ground'. James O'Kelly MP, one of the speakers at Belleek, said the advocates of landlordism claimed that 'the men of Ulster were satisfied with something they called the Ulster Tenant-right' – that it was a sufficient protection for the tenant farmer. He argued, however, that it actually protected the landlord. Parnell, speaking as a Protestant, appealed for unity among Catholics and Protestants.[161] After the Belleek meeting, Catholic and Protestant farmers from that area of Fermanagh 'united in sympathy' and moved on to Enniskillen on 10 November.

The next meeting was held later that month at Swanlinbar, County Cavan, at which many Protestants and Orangemen from Fermanagh attended. No emblems or colours were worn out of respect for them. The Land League was said to be determined that the Orangemen should forget 'past feuds and differences' and that nothing should oppose 'their united help with their fellow-countrymen'.[162]

James O'Kelly, on returning to Dublin, said he was happy to announce that there was not a single Ulster county without branches of the organisation, and that the Protestant element of the population was 'coming in rapidly' to the branches. They had had Orangemen, including deputy grandmasters, on their platforms at every meeting in the north. He had received a letter from Jeremiah Jordan, chairman of the Belleek branch, stating that he believed, within a month or two, 'there would be no distinction between Orangeman and Catholic in the north of Ireland.'[163] Jordan was the son of a Brookeborough farmer and was himself a large businessman.[164]

Prior to a proposed Land League meeting in Brookeborough, the landlords planned to hold a protest at the same time. A placard was posted which stated, 'Orangemen of Fermanagh, will you allow your county to be disgraced by letting a Land League meeting be held in Brookeborough on 7th December? Assemble in your thousands on Tuesday and give Parnell and his associates a "warm" welcome.'[165] By this time, many new Land League branches had been formed in Fermanagh, and many Protestants and Orangemen had joined.[166]

Between eight and ten thousand people, a considerable proportion of them Protestants, gathered in a field at Brookeborough for the Land League meeting on 7 December. The two chief organisers were both masters of Orange lodges.[167] Four magistrates had issued a proclamation banning the meeting amidst rumours that Newtownbutler Orangemen would disrupt the proceedings. When the people assembled in the main street, a force of military and police were dispatched.[168]

James O'Kelly and Andrew Kettle[169] were informed that the Riot Act had already been read twice and the meeting was prohibited. (The Riot Act was passed into law in 1763. It was enacted to deal with 'unlawful, riotous, tumultuous assembly'. It gave powers to Justices of the Peace, Sheriffs, Bailiffs, etc. to go to a location where such an assembly was taking place and read the act to those assembled there. If they failed to disperse, they would be apprehended.) Two Protestants had already been arrested for shouting, 'God save the Queen and down with the landlords.'[170] O'Kelly was ordered out of the field by the magistrate, Harvey, who refused to tell him what the geographical limits of the proclamation were. Eventually, the meeting went ahead about a mile outside Brookeborough, on the road to Maguiresbridge. Francis Little, master of the Grand Orange Lodge of Clabby, took the chair. He said he was proud to stand there 'as good a Protestant and Orangeman as any' on the Colebrooke estate.[171] On the following day, a Land League branch was formed at Enniskillen.[172]

Col. Irvine's agent, Edward Atthill, tried but failed to stop a Land League meeting that was set to establish a branch at Ederney on 10 December. Over a hundred new members were enrolled on that day.[173]

Shortly before Christmas, ahead of a planned Derrygonnelly meeting, fears were expressed that it would be banned. A rumour circulated that Orangemen of the barony on the opposite side of Lough Erne were going to cross the lake with Captain Mervyn Archdale at their head and attack the meeting. Captain Archdale duly arrived but returned home, as he couldn't bring himself to oppose the troops who were present.[174] He later called on all loyal Orangemen to drive the League out of Derrygonnelly.[175] Richard Breen, a Protestant and the president of the local Land League branch, presided; George Darragh and Mr Forde, two Methodist clergymen, were on the platform. Forde said nine-tenths of his people wanted a change in the land laws. After dark, some rioting occurred. Sticks and pistols were reported to have been used. Some of those attending were said to have been 'waylaid and attacked'.[176]

A large meeting of landlords was held in Enniskillen on 27 December. Members of the County Fermanagh Grand Orange Lodge, who were to meet at the same time, were asked to support the landlords' meeting but they refused. A placard convening the meeting was signed by the earls of Belmore and Lanesborough, Sir Victor Brooke and others. The notice announced that resolutions were passed expressing a wish for a satisfactory settlement of the land question – one that would ensure every tenant was protected from arbitrary eviction and unreasonable rent and would secure to him the value of his improvements. The landlords had stopped short of granting free sale, which they claimed would lead to Catholics taking over Protestant farms. The Earl of Enniskillen and Viscount Crichton refused to attend the landlords' meeting because they objected even to the limited programme suggested.[177] The meeting recorded a protest against the 'principles and tyrannical practices of the Land League, the avowed object of whose leading promoters is to drive all landlords out of Ireland as a step towards dissolving the union between Great Britain and Ireland.'[178]

In January 1881, further meetings were held at Tempo, County Fermanagh and Fintona, County Tyrone. Francis Little took the chair in Tempo, where the crowd was mainly composed of Protestants. Little had recently been expelled from his Orange Lodge.[179] At Fintona, a heavy fall of snow did not deter the tenant farmers of Tyrone and Fermanagh from attending. There the chair was taken by John Batten Gravally, a Protestant and a large tenant farmer and mill-owner.[180] By March, Fermanagh had twenty branches of the Land League.[181]

In the same month, the Protection of Persons and Property Act, or the Coercion Act, was implemented; it gave powers to intern suspects without trial and allowed for the arrest and legal detention 'of any person suspected of an act of violence or intimidation'.[182]

Undeterred, a large meeting was organised for Derrychara, Enniskillen, on 22 March at which between seven and eight thousand people were present. It was reported that the majority of the attendees were well-to-do farmers and Protestants, including three Methodist clergymen; many of them were Orangemen. Speaking at the meeting, T.P. O'Connor MP referred to the Marquess of Ely's[183] estate, which had withdrawn abatements (reductions in rent)[184] since the Coercion Act became law.[185]

Around that time, John Crichton, 4th Earl of Erne,[186] formed the Fermanagh Defence Association, urging local Protestants to 'resist the Nationalist invasion of Ulster' and not to employ Catholics.[187] He tried to incite the Protestant members by remarking that the Land League 'continues the agitation of 1641'.[188]

In July, the various Fermanagh branches of the Land League held a conference in Enniskillen Town Hall. Figures were produced which showed that the organisation there was in 'a flourishing state' and new members were joining daily. Rev. Harold Rylett and Francis Little were present from Central Branch. Little told those assembled that he 'had been thrown out "on the back of the ditch" and there was not a man dared to give me a night's lodging'.[189] This was a reference to the fact that he, his wife and three children had been evicted from the estate of Sir Victor Brooke at Colebrooke. An ejection action had been taken against him in May for non-payment of rent for eighteen months. His wife's former, late husband had been the actual tenant on the farm.[190] Nevertheless, Thompson argues that – possibly because of the strength of the league – eviction was not widely used by landlords in Fermanagh as a weapon against the Land League.[191]

Action was taken by landlords to try to have martial law proclaimed in areas in which the league was active. Mervyn Archdale and the agent of the Marquess of Ely wrote to Dublin Castle complaining about intimidation and outrages around Derrygonnelly and Belleek, urging that the areas be proclaimed.[192] Reports from resident magistrates, however, contradicted these claims. Fermanagh, in fact, had the lowest number of agrarian offences of any Ulster county during the months of the most intense league activity.[193]

Parnell and Andrew Kettle were arrested under the Coercion Act in October 1881 and were detained in Kilmainham Gaol. From prison, Parnell arranged for the 'No Rent Manifesto' to be published in his newspaper, the *United Ireland.* The 'No Rent Manifesto' called for a campaign of passive resistance, by the entire population of small tenant farmers, by withholding rents in order to obtain large rent abatements under the second 1881 Land Act. The intention was to 'put the Act to the test' and prove its inadequacy to provide for the core demands of tenants – fair rent, fixity of tenure and free sale.[194] This direct confrontation with the government led to the Land League being banned. On 20 October 1881, a proclamation was issued prohibiting meetings taking place under the title of 'Land League'.[195]

In the spring of 1882, Gladstone decided to negotiate directly with Parnell, resulting in the Kilmainham Treaty of 25 April whereby the government agreed to expand the 1881 Land Act to cover tenant farmers in arrears and to phase out coercion. Parnell, in return, agreed to withdraw the manifesto and bring violence to an end.[196]

After the imprisonment of Parnell and the other leaders, and the banning of the Land League, Ulster Protestant support for the organisation began to fall away. Now with a clear field, the landlords pressed home their exploitation of Protestant fears and eventually succeeded in causing divisions between Protestant and Catholic tenant farmers. Tenants in Fermanagh took immediate advantage of the 1881 Land Act and Protestant support was withdrawn.[197]

In August 1882, Viscount Crichton, Viscount Cole, William Archdale, Hon. Col. Crichton, Hon. Cavendish Butler, Edward Archdale and many other landlords presided at an Orange demonstration at Enniskillen. Viscount Crichton said Parnell had offered inducements to the Orangemen but they had been refused. He told the crowds that Parnell had a greater objective – Ireland for the Irish. They knew the object was to get rid of Protestants 'but the Protestants were not ready to go'. It was proposed that

> We, the Orangemen of the County Fermanagh desire to express our sentiments of sorrow and indignation at the disgrace brought upon our country by the murderous outrages committed by a disloyal section of the community in other counties and we pledge ourselves to uphold law and order to the utmost of our power and also to resist any attempt to sever the union between Great Britain and Ireland.[198]

In the autumn of 1882, Parnell disbanded the Land League and established in its place the Irish National League. The aims of the new organisation were more political than agrarian, the main objective being to assist the Home Rule movement.[199] This decision sounded the death knell to Protestant and Catholic cohesion around the land issue.

About a year later, in October 1883, two opposing meetings were held in Roslea – Orange and nationalist. Lord Crichton presided at the Orange meeting with Lord Rossmore, Sir John Leslie, Col. Lloyd, Major Saunderson and Captain Somerset Maxwell. Lord Crichton told his audience that the Parnellites 'had torn off the mask'. It was no longer talk about tenant rights and peasant proprietorship but 'the land for the people'. He warned that after the Parnellites had dispossessed the Protestants of their lands, they would go for a parliament in College Green and the establishment of an independent republic. [200]

At the Irish National League meeting half a mile away, Tim Healy MP said that the farmers of Ulster wanted to know from Lord Crichton what reduction Lord Enniskillen was making in his rents. He appealed to the Protestant tenants not to let religious differences prevent them from helping themselves and not to imagine that Catholics 'desired to interfere with any man's conscience'. He asked them to join their brethren in the other parts of Ireland in fighting for their rights.[201]

Sadly, the short-lived social cohesion and harmony between Catholics and Protestants had come to an end. Ulster's Catholics rallied to the banner of Home Rule, but faced with a clear threat, Ulster Protestants, particularly landlords and tenants, sank their differences to defend the union. The major landlords of the county had done all in their power to cause division between Protestant and Catholic tenant farmers, and eventually they succeeded when they could point to Parnell's new organisation as being political rather than agrarian.

Chapter 4

EARLY TWENTIETH CENTURY

HOME RULE, THE FIRST WORLD WAR AND THE EASTER RISING

Gradually, as the nineteenth century drew to a close and the twentieth dawned, Fermanagh became more segregated. When Gladstone introduced the third Home Rule Bill at Westminster on 11 April 1912, despite the derisory amount of power it offered to a devolved government in Ireland, it provoked such a hysterical reaction among unionists that, within a short time, it brought Ireland to the brink of civil war. Two days before the bill was introduced, Andrew Bonar Law, Conservative Party leader, with Edward Carson[202] by his side, reviewed a march at Balmoral, Belfast of 100,000 opponents to the bill. Carson began his campaign against Home Rule in Enniskillen in September 1912, when he, along with the Earl of Erne, was led into the town.[203] He was the first to sign the Ulster Covenant[204] at Belfast City Hall on 28 September.

A meeting of unionist clubs was held at Crom Castle, The Earl of Erne's estate, in early 1913; they discussed the formation of a volunteer force to oppose Home Rule while continual drilling was taking place there by more than seventy local farmers.[205] The Ulster Volunteer Force was established in January. In July, Rev. W.B. Stack was identified as a prime mover in the importation of arms into Fermanagh. The RIC County Inspector reported:

> At a secret meeting of five delegates of the UVF, held at Florencecourt, the Rev Mr Stack, organiser, is said to have stated that a number of arms have been received into the county, via Bundoran and Ballyshannon, and brought up to Kesh and Irvinestown by small boats.[206]

Stack acted as camp adjutant at a UVF camp in Crom Castle in November.[207] By mid-1914, almost 3,000 Fermanagh men had joined the Ulster Volunteer Force to oppose Home Rule.[208] The whole force was commanded by Viscount Crichton, Earl of Erne.[209]

On the nationalist side, Fermanagh became exposed to the Gaelic League and the Gaelic Athletic Association (GAA). The county's first GAA club was founded in Newtownbutler in 1887.[210] By 1911, the Irish language was being taught in all Catholic schools in the county, and one of the first battalions of the Irish Volunteers was formed in Fermanagh. This reflected the growing conviction that it was necessary to form a counter-organisation to the UVF.[211]

In the year before the First World War broke out, Barton argues, Fermanagh emerged more sharply divided on grounds of religion and politics than ever before in its recent history.[212] The political power and social leadership of the Anglo-Irish gentry was perpetuated and enhanced during this period. They continued to be looked up to as natural leaders, their military traditions and training essential in these turbulent years.[213]

When the war broke out, two hundred Fermanagh members of the UVF and the Redmondite National Volunteers immediately enlisted in the British Army while the breakaway Irish Volunteers, who disagreed with John Redmond, the leader of the Irish Parliamentary Party, chose not to do so. Thirteen battalions of the Royal Inniskilling Fusiliers took part in the war, including both Protestants and Catholics. Sir Basil Brooke served in France and Gallipoli.[214]

In terms of loss of life of Fermanagh men in the First World War, Jason Myers, a US historian, claims that 510 were killed from all regiments.[215] As a percentage of the male population of Fermanagh aged between 15 and 54 in the 1911 Census, the loss was 3.10 per cent. This compares with Down – 3.98 per cent; Derry – 3.81 per cent; Armagh – 3.74 per cent; Dublin – 3.69 per cent; Antrim – 3.37 per cent; and Carlow – 3.24 per cent. All other counties lost less than 3 per cent of their male population within this age range.[216] In terms of actual numbers lost, Fermanagh was well down the list. Antrim (including Belfast) lost 5,122; Dublin – 4,973; Cork – 2,226; Down – 2,056; Derry – 1,343; Armagh – 1,128; Tyrone – 1,073; Tipperary – 1,039; Limerick – 827; Mayo – 723; Donegal – 720; Galway – 683; Waterford – 648; Kildare – 567; and Wexford – 538. All other counties lost less than 500 men.[217]

The Easter Rising against British rule in Ireland began on Easter Monday, 24 April 1916, when the Irish Republican Brotherhood (IRB) and Irish Citizen Army seized key positions in Dublin and, from their headquarters in the General Post Office, declared a republic. At least twelve Fermanagh men fought with the rebels.

Three of the twelve were Protestants – George Irvine, William Scott and a man called Wilson. George Irvine, from Enniskillen, was the most prominent of the three. He was a member of the Church of Ireland and had been educated at Portora Royal School.[218] He trained as a teacher, and at the turn of the century, he moved to Dublin to take up a teaching post at a Church of Ireland school in Rathmines. He joined the Gaelic League in 1905 and became an ardent advocate of the Irish language. Two years later, he joined the IRB. During the Rising, he fought in the South Dublin Union under Éamonn Ceannt.[219] He was sentenced to death but had his sentence commuted. Like the other prisoners, he was released in 1917 and was chaired through the streets of Enniskillen. He attended a service in the Church of Ireland in his volunteer's uniform and refused to stand for the British national anthem.[220] He fought on the republican side in the Irish Civil War. He died in June 1954[221] and was buried in Mount Jerome Cemetery, Dublin.[222] Fermanagh County Museum recently acquired a Christmas card designed by him.[223]

William John Scott was also a member of the Church of Ireland and, in later years, joined the Plymouth Brethren. He was a bricklayer and a strong trade unionist. At the time of the Rising, he was living in the Dublin tenements. He was a member of James Connolly's Irish Citizen Army and fought under Constance Markievicz and Michael Mallin in St Stephen's Green.[224] He, too, is buried in Mount Jerome Cemetery, Dublin.[225]

Wilson (first name unknown) was a native of Enniskillen and reportedly kept a boot shop in East Bridge Street. When his shop was burned, he lost everything and moved to Dublin.[226]

Three Derrygonnelly men fought in the Rising – Patrick Maguire, Joe Duffy and a man called Meehan. Afterwards they were imprisoned in Stafford Gaol, Wormwood Scrubs and Frongoch Camp, respectively. John Joseph Scollan, a native of South Shields whose parents were both from Enniskillen,[227] served as a captain in the GPO and was complimented by Pearse and Connolly for the courage of his company during the fighting.[228]

He had previously moved to Enniskillen and worked for a time with the *Impartial Reporter* newspaper.[229] Two other men were Owen Greene from Mullaghdun, who fought at Boland's Mill, and Philip Cassidy from Letterbreen. Other men who took part were Michael Love, who fought at Jacob's Biscuit Factory, and brothers Rommy and Conway McGinn, who were first cousins of Michael Love.[230]

Owen Greene was in business in Dublin and later owned a farm and drapery shop in Kinlough, County Leitrim.[231] Phil Cassidy, at the time of the Rising, was also in business in Dublin. He died in 1938 and is buried in Arney cemetery.[232]

A conference was held in Belfast in June 1916 which was attended by nationalists from the six counties that were, at that time, being proposed to be exempted from Home Rule. By a vote of nearly two to one, it was decided to accept the plan but as a temporary measure only. The Fermanagh delegates opposed the plan and, in particular, the exclusion of Fermanagh and Tyrone from Home Rule.[233]

In the general election of 1918, Sinn Féin decided to contest both Fermanagh seats. In south Fermanagh they won the seat with a majority of 2,281 votes, but they narrowly lost the north Fermanagh seat to unionist Edward Mervyn Archdale,[234] by 532 votes. Overall, Fermanagh therefore voted for independence by 1,749 votes.[235] This was hardly surprising considering Catholics were in the majority in the county.

THE GOVERNMENT OF IRELAND ACT (1920)

When Britain was preparing to partition Ireland through the passage of the Government of Ireland Act in March 1920, Ulster unionists, led by the advocacy of James Craig (who would become the first Prime Minister of the new Northern Ireland), lobbied heavily to steer the British government away from recommending a nine-county Northern Ireland. The unionists were doubtful the northern parliament would be able to govern in areas where there was a nationalist majority and greatly preferred that the scheme should be limited to the six 'Protestant' counties.[236] The British government appointed a Cabinet committee to draw up a new home rule bill for Ireland, which was chaired by Walter Long,[237] the former Ulster Unionist

Party leader. Other members included the Chief Secretary, Ian Macpherson and the Lord Lt of Ireland, John French. The committee proposed the creation of two Irish home rule entities – northern Ireland and southern Ireland. The bill was finally passed into law in November 1920.[238]

Of the six so-called 'Protestant' counties, there were Catholic majorities in the city of Derry, and in counties Fermanagh and Tyrone. One-third of the population was nationalist, as was half of its territory. Although the British government favoured the nine-county option in order to maintain a religious balance, they agreed to legislate for the six-county option.[239]

This legislation saw unionists abandon their co-religionists in Donegal, Cavan and Monaghan in the rationalisation that a six-county state was the maximum territory they could control.[240] Having played a significant role in mobilising opposition to Home Rule, the approximately 70,000 Protestants[241] of these counties regarded Carson's and Craig's acceptance of a six-county northern state as the ultimate betrayal. During the Home Rule crisis, recruitment into the Ulster Volunteer Force had been higher in Cavan, Donegal and Monaghan than in Antrim, Down or Belfast relative to population.[242] The aim, thereafter, of the abandoned southern Protestants/unionists was to make the best of their lot and secure the most advantageous deal possible in the new Free State.[243]

Partition's major victims, however, were the nationalists who suddenly found themselves a minority within the new Northern Ireland, comprising just over a third of its population. By contrast, Protestants in the newly created Free State were much better placed than Catholics were in the new Northern Ireland. Donnacha Ó Beacháin observes that they were 'essentially a ruling elite imbued with the confidence that came from a history of economic, social and political dominance, and of governance'.[244] This mindset empowered them to make demands of the government. As a result, half of the seats in the senate were reserved for unionists and a proportional representation electoral system was introduced.[245]

It has been claimed that the Government of Ireland Act was allowed to pass relatively unchallenged due to the absence of nationalist representation in Westminster – only seven Irish Parliamentary Party members after the 1918 general election, and Sinn Féin maintained a policy of abstention.[246] The presence of Sinn Féin's elected members, however, would have made little difference, as Lloyd George's coalition held over 500 seats.[247]

Elections were held in both parts of Ireland in May 1921. In Northern Ireland, forty unionists and only twelve Sinn Féin and Nationalist Party[248] members were returned. This was a huge disappointment for Sinn Féin, as they had expected to win more than a third of the seats. The unionists, on the other hand, expected to win only thirty-three seats.[249] It is clear that unionists turned out in massive numbers – in Belfast, for example, the turnout was a remarkable 92 per cent.[250]

Sinn Féin and the Nationalist Party did, however, have a significant victory in Fermanagh and Tyrone. The two counties had been joined to form one eight-seat constituency. Four unionists, three Sinn Féin members and one nationalist were elected. The total unionist votes came to 37,935 while the nationalist votes were 45,766, a majority of 7,831 or 54.7 per cent. The nationalists of Fermanagh and Tyrone believed that their wish to be included under a Dublin parliament must be respected and so their successful Sinn Féin candidates took their seats in Dáil Éireann.[251]

After the overall election results, Sinn Féin and the Nationalist Party protested vehemently that the six-county voting area was gerrymandered in favour of unionism and that intimidation was practised on a large scale.[252]

In the aftermath, the *Irish Times* proclaimed triumphantly that 'North-East Ulster has voted overwhelmingly for the Government of Ireland Act'.[253]

James Craig moved quickly to introduce local government changes that removed proportional representation and reconfigured council areas in anticipation of a boundary commission being established. He was determined to maximise unionist representation in border areas and especially to subvert the nationalist claim of controlling Fermanagh and Tyrone county councils.

THE WAR OF INDEPENDENCE IN FERMANAGH

Fermanagh enjoyed relative peace during the War of Independence, particularly in its early days. There were a number of IRA raids on houses and barracks for arms and ammunition, but it wasn't until 1921, after the Government of Ireland Act had been passed, that more serious attacks occurred.

In April 1920, Captain Sir Basil Brooke set up Fermanagh Vigilance, a vigilante group, to provide defence against incursions by the IRA.[254] This militia, along with others in Antrim and Belfast, was incorporated into the Ulster Special Constabulary (USC), which also contained many UVF members.[255] Basil Brooke boasted that Fermanagh had the highest percentage of loyalists in the special police of any county in Ulster.[256] Men were also recruited from Orange lodges.[257] By 1922, there were 50,000 members of the police and Special Constabulary, constituting about one-sixth of the adult male Protestant population. The police were supplemented by sixteen battalions of the British Army. Generally, however, the regular army only had a permanent residence in large towns such as Omagh and Enniskillen. The USC, like the UDR later, were the most visible security agents of the state in rural areas, which was obviously very polarising for the community.[258]

The new state's military might was reinforced by the notorious Special Powers Act, enacted in March 1922, which provided for the death penalty, flogging, arrest without warrant and the prohibition of inquests.[259]

On 21 February 1921, the village of Roslea was practically razed, as Catholic-owned property was looted and burned by the B-Specials, a militia that was part of the Ulster Special Constabulary. This attack was a reprisal for the attempted murder of Constable George Lester as he opened his shop in the village. Livingstone claims that Lester had been searching Catholic children for IRA documents and persisted with this activity even after receiving a threatening letter from the IRA.[260] Revenge for the attempted murder came that same evening; B-Specials and UVF men descended on Roslea, attacking the Parochial House and burning ten Catholic-owned homes. The roads out of Roslea were filled with people carrying whatever possessions they could gather as they fled the flames that were engulfing the village.[261] The *Irish Times* reported that the attack began at around 10 p.m. when the houses of prominent residents were visited by armed men. The first house set on fire was that of Philip Trainor; Matthew Finnegan's shop was next.[262] Edward Burke, an academic and author, claims that loyalists from Crom Castle, the demesne of the Earl of Erne, were also involved in the attack on Roslea.[263]

Retaliation for the burning of Roslea came exactly one month later. Organised attacks against unionists were carried out on 21 March, when two B-Specials were shot dead and others were wounded. The two men killed were sergeants William Gordon of Rathkeevan and Samuel Nixon of Tattymore. Gordon was caretaker on the Madden property at Spring Grove, while Nixon was a farmer. Three houses were burned whereas others were wrecked.[264]

After the signing of the Treaty in December 1921, feelings ran high along the border. On 21 January 1922, the Ulster Gaelic football final between Monaghan and Derry was due to be played in Derry. On the previous evening, six carloads left Monaghan to transport the team. Many of the team were members of the IRA and were carrying their revolvers. They were stopped by a group of B-Specials en route, and when it was discovered that they were armed, ten men were arrested. One of the men was Dan Hogan, Officer Commanding (O/C) of the Fifth Northern Division, whose brother, Tipperary hurler Michael Hogan,[265] was shot dead in Croke Park on Bloody Sunday, 21 November 1920. The arrested men were brought to Omagh and were interned in Derry shortly afterwards. As a result, the IRA was just waiting for a chance of reprisal.[266]

They didn't have long to wait. Just a few weeks later, on 11 February, IRA volunteers stopped a group of B-Specials on a train in Clones en route from Belfast to Enniskillen. They too were armed. A gunfight began in which one IRA officer and four B-Specials were killed. The remaining constables were captured. The Specials, eighteen in number, were travelling to Enniskillen in order to strengthen three platoons that were engaged in patrolling the border. They had to change trains at Clones, and it was when they were seated in the Enniskillen train, ready for departure, that the incident began. Only six of the eighteen carried rifles. The *Irish Times* Clones correspondent described the scene:

> Commandant [Matt] Fitzpatrick [from Wattlebridge] and about 11 IRA men in uniform were on duty at the railway. When the train was about to depart, Fitzpatrick approached the carriage in which they [the B-Specials] were seated and ordered them to put up their hands. Some of the men obeyed the order and the Commandant remarked that, if the hands went up, there would be no shooting. A Special left another compartment and fired at the Commandant, who was shot through the head. Rapid firing then took place from rifles, revolvers and a machine gun.[267]

The four B-Specials who were killed were: Temporary Sergeant W.K. Doherty from Derry City, Constable McMahon from Belfast, Constable J.A. Abraham from Ballinamallard and Constable J. Lewis from Omagh.[268] Some of the Specials were taken prisoner, while others escaped across the border. Those being held were released the following day and made their way to Enniskillen.[269]

The last battle of the War of Independence was fought in Pettigo and Belleek. The battle took place between late May and early June 1922, almost six months after the Treaty was signed and shortly before the outbreak of the civil war. It was the largest military engagement between Irish and British forces since the Easter Rising.[270] It symbolised a final effort by republicans to contest Britain's continued presence in Ireland and was the very last time that pro- and anti-Treaty troops joined forces. There were fifty-five pro-Treaty Free State troops and thirty-one anti-Treaty IRA members involved.[271] At that time, many IRA volunteers from Tyrone and Fermanagh who had been forced to go 'on-the-run' had relocated to Pettigo and Belleek to be ready to participate in Collins's planned 'Northern Offensive', due to take place in May–June 1922. The offensive was designed to collapse the Stormont administration and force the British to renegotiate the Treaty. The presence of Irish forces in significant numbers in the area drew the ire of the unionist administration.[272]

On 27 May, about 100 B-Specials, led by Sir Basil Brooke, crossed Lough Erne in a pleasure steamer with a flotilla of small boats and landed near Belleek. They marched to Magheramenagh Castle, about 4 miles from Belleek, the residence of Catholic priest Fr Lorcán Ó Cíaráin, and ordered him to leave, which he did. They took up defensive positions there but soon realised their vulnerability to attack. They were forced by thirty IRA men to abandon the castle, from where they retreated to Buck Island on Lough Erne. Throughout the following week, the Irish forces fought off a number of attacks from a combined force of B-Specials, RUC and, later, British soldiers.[273]

On 31 May, word of the battle reached Michael Collins, who was meeting Winston Churchill in London. Churchill was incensed and demanded to know if Free State troops were involved. Collins denied that they were and, at that stage, believed it. However, he continued to deny their involvement even after he became aware of the facts when he returned to Dublin.[274] Churchill ordered British forces based in Enniskillen, including artillery, to attack Irish positions in Pettigo and Belleek. Hopelessly outnumbered, more than sixty members of the Irish force were evacuated from Pettigo. By 4 June, Pettigo was in the hands of the British, who then turned their attention to Belleek. They shelled Belleek Fort, which was soon evacuated by its IRA garrison. All was over by 8 June. Those killed on the Irish side were: Patrick Flood, Pettigo; Bernard McCanny and William Kearney, Drumquinn, County Tyrone; and William Deasley, Dromore, County Tyrone. It is unknown how many died on the British side.[275]

Liam Ó Duibhir observes that Collins believed the Irish force would be facing the Special Constabulary, but Churchill made the call to send in the military, which Collins had not anticipated. He noted that 'fewer than 100 Irishmen in their teens and 20s managed to keep the British Army at bay for almost a week.'[276]

Ninety-four years after the War of Independence, George Lunt, whose grandfather, Sgt William Gordon, was shot dead by the IRA on 21 March 1921, told his story in an oral history project – 'Border roads to Memories & Reconciliation':

> My mother was born on March 26 1921 in the townland of Scribby, in Clogh, near Roslea. Her father, William Gordon, was shot by the IRA on the night of March 21 in the family home in the townland of Rathkeevan, just a couple of miles along the road from Scribby. These were very difficult times for the families on both sides of the 'new' border. In 1920 the British Government passed the Home Rule for Ireland Act and a provisional border was drawn separating 6 counties of Northern Ireland from the remaining 26 counties of the rest of Ireland. The border had major implications for this area of Fermanagh and Monaghan. Neighbours and families were suddenly separated from each other and everyday tasks such as shopping, buying and selling livestock, going to school, going to church, suddenly took on a whole new dimension. My grandfather was active in the USC or B-Specials, a quasi-military militia set up in October 1920 as part of the 'defence' of Northern Ireland against the perceived threat from the impending separation of Ireland from the UK. Many of the Protestant families from the Roslea area strongly supported the B-Specials and saw them as a key element in protecting them from the activities of the Nationalist IRA. In February 1921, the local B-Specials carried out a major exercise in Roslea, turning many Nationalist/ Catholic families from their homes and 10 homes were burned, ironically there was only one death that day and that was a B-Special who accidentally shot himself. The raid was justified as a reprisal for the earlier attempted murder of one of the local shopkeepers, George Lester. Needless to say, the

> B-Specials found arms and ammunition in several homes and so far as the Protestant community was concerned, the raid was entirely justified. The local IRA of course took an entirely different view and planned a major reprisal which took place on the night of March 21 1921 when 16 Unionist homes were attacked and members of the B-Specials were especially targeted. My grandfather was shot that night as was a B-Special colleague of his, Sam Nixon. My grandfather had been an active member of the local Orange and Black Lodge and indeed was the Master. Sam Nixon was also an active Lodge member and both are commemorated in the Lodge banner [...]
>
> My grandparents [grandmother and step-grandfather] both made their final crossing from where they were carried across the border, round the spikes and the crater and into the church. On both occasions their coffins were carried by Protestant and Catholic neighbours alike. Despite years of troubles from these difficult days of the 1920s through the Troubles of the 60s, 70s and 80s, close neighbours put their differences aside and crossed the border together. Happily there is no trace of those borders now and it is inconceivable that they will ever return. How much better for all it would have been if the border had never been put in place at all and the island of Ireland had never been divided.[277]

THE ANGLO-IRISH TREATY

When negotiations on the Anglo-Irish Treaty began in London in October 1921, a boundary commission formed part of the discussions. Arthur Griffith[278] reported to Dublin that it would be 'a Boundary Commission to delimit the six-county area so as to give us the districts in which we have a majority'.[279]

During the negotiations, Michael Collins told Lloyd George that he (Lloyd George) was faced with the coercion of half of the area of Northern Ireland. Collins proposed that Tyrone, Fermanagh, more than half of Armagh, a great deal of Derry and a strip of Antrim 'would go with the authority they prefer'.[280] He was left with the impression, which was nowhere to be found in the subsequent written agreement, that the Boundary Commission would deliver vast territorial tracts to the south. He believed that what would remain in the north would not be viable and that it would be forced, for economic reasons, to seek unity with the rest of Ireland. Rankin argues that his belief was based on the misconception that mere physical size would dictate the economic viability of the north. As it was not a separate state, its ultimate viability would be decided by Britain, regardless of size.[281]

The text of the article to be included in the Treaty was altered by the British side, to the detriment of the Irish delegation, with a selectively inserted clause, which, although inspired by the Treaty of Versailles, diverged subtly from it. The article (Article 12 of the Anglo-Irish Treaty) with the new clause inserted read as follows:

> A commission shall be appointed by the British Government to determine in accordance with the wishes of the inhabitants, *so far as may be compatible with economic and geographical conditions* the boundaries between Northern Ireland and the rest of Ireland and for the purposes of the Government of Ireland Act 1920 and of this instrument, the boundary shall be such as may be determined by such Commission.[282] [Emphasis added]

This wording suggesting that the wishes of the inhabitants could be subordinated to other considerations was reinforced by the omission of provision for a plebiscite to determine local preferences.[283]

Griffith was warned that the clause was too vague and ambiguous, and that some geographical unit should be specified (e.g. barony or electoral division) – that a vote should be taken in this unit and the unit would automatically come to the Free State or remain in the north according to the majority of the votes.

However, the wording was not changed and Lloyd George intensified the pressure on the Irish delegates with a threat of 'immediate and terrible war' within three days if they refused to accept. The Anglo-Irish Treaty was signed on 6 December 1921. Article 12 specified that three commissioners should be appointed – one by the Irish government, one by the Northern Ireland government and one by the British government. The British appointee would also serve as chairman.

Article 12 could be interpreted in a variety of ways, but it crucially secured the signing of the Treaty and sustained the nationalist aspiration to remove partition.

From a nationalist perspective, its flaws were as follows:

- There was no contingency for Northern Ireland's refusal to appoint a commissioner – this should have been foreseen, as Northern Ireland was not a signatory to the Treaty.
- With regard to the geographical perspective, there was the failure to adopt a territorial framework – county, barony, electoral division. As would be proved in the gerrymandering of local council areas, geographical majorities and minorities could be easily manipulated.
- There was no contingency for plebiscites.
- No date was set for when the commission would meet and begin its work. Attempts by Collins to have it established were rejected on the basis that the political situation was too volatile. This was compounded by the escalation of the civil war, which claimed Collins's life. Later it was again delayed because, as Craig had refused to appoint a commissioner, legislation had to be passed in Westminster to enable the British Prime Minister to appoint a commissioner on its behalf.
- The commission was internal rather than international, which was a huge drawback in terms of its independence.

Aggravating these flaws, the Free State government imposed customs barriers that entrenched the existing boundary before the commission had even been established.[284]

The failure to recognise these problems exposed the inexperience and naivety of the Irish delegation in placing their trust in a British government that had vast experience in negotiations of this kind and had parsed every word of the article to their advantage. They were ill-prepared and no match for the likes of Lloyd George, Austen Chamberlain, Lord Birkenhead and Winston Churchill. [285] One of the Irish negotiators, Robert Barton, recorded:

> We Irishmen were nervous and ill at ease, it was our first introduction to Diplomacy. The English were at home and confident in surroundings where they had met and out-manoeuvred or intimidated their opponents in a hundred similar struggles. On the walls hung portraits of past prime ministers, the builders of Britain's Empire. Opposite to me was the portrait of Sir Robert Walpole and beneath it sat Winston Churchill.[286]

Collins and Craig met in January 1922 to try to reach agreement on the future boundary. Their views were, however, so divergent that no such agreement could be reached. Craig said Collins had shown him a map suggesting he had been promised 'almost half of Northern Ireland, including the counties of Fermanagh and Tyrone, large parts of Antrim and Down, Derry City, Enniskillen and Newry'.[287]

On 16 February 1922, Churchill, in the House of Commons, delivered his famous rhetorical speech on the 'dreary steeples of Fermanagh and Tyrone' emerging from the deluge of the First World War with 'the integrity of their quarrel' unaffected by the cataclysms of Europe. The speech was delivered in the context of the reading of the bill that would give effect to the Treaty.[288] Hints are to found in that speech regarding his preferred outcome of the proposed Boundary Commission's deliberations. He prefaced his comments by noting that 'when the time comes, Article 12 will have to be interpreted in the manner prescribed in the Treaty', and he observed that the trouble regarding boundaries related specifically to those of Fermanagh and Tyrone. He observed that the 'one weak point in the strength of Ulster' was that districts of these two counties might prefer to join the Irish Free State, and he warned that the outcome of the Boundary Commission might affect the existing frontiers prejudicially to 'the Ulster Government'.[289]

He informed the House that they had agreed to the commission 'knowing well that [...] there are also Protestant districts of great importance and considerable population and dimensions which [...] must be taken into consideration in the general question of rectifying the boundaries which is entrusted to the Boundary Commission.' He clarified that these Protestant districts were located in Donegal, Cavan and Monaghan.[290] He was anxious that the Treaty should come into force as soon as possible so that 'the Republic can be disestablished and completely put aside.'[291]

Collins regarded the Treaty as a stepping stone to full unity, and in the early months of 1922 he was doing his utmost to destabilise the northern state. Ó Beacháin believes he had 'embarked on a high risk policy with the aim of forcibly bringing down the Belfast Government and protecting the northern nationalist population.'[292]

In August 1922, Collins complained in vain that Churchill 'intended to paint Tyrone and Fermanagh with a deep orange tint' in anticipation of the operation of the Boundary Commission and to try to defraud these people of the benefits of the Treaty. Collins was killed only days later, which removed the only leader in the Irish government who had consistently made partition and the plight of northern nationalists a proactive concern.[293]

As an exercise in boundary making, the Irish example had little semblance of democratic credibility and departed from the recent precedents with which Britain was involved in post-war Europe.[294] The Versailles precedents provided adequate templates for enshrining the principle of self-determination. In Ireland, however, the people were never given a chance to vote on the issue.

Academics Thomas Leahy and Niall Ó Dochartaigh argue that the territorial settlement gave greater weight to the views of those who favoured the constitutional *status quo* – the Protestant and unionist community that asserted a strong cultural identification with Britain and the empire. The strongest indication of this partiality, they claim, was the inclusion of Fermanagh and Tyrone in Northern Ireland.[295] They contend that it was also reflected in the Boundary Commission's 'working principles, which effectively stated that no district with a significant Protestant minority would be transferred out of Northern Ireland'.[296]

Chapter 5

PARTITION CONSOLIDATED: DISCRIMINATION IN THE NEW NORTHERN STATE

At last, the Boundary Commission was established. The British government appointed Richard Feetham of the South African Supreme Court as chairman on 5 June 1924. South Africa, at the time, was a British dominion. Joseph Fisher was appointed as the Northern Ireland representative on 24 October 1924. He was a Belfast barrister and former editor of the unionist *Northern Whig* newspaper; he was a 'staunch Ulster Unionist' who had privately advocated the inclusion of Donegal into the northern statelet.[297] The Free State government appointed Eoin MacNeill, an academic, a former university professor and the serving Minister for Education, who, unlike the other two, had no legal training. Because of his duties as a minister, he was unable to devote the necessary time and energy to the commission, which, in hindsight, was a drastic mistake. Joseph Lee argues that W.T. Cosgrave and his Cabinet colleagues were aware of the forthcoming disaster and sought MacNeill as a scapegoat.[298]

Shortly after the Commission's establishment, the Free State government made a submission to the commission underlining how the wishes of the inhabitants should be ascertained. The necessity for plebiscites was emphasised. Feetham argued that such wishes could be deduced from previous elections and the census results. The Free State objected on the grounds that the council areas had been reconfigured by Craig.[299] Nevertheless, their complaints fell on deaf ears. Feetham declared that a nationalist majority in a given area did not guarantee an alteration of the border.

With regard to Fermanagh, there were submissions from the Nationalist Committee and the almost-entirely unionist Fermanagh County Council. The Nationalist Committee claimed that, in view of the fact that the 1911 census (on which Feetham had stated he was relying) showed a Catholic majority of 7,644, the county as a whole should be transferred to the Free State. The committee supported this claim by reference to the parliamentary election of 1918 in which 18,041 votes were given for nationalist candidates as against 11,292 for unionist candidates; they also made reference to local government elections of 1920, when fifty-two nationalist members were elected on the three district councils and one urban council as against forty-eight unionist members.[300] The committee submitted that the inclusion of the county in the Free State would remove the numerous economic and geographic inconveniences caused by the existing border. It urged that the county, being economically and geographically a natural unit, should not be divided by the new boundary.

Fermanagh County Council, on the other hand, contended that the county should be wholly retained within Northern Ireland, and in order to remedy economic and geographic inconveniences caused by the existing border, certain portions of the adjoining Free State counties should be transferred to Northern Ireland, notably the town and neighbourhood of Pettigo, the bridge and sluice gates at Belleek and the district electoral division of Drummully, County Monaghan, which was practically enclosed by County Fermanagh. The council claimed that the 1911 census did not accurately represent the present proportion of Catholics and Protestants, as there had been a considerable Protestant migration into Fermanagh from the Free State, and recent elections had shown that the county was about equally divided between nationalists and unionists. Evidence was provided in support of this recent migration. The names and addresses of several hundred Protestant families were submitted to the commission containing a total of 2,117 persons who had settled in the county since 1920. The commission noted that it was not possible to determine how far this migration constituted a net increase of the Protestant population.[301]

Academic and author, Terence Dooley,[302] provides the names, former addresses and occupations of all the families contained in this private census. He claims that 25 per cent of the movement northwards could be accounted for by the withdrawal of the British Army from the Free State and the disbandment of the RIC.[303] There were other factors discouraging Protestants from remaining in the Free State – separation from Britain, the burning of the Big Houses and intimidation.

Unionists were totally opposed to the establishment of the Boundary Commission. Thousands of Orangemen in Tyrone and Fermanagh prepared to resist any of its findings. They had met the commissioners in Omagh 'as a matter of courtesy' and informed them that they did not recognise their powers. Their spokesman was Captain Fyffe, who claimed to represent almost 40,000 Orangemen. He remarked that the northern government was not bound to accept their findings, whereas the Free State was bound to do so, and he informed them that the Orangemen also 'wanted east Donegal and north Monaghan'.[304]

When it eventually came to writing their report, the Boundary Commission recommended that territory be transferred both to and from Fermanagh.

The following land was to be transferred to Fermanagh from Donegal: the whole of Grousehall, a portion of Pettigo, a portion of Templecorn and the Belleek Island portion of Carrickboy. A portion of Drummully, previously located within Monaghan, was also to be transferred to Fermanagh. A total of 11,849 acres was to be transferred from the Free State to Fermanagh.

The following transfers were to be made to the Free State from Fermanagh: portions of Mallybreen, Castlecauldwell, Belleek, Inishmacsaint, Church Hill, Roogagh, Doagh, Old Barr, Glenkeel and Gortahurk; the whole of Garrison, Lattore, Holywell and Gardenhill; portions of Cuileagh, Derrylester, Kinawley, Springtown, Doon, Aghyvule, Crum, Derrysteaton, Newtownbutler, Clonkeelan, Magheraveely, Dresternan and Roslea. A total of 86,440 acres was to be transferred from Fermanagh to the Free State.[305]

The total acreage to be transferred from the Free State was 49,242 acres, while 183,290 acres were to be transferred to the Free State – a net gain of 133,448 acres for the Free State.[306] The overall effects of the Boundary Commission's recommendations would have seen the transfer of 286 square miles to the Free State and 77 square miles to Northern Ireland. It would have shortened the border by 51 miles.[307]

On 7 November 1925, however, before the Boundary Commission report could be published, an English conservative daily newspaper, the *Morning Post,* published leaked notes of the negotiations, including a draft map, which were largely accurate. It is thought likely that the leak came from Fisher. It caused panic in the Dublin Cabinet, which had never envisioned losing territory – particularly part of Donegal – to Northern Ireland.[308]

Nevertheless, they should have been aware of this possibility because, as has been noted, Churchill had hinted at such an outcome in February 1922. They must also have been informed that evidence had been gathered by the commission from residents in Donegal and Monaghan.[309] The leak was a huge embarrassment to the Free State government – there was outrage among the nationalist population that tracts of land were to be transferred to Northern Ireland. There was also consternation that Newry, which was 75 per cent Catholic, was being retained within Northern Ireland. The entire Treaty settlement hung in the balance.[310]

The issue was raised in Dáil Éireann on 19 November by Denis McCullough, an Independent deputy for Donegal. He was deeply concerned at the suggestion that tracts of east Donegal would be transferred to Northern Ireland.[311] He also noted that several towns, which 'desire by a majority of their population to be transferred under the jurisdiction of this government: Newry, Omagh, Strabane, Derry and Enniskillen', would remain in the northern state. P.J. McGoldrick, a Cumann na nGaedheal TD for Donegal, said he had voted for the Treaty in January 1922 but did so 'mainly because it contained Article 12'. He said many others did the same and observed that the Treaty would have had no possibility of being accepted if Article 12 had not been included.

On the British side, this view was echoed in the House of Lords by the Earl of Birkenhead on 9 December when he said:

> I state plainly to your Lordships that there was no signatory of that Treaty but knew that in Article 12 there lurked the elements of dynamite. We knew it well. It was forced upon us in this sense, that whether it was for good or for bad that the Treaty should be signed, it never could have been signed, it never would have been signed, without Article 12.[312]

John White, of the Farmers' Party, also representing Donegal, blamed the government 'for binding themselves in advance to accept the decision of the [Boundary] Commission under these circumstances'.[313]

On 21 November, the *Belfast Newsletter* quoted from the *Morning Post* article that Mr Cosgrave was 'none too well pleased' with their forecast of the report of the Boundary Commission and that 'the zealots of Sinn Féin have been vowing that nothing would content them but Fermanagh,

Tyrone and Londonderry.' The article highlighted the fact that Cosgrave had agreed to accept the Boundary Commission's decisions.[314]

Eoin MacNeill resigned from the commission and from his Cabinet post on 20 November.[315] Four days later, he made a statement in Dáil Éireann setting out the reasons for his resignation from both posts.[316] He accused the commission chairman of having introduced a new condition into Article 12 that did not appear in the terms of the article. The chairman, in explaining how the decisions regarding the awards were reached, had written that

> Northern Ireland must, when the boundaries have been determined, be recognisable as the same provincial entity; the changes made must not be so drastic as to destroy its identity or make it impossible for it to continue as a separate province of the UK, with its own parliament and government for provincial affairs under the Government of Ireland Act.[317]

MacNeill contended that this was a political consideration designed to override the wishes of the inhabitants. He noted that he had scrupulously observed the agreement to confidentiality which others had broken. By his own admission, he appears to have been a poor negotiator who failed to intervene at crucial times in seeking a more favourable outcome.[318]

Facing a no-confidence motion, W.T. Cosgrave headed to London the next day and was followed by a delegation forty-eight hours later, which included Kevin O'Higgins, Vice President of the Executive Council and Minister for Justice; Ernest Blythe, Minister for Finance; John O'Byrne, Attorney General; and Diarmuid O'Hegarty, Secretary to the Executive Council.

On 3 December, an agreement was reached – in the form of the Treaty (Confirmation of Amending Agreement) Act, 1925 – between the British, Free State and Northern Ireland governments that amended the Treaty of 1921. Under its terms, Article 12 was revoked, and the Free State, to its own embarrassment, was to assume responsibility for the cost of the War of Independence and would have to pay compensation for 'malicious damage' in the period from the truce to the end of the civil war. Other clauses provided for the continued payments of land annuities to the British government and the transfer of Council of Ireland powers to the Northern

Ireland government. The Free State secured some concessions regarding Article 5 of the Treaty, which committed the Free State to a share of the UK's national debt. Ó Beacháin argues that the amount the Free State was still liable to pay Britain annually 'was proportionally greater than the reparations that Germany had to pay under the Treaty of Versailles'. O'Higgins believed that this concession could 'deaden in the 26-counties the echo of the outcry of the Catholics in north-east Ulster'.[319] From an Irish perspective it was, in reality, a poor result.

Kevin O'Higgins had argued that a possible solution would be to announce far-reaching concessions to northern Catholics who had endured serious infringements of their rights over the previous three years and were, at that moment, experiencing the full weight of the B-Special mobilisation. The B-Specials had been mobilised at that time in anticipation of the publication of the Boundary Commission's report, which might be expected to lead to protests by northern nationalists. Concessions such as the restoration of proportional representation in local elections and greater equity in public appointments would help to diffuse northern Catholic anger. A recalcitrant Craig, however, refused to budge on proposal after proposal put to him by the southern delegation – the disbandment of the B-Specials, the reinstatement of proportional representation and the ending of discrimination.[320]

The agreement was debated over three days in Dáil Éireann, between 7 and 10 December. One of Cosgrave's own Cumann na nGaedheal members, Prof. William Magennis, was his main adversary. On 10 December, the final day of the debate, Magennis noted that the new settlement was the boundary drawn in 1920, 'minus all the considerations that made it not wholly unpalatable to the politicians who were in charge at that date.' He continued, 'Now, what were we talking about all those years when we protested against the partition of our beloved country.' He described the border in emotional terms as 'this red scar branded across the face of our motherland.' [321]

Even before the new agreement was voted on, Cosgrave and other Cabinet members began to distance themselves from northern nationalists. A delegation had arrived seeking a hearing of their grievances before the Dáil, but this was refused and they were sent away empty-handed. Cosgrave commented caustically that 'An occasion may arise in future in which some of our own citizens, for whom we have a direct responsibility, may have a case if a precedent has been made in respect of those for whom we only act as trustees.'[322]

The vote on the Treaty (Confirmation of Amending Agreement) Act 1925 was passed in Dáil Éireann by 71 votes to 20. The fourteen Labour Party members, four Cumann na nGaedheal deputies, one Farmer's Party member and one Independent deputy voted against the agreement. There were fourteen abstentions.[323] The Labour Party leader, Tom Johnson, encouraged Sinn Féin to enter the Dáil in order to vote against the agreement but to no avail. It is clear that their forty-seven members would not have changed the result, and political scientist Brendan O'Leary is incorrect when he contends that had they agreed, 'the Treaty would not have been ratified.'[324]

Northern nationalists had long suspected betrayal, and now their worst fears were confirmed. The claim that they had been 'thrown to the wolves' was echoed across the nationalist north, and particularly in the newspapers of the border regions. This bitterness is reflected in a comment made by Cahir Healy, the MP for South Fermanagh and a Sinn Féiner from pre-1916 days, 'John Redmond was driven from office for accepting partition for five years. Our present leaders have accepted it forever.'[325] Enda Staunton argues that the 1925 Agreement denied the legitimacy of Ireland's independence struggle, recognised partition and abandoned northern Catholics to decades of discrimination.[326]

A sense of that bitterness and disillusionment is reflected in a letter to the *Donegal Democrat* from Eugene Coyle, the parish priest of Devenish, County Fermanagh. His letter is truly a *cri de coeur*. Writing in January 1926, he claimed that it was the first time in Irish history that Irishmen had consented to and signed a pact 'permanently cutting Ireland in two'; at the same time, he wrote, they were betraying the nationalists of Ulster, of whose rights they were the guardians and trustees. This was done, he noted, by three Irishmen, W.T. Cosgrave, Kevin O'Higgins and Ernest Blythe, without consulting the Irish people. He proclaimed that John Redmond 'never did this' and 'certainly poor Collins and Griffith never did it but our latter day statesmen have done it.' He expressed the view that the whole Boundary Commission, from start to finish, was a gigantic act of treachery and deception. He echoed many others when he wrote that without Article 12 of the Treaty, there would not have been a treaty; that thousands of Irishmen had accepted the Treaty only because it included Article 12.[327]

THE CIVIL AUTHORITIES (SPECIAL POWERS) ACT (NORTHERN IRELAND) 1922

As soon as the Anglo-Irish Treaty was put into effect, the Special Powers Act (SPA) was enacted – on 7 April 1922 – by the Northern Ireland government. This act was regarded as one of the most draconian pieces of legislation ever passed in a liberal democracy.[328] The act's sweeping powers were seen by the nationalist population as a tool of unionist oppression.[329] It was used throughout the whole tenure of the Northern Ireland parliament, up to its prorogation in 1972.[330] It was initially presented as emergency legislation and had to be renewed annually.[331] In 1928, however, it was renewed for five years, and at the end of that period, in 1933, the act was made permanent.[332] In its early years it was used to return civil order, but as the violence declined, the government began to use its powers to prevent the expression of republican ideals. Any attempt to garner support for a united Ireland was regarded as an attack on the northern state. The act was used almost exclusively against the nationalist population.[333]

Its powers included internment, flogging, curfew, the closure of roads, restrictions on flying the Irish tricolour, the power to prohibit inquests – a power that prevented the investigation of illegal killings by the security forces[334]– the closure of licensed premises and the introduction of stringent requirements for the possession of firearms, explosives and petrol.[335] It also allowed for the banning of publications, newspapers, parades, meetings, the singing of rebel songs – particularly 'The Soldier's Song' – the wearing of the Easter Lily, the wearing of uniforms, the erection of republican monuments and the congregation of individuals in camping areas. Events such as commemorations of the Easter Rising and the 1798 Rebellion were banned, as were St Patrick's Day celebrations, Gaelic sports events, anti-partition meetings, unemployed workers' gatherings, céilidhís for released public representatives and various Ancient Order of Hibernians' functions.[336]

The Minister for Home Affairs in the Northern Ireland government, and members of the RUC acting at his discretion, held virtually unlimited powers of search. No distinctions were made between republicans and nationalists.[337]

In 1933, the Prime Minister, James Craig, when making the SPA permanent, said:

> We are not yet satisfied that those malcontents in our community have yet learned the lesson that Ulster will not stand for further outbreaks or disorders [. . .] although peace prevails throughout the province and law and order have rapidly improved in recent years, it is desirable to avoid as far as possible the yearly debates which have taken place on this particular measure during recent years.[338]

An example of the SPA in action was the case of two young Catholic men, Hugh McGauran of Belleek, a well-known Gaelic footballer and a former member of the Fermanagh county team, and Stephen O'Reilly, Newtownbutler; they were charged in June 1936 with unlawful assembly at an Easter commemoration in Tempo. It was alleged that a baton charge was made by the police while prayers were being recited over the grave of Volunteer Phil Breen, who was killed by northern forces following a raid on Tempo Barracks in 1922. Both defendants, who did not appear in court and were not legally represented, were sentenced to three months' imprisonment and were further ordered to enter into a bail bond at the end of the prison term or, in default, to serve a further three months in gaol.[339]

Efforts to hold a nationalist meeting in Newtownbutler in November and December 1938 were persistently thwarted by the authorities, with the town being made the subject of four banning orders issued over a three-week period and covering eight separate days.[340]

The power to control inquests was very significant. In order to avoid controversial findings, the government retained the power to appoint its own coroner and coroner's jury; particular inquests could be prevented from taking place, and inquests in any part of Northern Ireland could be prohibited. The government observed that not all coroners had the political inclination of the majority in the parliament (each county had at least one coroner – some counties had more than one). The power was designed to protect the security forces from prosecution while they exercised other powers under the act. One of the 'unsatisfactory' coroners was said to be that of Fermanagh.[341]

In 1936, a commission of inquiry was appointed under the auspices of the National Council for Civil Liberties of Great Britain 'to examine the purpose and effect of the Civil Authorities (Special Powers) Acts (Northern Ireland) 1922 and 1933'. The commissioners concluded that the acts were being used overwhelmingly against one section of the population, namely the nationalists. They noted, 'It is sad that in the guise of temporary and emergency legislation there should have been created under the shadow of the British Constitution a permanent machine of dictatorship.'[342]

In April 1963, the South African Minister for Justice, Balthazar Johannes Vorster, when introducing some new apartheid laws, stated that he 'would be willing to exchange all the legislation of this sort for one clause of the Northern Ireland Special Powers' Act'.[343]

POVERTY IN ESHNADARRAGH IN THE 1920S

During the period when the boundary commissioners were undertaking their consultations across the six counties, a situation of extreme poverty arose in the townland of Eshnadarragh in Clones parish (the Clanelly portion). The extent to which the Boundary Commission was flawed is thrown into sharp relief by the way in which the crisis was dealt with. The townland contains 819 acres and is situated on the Fermanagh–Monaghan border. It is a mountainous region and, at that time, was exclusively Catholic. The crops, including the potato crop, had failed due to a combination of poor land and wet weather. The people had no food, crops, seed or fuel.[344] A special meeting of Lisnaskea Board of Guardians was held in early February 1925 to seek powers from Fermanagh County Council to enable it to grant outdoor relief to those who were not entitled to access relief under the existing regulations. The possibility of initiating relief works – new roads and the widening of existing lanes, so as to provide employment and improve communications in the locality – was also discussed.[345]

Eshnadarragh was at one time a great centre for lace-making – it was in this district that the famous Clones lace was produced, but after the First World War, the industry was in rapid decline, which exacerbated the poverty of its people.[346]

The concern of some members of the Board of Guardians and Lisnaskea Rural Council was that they might initiate 'elaborate' relief schemes only to find that the people of Eshnadarragh were against the 'northern system of government' and might go into the Free State within a short time. They sought reassurances from the Secretary of the Eshnadarragh Relief Committee, one Joseph McMahon, that if the boundary commissioners came there to take evidence, the inhabitants would not express a desire to join the Free State. McMahon replied that, as they were simply a relief committee, they could not speak for the Eshnadarragh district or give any guarantee on behalf of the people.[347]

Despite this despicable attempt to bribe impoverished people, the more humane members decided to grant outdoor relief in food and fuel to the value of twelve shillings and sixpence a week maximum for a family.[348] One of the guardians, Mr Kirkpatrick, advised that political matters should not be a factor and said they were bound to provide for the people, irrespective of politics or religion. He noted there was 'real distress' in two out of every three houses in the Eshnadarragh district.[349] A decision was also taken to build a road from Jenkin Hill to Corraleek Mill.[350]

The local parish priest, Rev. Gormley of Roslea, reported that a relief officer had visited a house where there were three adult invalids with no visible means of support. The family had previously been evicted and had to go into service. They were now almost 'doubled up' from hard work and starvation. A poor brother of theirs, who hadn't much for himself, was trying to keep them alive.[351]

The *Sunday Independent* reported that an objection had been lodged with the Board of Guardians against relief being given to a woman because her son was getting a college education. This poor woman had travelled 'all the way from her little home in the mountain' to explain her circumstances to the guardians. Her husband had died, and she had eight children dependent on her. Her crop was a failure and the only means she had was six shillings a week, which she received from a teacher for the rent of a room in her house. Her eldest son had won a scholarship, and through the influence of the Catholic bishop of Clogher, he was admitted to the Diocesan college. It was agreed to allow the woman seven shillings and sixpence per week.[352] This was well below the maximum of twelve shillings and sixpence allowed.

Despite these efforts, Joseph McMahon, Secretary of the Relief Committee, later denounced the Lisnaskea Rural Council, which he claimed was 'blinded by political prejudice', and accused it of tardiness in relieving the destitute people.[353] He provided proof that three members of the council had tried to extract a guarantee from the relief committee 'that the people would vote in a certain way in the event of the Boundary Commission coming to the district to take evidence, thus taking advantage of the pitiable plight of the people to further its own ends.' He praised the northern government for their suggestion that a scheme of seed distribution be put in place, but he said that the Lisnaskea Council 'remained adamant in their determination to do nothing.'[354]

By May 1926, it would appear that the crisis had eased, as there is a reference in the *Fermanagh Herald* to money being repaid by Fermanagh County Council to Lisnaskea Rural Council for the 'special outdoor relief' that had been made to residents of the Eshnadarragh district.[355]

ASPECTS OF DISCRIMINATION UNDER THE NEW REGIME

Gerrymandering

During the period between partition and Operation Harvest,[356] discrimination became systemic. In Northern Ireland's earliest days, as has been shown, it had very nearly lost the western counties of Fermanagh and Tyrone, as well as Derry City. In local elections held under a proportional representation system in 1920, just before partition, Sinn Féin and other nationalists won control of Derry City and the county councils of Fermanagh and Tyrone.[357] As late as mid-1922, these councils were still giving their allegiance to the new Irish Free State government in Dublin.

There was a real danger that these areas would secede to the south. So when power was devolved to the new unionist government at Stormont, it wasted no time in bringing about change through gerrymandering. For the local elections of 1924, it redrew the electoral boundaries of Derry City, Fermanagh and Tyrone (among other areas) and reintroduced the first-past-the-post system of voting so that a minority of unionist voters now had a majority in a large number of wards and thus elected more representatives than nationalists.[358] Leahy and Ó Dochartaigh argue that by 'the creation of these new internal boundaries, the inequality that was embedded in the external border was diffused throughout the territory of Northern Ireland.'[359]

A number of public remarks made in the early 1930s by members of the unionist establishment had increased the alienation of Catholics. A senator in the Northern Ireland parliament, John Porter-Porter, said at a Twelfth gathering at Lisnaskea on 12 July 1931, 'The Northern Government is a Protestant Government, put into power by Protestants and the welfare and safety of the Protestants should be its first consideration.'

On 12 July 1933, Sir Basil Brooke MP, then junior government whip, advised employers not to employ Catholics at a Twelfth celebration in the overwhelmingly nationalist village of Newtownbutler. He remarked that there were a great number of Protestants and Orangemen who employed Roman Catholics. He felt he could speak freely on this subject, as 'he had not one' about his own place which was responded to with cheers. He appreciated the great difficulty experienced by some employers in procuring suitable Protestant labour, but he pointed out that the Roman Catholics were 'endeavouring to get in everywhere and were out with all their force and might to destroy the power and constitution of Ulster'. He appealed to loyalists, therefore, wherever possible, 'to employ good Protestant lads and lassies'.[360] According to journalist and author, Susan McKay, he recommended to Derry's Unionist Association that loyalists should not employ Catholics, '99% of whom are disloyal. If you don't act properly now, before we know where we are, we shall find ourselves in the minority instead of the majority.'[361]

On 20 March 1934, Sir James Craig, then Prime Minister of Northern Ireland, replied to a question in the Stormont parliament from Cahir Healy, the MP for South Fermanagh, on what the government's policy was in relation to the employment of Catholics. Craig referred to Sir Basil Brooke's speech the previous year. He said there was not one of his own colleagues who did not entirely agree with Brooke, and he would not ask him to withdraw one word he said.[362] Craig went on to state 'it is undoubtedly our duty and our privilege, and always will be, to see that those appointed by us possess the most unimpeachable loyalty to the King and Constitution. That is my whole object in carrying on a Protestant Government for a Protestant people.'[363]

Also in 1934, Sir Basil told the Northern Ireland House of Commons of how, when he was in the Ulster Special Constabulary, he was informed of a plot to kidnap his eldest son. As a result, 'taking every precaution', he got rid of 'every man in the place who I thought might betray me'. By inference, he meant every Catholic.[364] Academic and author Thomas Hennessy argues that the unionist perception of the nationalist enemy 'within and outside the statelet remained a core facet of the Ulster unionist sense of siege'.[365]

At an April 1948 meeting in Enniskillen, Ernest Cecil Ferguson, the Unionist MP for Enniskillen,[366] made disturbing remarks:

> The Nationalist majority in the county notwithstanding a reduction of 336 in the year stands at 3,604. We must ultimately reduce and liquidate that majority. The county, I think it can be safely said, is a Unionist county. The atmosphere is Unionist. The Boards and properties are nearly all controlled by Unionists. But there is still this millstone [of a Nationalist majority] around our necks. I would ask the meeting to authorise their executive to adopt whatever plans and take whatever steps, however drastic, to wipe out this Nationalist majority.[367]

Decades later, the Fermanagh branch of NICRA claimed Ferguson had been attempting to eradicate the Catholic population from the county. They maintained that the drop in Fermanagh's Catholic population between 1951 and 1961 proved the efficacy of what they called Ferguson's 'Campaign of Liquidation'. The Catholic population did indeed decrease from 29,492 in 1951 to 27,414 in 1961, a drop of 2,078; the Church of Ireland population also decreased by 238, but this was offset by an increase of 206 in the Presbyterian population and 58 in the Methodist community. Other denominations, and 'denomination unstated', also increased by 539. Clearly, Ferguson's campaign had a major detrimental effect on the Catholic population, but other factors, such as a fall in agricultural occupations, may also have contributed to the decrease. For the first half of the twentieth century, up to 1951, the Catholic population had maintained a steady 55–56 per cent, yet by 1961, it had dropped to 53.2 per cent. When Catholics reached employment and marriageable age, they were often forced to leave the county in large numbers because discrimination in housing and jobs was rife.

Canadian academic Eric Kaufmann claims that, though they formed just 35 per cent of Northern Ireland's population, Catholics made up 60 per cent of its emigrants.[368] He observes that 'Protestants acted on several levels to make life difficult for Catholics, which encouraged emigration.' At grassroots level, Protestants tried to prevent 'Protestant land' being sold to Catholics. Protestants who did so faced sanction from their community.[369] For Orangemen, according to Paul Morland, this included expulsion from the order.[370] The County Fermanagh Grand Orange Lodge, in 1938, developed a 'Land Fund' to purchase land for Protestants. The scheme was soon copied elsewhere and, according to Kaufmann, was still in place in 1996.[371] According to Edward Burke, it was still in operation as recently as 2015.[372]

As well as driving Catholics out, the Unionist party also encouraged Protestants to come in from the republic. John Miller Andrews MP, who had served as the second Prime Minister of Northern Ireland (1940–6), addressing the Grand Orange Lodge of Ireland in 1950, said:

> I fear we could not introduce a measure openly to debar Catholics from Eire and admitting Protestants from Eire to come and reside in Northern Ireland, Clause 6 of the Government of Ireland Act forbade a privilege of preference on account of religion. But a good deal can be done administratively.[373]

At his address to the Fine Gael Árd Fheis on 6 February 1957, the Taoiseach, John A. Costello, told the delegates that discrimination in the six counties was 'constant, deliberate and manifestly unjust and has continued ever since the area became a separate political entity'.[374]

Housing

As the welfare state was established in the aftermath of the Second World War, the British Labour government provided funding for a huge public housing programme in Northern Ireland.[375] Under this development, everyone living in substandard housing was to be provided with a new house funded by the state and had to pay rent to a public body or housing trust that would ensure stronger protections and higher quality housing.[376] Ironically, this gave the unionist-controlled councils a unique opportunity – the newly established housing trust could only build with the permission of local authorities, which, Leahy and Ó Dochartaigh contend, gave the local authorities control over 'a novel and huge source of patronage' that led to large-scale discrimination in order to bolster their control.[377]

Over the following decades, there were many instances of individual discrimination against Catholics reported in the nationalist press. None, however, is more shocking than the eviction of Margaret Nolan. Margaret was a single woman, 50 years of age, who lived in a council cottage in the townland of Tonyloman, Belnaleck, Enniskillen.[378] The cottage was built for her father and his family in around 1908. The family had lived there for many years until, eventually, Margaret's parents died and her other two siblings had moved away. She was the only family member left in the home.

After her father's death in 1951, Enniskillen Rural Council was granted an order by the town's quarter sessions whereby Miss Nolan was to be removed from her home.[379]

She appealed to the Northern High Court against the decision and won her appeal on the grounds that the ejectment proceedings should have been taken at petty sessions. Enniskillen Rural Council again took proceedings against her, and an order for possession was again granted at Letterbreen petty sessions. Nolan again appealed, this time to Enniskillen quarter sessions, where her solicitor made the case that 'she was being penalised because of her religion, the decision to eject her and give her house to a Protestant having been reached by the Council on a strictly party vote of unionists against the nationalist minority on the council'.[380] Nevertheless, she lost this appeal. The council decision led to several heated exchanges at council meetings, where nationalist representatives protested strongly against the bigotry manifested in the decision to eject her from her home.[381]

On 29 May 1953, two sheriff's bailiffs, Henry Coalter and Thomas Higgins, arrived at the cottage in order to evict Nolan. A welfare officer was also in attendance. When the reporter from the *Fermanagh Herald* arrived at the scene, two policemen were standing on the roadside. Inside the cottage plot of ground were the two bailiffs, who were removing her pieces of furniture. The reporter described Margaret's sadness as she watched her furniture being removed and left out in the open. She told the reporter that the welfare officer had enquired if she had anywhere to go and she had replied in the negative. Also present at the scene was Cahir Healy MP.[382] When the cottage was vacated, the door was locked and the key handed to the bailiff. The furniture, the pictures, the beds and bed clothes, and Margaret, were left on the roadside.[383]

Eventually, a kind neighbour provided a lorry to take her and her belongings to the overcrowded home of her [Margaret's] sister, who lived 'in a shocking hovel' with her husband and four children in Queen Street, Enniskillen. Margaret's other sister had entered the convent and become a member of the Sisters of Mercy order in Belfast.[384] Her married sister had been trying, futilely, to secure a house in Enniskillen for years.[385]

In the meantime, the cottage at Tonyloman was offered to two Protestant tenants, neither of whom had taken up the tenancy. One of them had since been allocated a new council house in Derryaghanagh. For a considerable amount of time after the eviction, the cottage was under 24-hour police guard.[386]

Margaret's heart-wrenching story seems to have had a happy ending, however, in that she was given private tenancy of a house in Drumbrochers, Macken, by its Catholic owner.[387] Then, in November 1954, eighteen months after her eviction, she married Thomas McAloon from Arney.[388]

It is clear from this analysis that discrimination in all walks of life – in politics, employment and housing – was institutionalised quickly and became reinforced in the new state during these thirty years, and it continued for a further two decades, buttressed by the draconian legislation of the Special Powers Act.

Chapter 6

FROM OPERATION HARVEST TO THE CIVIL RIGHTS MOVEMENT

OPERATION HARVEST (THE IRA BORDER CAMPAIGN, 1956–62)

After the Second World War, Cahir Healy MP was involved in the launching of the Anti-Partition League (APL), which, according to Eamon Phoenix, for a time in the 1940s and 1950s, secured the support of all parties in the south in its campaign 'to mobilise public and political opposition to partition' in Britain and the United States.[389] It reached a climax in the 1949 Stormont election when, backed by Dáil speakers and a 'fighting fund' raised at Catholic church gate collections throughout Ireland, the APL contested seventeen of the fifty-two Northern Ireland constituencies. In Fermanagh, the league contested all three seats, but the results only confirmed the effectiveness of the unionist gerrymander. Healy was returned with a 4,000 majority in nationalist South Fermanagh, but the two candidates in Lisnaskea and Enniskillen were defeated by unionists.[390]

The APL had the contrary effect of consolidating border unionism and served to entrench Fermanagh's unionist leaders in their determination to dilute the influence of the county's nationalist majority.[391] It led to an intensification of discrimination against nationalists in local government employment and in the allocation of council houses.[392]

According to Diarmaid Ferriter, Sir Basil Brooke, in 1948, was concerned about the repeal of the External Relations Act, which was the Free State's last remaining formal link with the British Commonwealth. Just months before Ireland was declared a republic, Brooke worried that the constitutional position of Northern Ireland could be prejudiced by 'Éire's ceasing to be a member of the Commonwealth'. The British Prime Minister, Clement Attlee, assured him that it would have no effect but rejected Brooke's request that the name 'Northern Ireland' should now be changed to 'Ulster' and that the south's proposed new title, 'The Republic of Ireland', should not be recognised.[393]

The British Labour government's enactment of the Ireland Act (1949), which reinforced partition by giving a veto over constitutional change to the Northern Ireland parliament, struck a fatal blow to the APL while the collapse of the Costello-led Irish coalition government in 1951 saw the eclipse of Seán MacBride's Clann na Poblachta party. (Clann na Poblachta was a radical republican party founded by MacBride, a former Chief of Staff of the IRA, in 1946. It was comprised of many who had taken the anti-Treaty side in the civil war and who had not joined Fianna Fáil. They were the driving force behind the anti-partition campaign.) These changes increased northern nationalists' sense of isolation by the early 1950s.[394]

Despite the fact that Ireland had joined the United Nations in December 1955, Costello's government, and successive governments, seemed strangely reluctant to use this important international forum to highlight the injustice of partition. Ó Beacháin argues that 'any hope that the UN might provide a platform to further an anti-partition agenda had to be counterbalanced with the reality that, institutionally, the UN was weighted in favour of a small club of states that had emerged victorious from the Second World War.'[395] Notwithstanding the slim chance of success, it could be argued that the use of the UN as a platform was an opportunity to keep the issue at the forefront internationally.

In January 1956, the Northern Ireland Government published a pamphlet entitled *Why the Border Must Be: the Northern Ireland case in brief* with contributions from Prime Minister Viscount Brookeborough; Minister of Finance, Brian Maginess QC; and Minister of Home Affairs, George Hanna QC.[396] It was described as a 'world-wide drive aimed at countering anti-partitionist propaganda' and would be 'circulated to all parts of the English-speaking world'.[397] It is hardly a coincidence that it was published hard on the heels of Ireland's entry into the UN a few weeks earlier. Indeed, the *Belfast Telegraph* warned that 'Ireland's entry into the UN is likely to be exploited for its own political ends.'[398]

The pamphlet portrayed Northern Ireland as a utopia where democracy reigned supreme – where, according to Brookeborough, 'the union with Great Britain is preserved not by a British garrison but by the declared will of the Northern Ireland people, expressed through their elected parliament.'[399] There is, assuredly, no mention of gerrymandering or the Special Powers Act.[400]

Maginess and Hanna focused on Northern Ireland's 'record of freedoms' – of thought, expression and worship, and from censorship – and they contrasted these freedoms with the 'South'. While there was, undoubtedly, censorship in the republic, there must have been much hollow laughter among nationalists when they read the publication, as they were only too well aware of the extraordinary powers that the Northern Ireland government imposed upon them and which were implemented by their militia, the B-Specials.

Hanna also stressed the 'unity of outlook of the United Kingdom and the USA' as being 'essential to the preservation of democracy in the world'. He noted that 'the backward policy of the South' was exemplified by their efforts 'to revive what is to us a dead language instead of a tongue that is almost universal'.[401]

Harry Diamond, Republican Labour MP, complained in parliament that there was no mention in the pamphlet of the widespread discrimination in both public and private employment. Cahir Healy remarked that one of the new industries brought to Northern Ireland was requesting applicants for jobs to state their religion. He also noted that letters were being censored in a room in Belfast Post Office.[402]

The vacuum caused by the collapse of the APL was filled in the mid-1950s by the revival of the IRA and the formation of a number of republican splinter groups in Fermanagh and other border counties.[403]

In the UK general election of 1955, Sinn Féin made an electoral breakthrough when two of their candidates were elected as MPs for the mid-Ulster and Fermanagh and South Tyrone constituencies with a total of 152,310 votes.[404] This show of support, together with the collapse of the APL, may have encouraged the IRA to consider an armed campaign against the partition of Ireland. A further impetus for the decision to start a campaign was the growing discontent of some members at the lack of activity – indeed, an IRA survivor of the campaign told the author that there was mounting pressure from the volunteers to begin armed actions.[405] There was fear that such members might join breakaway groups that would usurp the IRA. One such group, Saor Uladh, had carried out a raid on Roslea Barracks on 26 November 1955, during which one of their volunteers, Connie Green, had been killed.[406] Before the campaign had even begun, however, the Dublin unit was depleted. Joe Cristle, a lawyer and well-known racing cyclist, held a meeting in Dalkey where he split from the main organisation and formed a splinter group. Most of the Dublin volunteers joined his group, leaving only about forty poorly trained members in the Dublin unit.[407]

The IRA border campaign strategy was to repeat the tactics used by the flying columns in the War of Independence. They would wage a guerrilla war in the predominantly Catholic areas of Northern Ireland around the border in order to create 'liberated areas'. Operations were controlled from Dublin and, more locally, from Monaghan. Most of the volunteers came from south of the border, with northern units used mainly as support and sources of local intelligence. By then, the splinter groups had quickly patched up their differences but were not under the control of the main organisation.[408]

The attacks, particularly in the early days of the campaign, focused on Fermanagh for a number of reasons: the county had a majority nationalist population that could provide safe houses and other assistance, and it had a very long border, surrounded on three sides by Monaghan, Cavan, Leitrim and Donegal. Tyrone, the only other county with a nationalist majority, by contrast, had only a short border with Monaghan.

The campaign, codenamed Operation Harvest, began without warning on 12 December 1956. During the early hours of that morning, attacks were carried out in five of the six counties of Northern Ireland; in Fermanagh, heavy explosions damaged Lady Brooke Bridge, west of Newtownbutler, and Cary Bridge, at Inishmore Island on Lough Erne. A Territorial Army building at Enniskillen, which was under construction, was also damaged.[409]

Two nights later, on 14 December, a large party of armed men of the IRA's Pearse Column, led by Seán Garland, attacked Lisnaskea Barracks at 1 a.m.[410] A high explosive charge was set off at the front of the building, blowing in the front door and causing other damage to the structure.[411] Daithí Ó Conaill opened fire on the station with his Thompson gun, but their Bren gun malfunctioned[412] and they were badly exposed as a gun battle broke out in the main street. Immediately, Garland ordered a retreat, and the unit headed for the border, abandoned their lorry and eventually made it to Monaghan on foot.[413] About half an hour later, Derrylin RUC Station was heavily attacked from front and rear by machine gun fire. The police returned fire, causing the raiders to flee.[414] On 17 December, at Nutfield Cross, about 2 miles from Lisnaskea, RUC Constable Ferguson was injured in a shootout with the IRA.[415]

On the same date, the British Ambassador reported that the Taoiseach, John A. Costello, during a conversation about the recent attacks, had 'branched off into a highly emotional account of the passionate feeling aroused throughout the country by partition'. Costello complained that, because no progress towards a solution had been made after thirty-five years, it was 'small wonder' that the younger generation 'got desperate'. At the very least, he suggested, the British should give up Fermanagh and Tyrone; nevertheless, he was committed to taking the gun out of politics and stood by his doctrine of 'no violence'.[416]

On 21 December, the Northern Ireland Prime Minister, Basil Brooke, interned several hundred republican suspects under the Special Powers Act, and over 100 men were arrested on 12 January 1957.[417] These actions seriously limited the IRA's capacity to build up units within Northern Ireland.

An armed attack took place at Derrylin RUC Station on 30 December in which a Catholic RUC constable, John Scally, was killed – the first fatality of the campaign. Considerable damage was caused to the building. The military were called out, and the B-Specials and RUC arrived from Enniskillen and Lisnaskea. A cordon was thrown around the area, and at dawn next morning, the security forces made a sweep through the Doon Mountains to the Cavan border but the IRA unit had escaped.[418]

Two days later, the next and most famous attack took place during the evening of New Year's Day at Brookeborough RUC Station. All stations in the Lisnaskea district had been alerted to cover defence points at stations in order to be prepared for an attack.[419] Fourteen IRA volunteers were involved in the raid. The leader was Seán Garland, and the other participants were Daithí Ó Conaill, Phil O'Donoghue, Michael O'Brien, Paddy O'Regan, Seán Scott, Harry Goff, Liam Nolan, Mick Kelly, Seán South and Fergal O'Hanlon – all from south of the border. The three northerners were Vincent Conlon of Armagh and two Fermanagh men, Pat Connolly and Packie Tierney.[420]

Most of the men set out from Dublin on St Stephen's Day, 26 December 1956. They travelled north to Monaghan in a Ford 10 van and a Volkswagen Beetle.[421] The fourteen volunteers gathered at the O'Hanlon home in Monaghan town before setting out for Fermanagh the following day. According to his sister, Fergal requested his mother to make a good meal for all of them, declaring that 'there were faces here you won't see again'.[422] Ironically, as it turned out, his was to be one of them. They collected their weapons from a house in Knockatallon and crossed the border by foot into Fermanagh on 28 December. They stayed in a safe house there until New Year's Day.[423] The local volunteers acquired a lorry from Newtownbutler, the property of P. Clarke & Sons.[424] According to the testimonies of the IRA men who were present, their objective was to attack the barracks and take their weapons and ammunition – not to take on the RUC.[425]

They drove into Brookeborough at precisely 7 p.m., and as they made their way down the main street, Daithí Ó Conaill jumped out of the lorry when he spotted Sgt Cordner crossing the street. Ó Conaill chased him, but the sergeant made it safely into the station, slamming the door behind him. Ó Conaill fired his Thompson submachine gun (SMG), directing it at the front door.[426] Sgt Cordner, who may have been slightly wounded, was able to proceed upstairs, where he fired a .22 rifle through a bedroom window.[427] Meanwhile, Seán South was operating a Bren gun from the rear of the lorry, firing at the station. A grenade was also thrown but it landed in the street and injured Phil O'Donoghue slightly in the forehead.[428] Sgt Cordner moved into the front bedroom, which overlooked the street, and where a Bren gun was already mounted and loaded. He directed his fire towards the red lorry and emptied an entire magazine into it. The lorry moved off slowly, and the police considered it most unlikely that it could reach the border because it appeared to be seriously damaged.[429]

A police car at Colebrooke pursued the lorry and found it abandoned at Altawark between Roslea and the border. The police reported that it contained a Thompson SMG, a large quantity of ammunition, gelignite and a first aid kit, as well as Molotov cocktails. Most of the items were contained in canvas haversacks.[430] The survivor who spoke to the author, who was involved in this operation, had no knowledge of the first aid kit and said that even if there had been such a kit, they would have been unable to use it because of the tilting of the damaged lorry.[431] The police followed a blood trail to a byre at the side of a dwelling house. Head Constable Rodgers and Sgt McGregor entered the byre and found two dead men attired in khaki battledress. They were, however, unable to establish their identity at that point.[432]

It transpired that the dead men were Seán South, 28 years of age and a native of Limerick, and Fergal O'Hanlon, 20 years of age, from Monaghan. Over 50,000 people attended their funerals in both counties.[433] The funeral procession began in Monaghan when the two coffins were brought into the town. The pall bearers included members of the GAA and local councillors.[434] In Limerick, Seán South's funeral attendance included the Mayor, a senator and a number of councillors.[435] The two men were immortalised in ballads as IRA martyrs.

Four IRA men were injured in the attack on Brookeborough, including the group leader, Seán Garland, who was shot while climbing back into the lorry. He had raided Gough Barracks, Armagh in June 1954 and had escaped with a significant number of weapons.[436] He was, at that time, a serving member of the British Army. The other three who were injured were Vincent Conlon, who was shot in the foot, Phil O'Donoghue, who was slightly injured in the stomach and forehead, and Paddy O'Regan, who was shot in the back and hip. The attack had lasted for only about five minutes.[437] Phil O'Donoghue believed that the bullets that grazed his stomach then hit and killed Fergal O'Hanlon.

The British Ambassador, Alex Clutterbuck, made notes of a 'top secret' conversation between Lt General Sir Brian Kimmins, General Officer Commanding (GOC) Northern Ireland District, and General Richard Mulcahy, the Irish Minister for Education, on 26 January 1957 – a conversation that, Mulcahy insisted, was 'on no account to be quoted'. Kimmins had come to Dublin incognito; he attended a rugby match against France, and afterwards he and Mulcahy attended a quiet dinner at the home of the British Ambassador, where the discussion took place. Mulcahy feared that news of the meeting and his discussions with the GOC would be leaked.[438] He informed Kimmins that the events of 12 December had taken the army, police and government by surprise.[439] He suggested that the activities of the splinter groups had forced the IRA to take action to reassert themselves. Even so, the government would have expected to have had an inkling that something 'was in the wind', but they had heard nothing.[440]

In the first shock of surprise and dismay, Irish ministers were divided as to how the situation should be handled, but they soon accepted the necessity of stamping out these activities quickly. Forty men were arrested and were awaiting trial. Documents were captured while arrests were being made. Of major interest was a document on the programme of operations drawn up by Seán Cronin, the IRA Chief of Staff.[441]

Mulcahy intervened with the Minister for Justice and the Taoiseach so that the document could be read out in court, which was the only way of informing the British surreptitiously of its contents.[442] Another document listing the names of helpers and sympathisers in the north was prevented from being read out in court by the presiding judge. Mulcahy's assessment was that if further incidents were to take place, the likelihood was that they would be confined to areas where the local population would be sympathetic – Fermanagh, Tyrone and parts of Derry.[443]

Before January was out, Costello's public opposition to IRA violence prompted Fine Gael's coalition partner, Clann na Poblachta, to mount a motion of no confidence, and rather than face parliamentary defeat, Costello dissolved the Dáil and called a general election.[444]

Fianna Fáil returned to power with a large majority and introduced internment on 6 July.[445] In the election, Sinn Féin won four seats and over 10 per cent of the vote in the nineteen constituencies it contested.[446] It made little impact, however, because of the party's abstentionist policy. With few resources, with internment on both sides of the border and with unapproved border roads blocked, the IRA found it almost impossible to continue their campaign. Subsequent incidents were on a much smaller scale.

At the beginning of the border campaign, while the British Army and the RUC were regarded as fair game, the B-Specials were not considered 'legitimate targets'. Seán Cronin's military directive considered them to be 'Protestants in uniform'; targeting them was seen as opening the door to sectarian warfare, which he abhorred. He hoped to persuade all denominations that their future lay in a united Ireland. This order was incomprehensible to northern IRA members, who suffered harassment from the B-Specials on a regular basis, and it demonstrated to them how out of touch the south had become regarding Northern Ireland issues. They believed emphatically that the B-Specials should be regarded as legitimate targets, but despite their opposition, they continued to obey the directive.

The directive was overturned on 1 September 1958 after James Crossan, a Sinn Féin organiser for County Cavan, was shot dead on the Cavan–Fermanagh border. He was, reportedly, last seen with a B-Special; republicans suspected he was killed in a failed attempt to abduct him across the border so he could be arrested in Northern Ireland. From then until the end of the campaign, on-duty B-Specials were regarded as 'legitimate targets'.[447] Several were injured but none were killed during Operation Harvest.[448]

As it turned out, 1957 was the most active year of the campaign. When, on 11 November, four IRA men and the owner of the house[449] in which they were staying were killed in a premature bomb explosion in Edentubber, County Louth, the campaign was virtually at an end, although it limped on for several years until it was officially called off on 26 February 1962. At the end of the campaign, the death toll was twelve republicans and six RUC constables.[450] A total of 256 republicans had been interned in Northern Ireland while 150 were held without trial in the republic.[451]

The campaign was politically naïve and a complete failure, but from the IRA's perspective, it succeeded in passing on the republican mantle to a younger generation and kept the issue of the partition of Ireland alive.

THE FERMANAGH CIVIL RIGHTS ASSOCIATION

If we examine the demographics and economy of Fermanagh, a picture emerges of a sparsely populated rural county with few job opportunities, especially in the south of the county, close to the border.

When a new Labour government was elected in 1964, Cahir Healy MP, perhaps expecting a more sympathetic ear, made representations to Prime Minister Harold Wilson about discrimination and gerrymandering against the nationalist majority of Fermanagh. Citing the case of the Catholic McManus family of twelve children who had been forced to live 'in a dilapidated caravan in a bog', he invited the Prime Minister to visit the area to witness conditions for himself. Nonetheless, the Wilson government, like its predecessors, declined to intervene in Stormont affairs and refused to meet a nationalist deputation on the issue.[452]

Around this time, Northern Ireland politics was undergoing a major shift and old-style nationalism was giving way to a new, educated and articulate

Catholic middle-class that was demanding full equality of citizenship. This was made possible by the Education (Northern Ireland) Act of 1947, which provided access to secondary and university education for people from less privileged backgrounds. With the opportunity of a higher-level university education, a new generation of political activists emerged. This led to the rise of the civil rights movement.[453] There was fierce Orange Order and populist Protestant opposition to the act's provisions to increase funding to the Catholic school sector, but to his credit, Sir Basil Brooke stood his ground and pushed the legislation through.[454]

This new-found confidence among nationalists led indirectly to the formation of the Northern Ireland Civil Rights Association in Belfast on 9 April 1967. Its aims were to achieve reform by publicising, documenting and lobbying for an end to discrimination in elections, public housing and alleged abuses of the SPA. Its leaders were inspired by the American civil rights movement, and one of them referred to northern Catholics as 'white negroes', a term that gained publicity in the world's press.

Soon, branches sprung up in many areas, including Fermanagh. Those involved in the local branch included Frank McManus, who was elected as an MP in 1970, and Fergus McQuillan, who later became a member of the Social Democratic and Labour Party (SDLP). The organisation in Fermanagh accused the unionist government of:

- The gerrymander of the Stormont electoral boundaries;
- The gerrymander of local government electoral boundaries;
- Discrimination, religious and political, in the allocation of employment;
- Discrimination, religious and political, in the allocation of council houses;
- Discrimination, religious and political, in the siting of industries;
- A deliberate effort to eradicate the Catholic majority of County Fermanagh;
- Having proved themselves unfit to hold any power in a state that claims to be democratic.

For these reasons, they demanded their immediate removal from power.[455]

In 1969, the Cameron Inquiry[456] reported that in Fermanagh no senior council posts (and relatively few junior ones) were held by Catholics – this was rationalised by reference to 'proven loyalty' as a necessary test for local authority appointments. Among about seventy-five drivers of school buses, at most seven were Catholics, which would appear to be a very clear case of sectarian and political discrimination.[457]

Council appointments to committees reflected its undemocratic nature. In the late 1960s, according to NICRA, of twenty-four county officers, twenty-two were Protestants; among the Educational, Management Advisory, Finance, Health, Housing, Library, Planning, Public Works, Welfare and Agricultural Committees there were seventy-three Protestants and thirty-two Catholics.[458]

Figures for council employment were provided, broken down by religion – they were based on pay sheets for the month of April 1969. Of a total of 370 employees, 338 were Protestants while only 32 were Catholics.[459]

Local government was reorganised in Fermanagh in 1966–7. Gerrymandering, however, continued. For example, in the Newtownbutler area, Catholics were in a majority of thirty-seven people.[460] In order to prevent the election of a nationalist representative, the Unionist party was prepared to go to extraordinary lengths. They created a new village at Donagh, 4 miles from Newtownbutler, specifically to rehouse Catholics from the Newtownbutler area. Donagh just happened to be in a different division: Derrylea, where there was already a Catholic majority.[461] This was done despite the fact that the people of Newtownbutler had no desire to move to Donagh, and they were not consulted. What's more, Fermanagh County Council already owned sufficient suitable land to build houses in Newtownbutler, which had easy access to sewerage, water and electricity. The site at Donagh had no drainage, which had to be installed at considerable cost to the ratepayers.[462]

Industry, or lack of it, was also a focus of NICRA. They perceived that it was unionist policy to make little effort to attract industry to Fermanagh. In terms of the distribution of what industry did come to the county, it went exclusively to the two unionist constituencies of Enniskillen and Lisnaskea. No industry had been located in the nationalist constituency of South Fermanagh since the establishment of Belleek Pottery more than a century earlier.[463]

As has been noted, housing was a particular area of discrimination against Catholics. George Elliot, a unionist member of Enniskillen Borough Council, declared, 'We are not going to build houses in the South Ward and cut a rod to beat ourselves later on. We are going to see that the right people are put into these houses, and we are not making any apologies for it.'[464]

NICRA alleged that, in the past, the housing authorities discriminated by refusing to house Catholics, and when, eventually, the new county council decided to house Catholics, many of whom had lived in deplorable slum conditions for years, it did so by creating religious ghettos. NICRA claimed that between 1945 and 1967, 195 houses in Fermanagh were allocated to Catholics, while 853 – over four times as many – went to people of other denominations.[465]

Another continuing source of grievance for the nationalist population throughout the north, including Fermanagh, was the B-Specials. It was Basil Brooke, who was also a Fermanagh landlord, a veteran of the First World War, and later Prime Minister of Northern Ireland, who founded the Ulster Special Constabulary. As was noted earlier, he began by raising a vigilante force of ex-soldiers who had survived the war, many of whom were former UVF members. This force evolved into the USC and Brooke became their commandant. After the autumn of 1922, and the A- and C-Specials had stood down, only the B-Specials remained. The B-Specials were about 20,000 strong, part-time and unpaid. Their purpose was to safeguard their own areas against nationalists.[466] Ellison and Smyth claim that the B-Specials were the private militia of the unionist government – their sole function being the suppression of nationalist dissent. The nationalist community detested the organisation, regarding it as sectarian and brutal.[467]

Séamus Heaney, in his poem 'Ministry of Fear', describes them as, 'crowding round / The car like black cattle, snuffing and pointing / The muzzle of a Sten gun in my eye'.[468] Henry Patterson, author and historian, writes that

> border areas were where the B-Specials were present in large numbers and where their role was a source of considerable resentment and, at times, trepidation amongst Catholics. The civil rights' demand for the abolition of the B-Specials was, therefore, a source of deep communal division in border areas where, whatever the fears and animosities of Catholics, the force was seen by Protestants as an effective bulwark against the IRA.[469]

From 1921 to 1969, every prime minister of Northern Ireland and all but three cabinet ministers were Orangemen. In Fermanagh, where the Catholic and Protestant populations were close to parity, membership of the Orange Order in 1971 was three times higher than in the more Protestant counties of Antrim and Down.[470] Kaufmann cites two reasons for this apparent anomaly: the Church of Ireland was the established Protestant denomination in rural west Ulster, and their members were more likely to join the pro-landlord Orange Order in the nineteenth century than other denominations, which were more numerous east of the Bann; secondly, membership of the Orange Order was historically lower in areas where Protestants were in the majority and vice versa.[471] The higher membership in Catholic-majority areas reflected the Protestant siege mentality, where they felt threatened by their minority status.

By 1968–9, Fermanagh Catholics, despite the fact that they constituted a majority, had long been nursing a sense of grievance because of the history of gerrymandering (of both Stormont and local government boundaries) and discrimination in jobs, housing and the siting of industries. Their historical legacy also included sectarianism, alienation and forced emigration.

POPULATION CHANGES, 1951–2011

In 1951, the total population of Fermanagh was 52,089, comprising 29,492 Catholics (55.6 per cent) while the Protestant figure was 22,597 (42.6 per cent). In 1961, the total population was 50,037, comprising 27,414 Catholics (53.2 per cent) while the Protestant population was 22,623 (43.9 per cent).

The population declined to an all-time low of 49,000 in 1966. It has since recovered to 61,805 (Census 2011) but still remains very much the poor relation of the other counties of Northern Ireland. It took 100 years for the county's population to get back to the 1911 level. It was reported as recently as 2017 that Fermanagh was the worst-performing county in all of Ireland with regards to job creation, and it had the lowest number of job vacancies out of all thirty-two counties, accounting for just 1.19 per cent of available jobs in Ireland.[472]

A breakdown, by religion, of the census figures for 1971 in the early days of the conflict shows that out of a total population of 50,658, there were 24,051 Catholics (47.5 per cent), 15,919 Church of Ireland members (31.4 per cent), 3,135 Methodists (6.2 per cent), 1,757 Presbyterians (3.5 per cent), 1,419 were other denominations (2.8 per cent) and 4,377 were not stated (8.6 per cent). Therefore, if the unstated figure is excluded, the total Protestant population was 22,230 (43.9 per cent).[473]

These figures show a continuing decline in the Catholic population between 1951 and 1971 while the Protestant population held steady. It is important, nevertheless, to strike a note of caution here, as many Catholics refused to state their religion in the 1971 census.

By 2001, the Catholic population was back to 1951 levels. It had reached 31,937 (55.52 per cent) while the Protestant population had dropped to 20,779 (36.12 per cent). By 2011, out of a total population of 61,805, 33,391 were Catholics (54.9 per cent), 21,199 were Protestants (34.3 per cent) and 6,675 were not stated (10.8 per cent).

Chapter 7:

THE CONFLICT IN FERMANAGH (PART 1)

In the first two years of the conflict, Fermanagh escaped relatively unscathed and death-free. In the twenty-three-year period between 1971 and 1994, 114 people were killed in conflict-related attacks, and a survivor of the 1987 Enniskillen bomb, who had been in a coma for thirteen years, passed away in December 2000, bringing the total to 115. The gender breakdown is 102 males and 13 females. The classification of those killed is as follows: 21 UDR members, 22 RUC/RUCR officers, 21 British soldiers, 1 Garda Inspector, 28 Protestant civilians (this figure includes five former UDR members and two former RUC members), 14 Catholic civilians and 8 IRA members. No loyalist paramilitaries were killed.

Measuring these deaths in Fermanagh as a percentage against the total number that died across all counties, it amounts to 9.7 per cent of all UDR deaths, 4.3 per cent of all RUC deaths, 4.2 per cent of all British Army deaths, 3.9 per cent of all Protestant civilian deaths, 0.5 per cent of all Catholic civilian deaths and 2 per cent of all republican deaths. In terms of security force deaths, the only county with a lower number is Antrim (excluding Belfast).[474] The breakdown of responsibility for the deaths is: 100 killed by the IRA, 9 by the British Army, 4 by loyalists, 1 by the UDR and 1 by the RUC.[475]

In this book, sectarian killings and attacks are defined as those in which individuals are targeted deliberately, solely on the basis of their religious beliefs – specifically, Protestant and Catholic civilians.

KILLED BY IRA

The following is a breakdown of those killed by the IRA. Note that one British soldier was killed by the Official IRA; all others were killed by the Provisional IRA.

- 20 UDR members – 19 Protestants and 1 Catholic.
- 22 RUC/RUCR officers – 21 Protestants and 1 Catholic.
- 21 British Army soldiers.
- 1 Garda inspector.
- 28 Protestant civilians – this figure includes 10 killed in the Enniskillen bombing, 5 former members of the UDR and 2 former members of the RUC (one of whom was killed in the Enniskillen bombing).
- 6 Catholic civilians – one of whom was an alleged informer.
- 2 IRA members – one was killed when a landmine he was laying near Roslea exploded prematurely; the other was alleged to be an informer.

Of the twenty serving UDR members killed by the IRA, only four were on-duty at the time; fifteen of the sixteen off-duty members were killed at, or near, their homes, their places of work or while making deliveries. By contrast, of the twenty-two serving RUC and RUC Reserve (RUCR) members killed by the IRA, fourteen were on duty when they lost their lives, while the remaining eight were off-duty. Of twenty-one British soldiers killed, three were shot in ambushes while four were killed in gun battles; the remaining fourteen died in bomb explosions.

Fifty-eight of the 100 killed by the IRA died at, or near, the border, which demonstrates the extensive use made of the border in carrying out many attacks. Forty-two people were shot dead in ambushes, while four were killed in gun battles and two were killed as alleged informers; five were killed in under-car bomb explosions, while a further forty-two were killed by landmines and other bomb explosions; three bomb disposal ammunition technical officers (ATOs) were killed while attempting to defuse bombs and two civilians died of heart attacks during gun and bomb attacks.

KILLED BY BRITISH ARMY

31/05/1972	UDR member was shot accidentally on a firing range.
23/10/1972	2 Catholic civilians – so-called 'Pitchfork murders' (stabbed by soldiers of the Argyll and Sutherland Highlanders).
20/01/1975	IRA member (shot by undercover soldiers).
25/11/1981	Young Catholic woman (shot by off-duty member of the Royal Anglian Regiment).

02/12/1984	IRA member (shot by SAS).
02/12/1984	IRA member (drowned while escaping from SAS in the same incident).
08/04/1985	Catholic civilian (sectarian motive – shot by a soldier on leave, gun supplied by UDR member).
26/04/1986	IRA member (shot by SAS).

KILLED BY RUC

17/05/1973	Catholic civilian (shot in car chase).

KILLED BY UDR

06/02/1992	IRA member (shot in self-defence).

KILLED BY LOYALISTS

16/12/1972	IRA member.	21/04/1974	Catholic civilian.
24/07/1974	Catholic civilian.	27/05/1975	Catholic civilian.

Of the fifteen people killed by the security forces and loyalists, one was a member of the UDR, six were IRA volunteers and the remaining eight were Catholic civilians; three of the latter were members of NICRA). An attempt was made on the life of a fourth NICRA member.

All four victims of loyalist paramilitaries were shot at, or near, their place of work. A UDR member shot an IRA member in a gun battle in self-defence; an RUC officer shot a young Catholic man in a car chase in disputed circumstances. Of the nine people killed by the British Army, five were shot, two were stabbed and one drowned while escaping.

CHRONOLOGY OF DEATHS (1971–1979)

1971

Two security force members – one UDR member and one British soldier – were killed by the IRA in late 1971.

Pte Francis Veitch (23): On 3 September Francis Veitch, a 23-year-old UDR member, former B-Special and only son of a farmer, became the first victim of the conflict in Fermanagh; he was the first member of 4 UDR (4th Battalion) to be killed and the second UDR man to be killed in the conflict. He was also a member of the Orange Order.[476] He was shot outside Kinawley RUC station; the gunmen opened fire from a car, hitting him with at least five bullets, one of which struck him in the neck. After the shooting, the killers sped off towards the border.[477]

Cpl David Powell, 16/5 Lancers (22): The second fatality in Fermanagh that year was a British soldier from Stoke-on-Trent. He was killed on 28 October near Kinawley by an IRA bomb. Several other soldiers were injured in the blast. His wife and baby daughter were living in married quarters in Omagh at the time.[478]

1972

Security forces deaths increased sharply in 1972. A total of twenty people died in conflict-related attacks in Fermanagh – seven UDR members, two RUC officers, five British soldiers, one Garda inspector, two Protestant civilians, two Catholic civilians and one IRA member. Sixteen of them were killed by the IRA; the two Catholic civilians were killed by the British Army, the IRA member was killed by the UVF or Ulster Defence Association (UDA), and one of the UDR members was killed by a British soldier.

Pte Thomas Francis McCann, Royal Army Ordnance Corps (19):[479] On 13 February a body was found in a ditch in Newtownbutler with a brown paper bag over his head.[480] He had been shot in the back of the head, he was hooded[481] and his mouth had been bound with masking tape. He was identified as Pte Thomas Francis McCann; he had been on compassionate leave in his native Dublin to visit his widowed mother, who was sick.[482] He was abducted and shot by the Official IRA.[483]

Pte Thomas John (Johnny) Fletcher (43): On 1 March at Frevagh, near Garrison, as he was driving to work, Pte Fletcher, a UDR member, was accosted by four armed men when he stopped his car at the gate of the laneway outside his home. He was ordered out of the car and marched back to his house. As he was held outside at gunpoint, the men searched his home and found a pistol and a shotgun. They quizzed Pte Fletcher about the location of his UDR rifle. He told them it was held at his depot in Enniskillen, but when they searched his barn, they found the rifle hidden there. They told his wife they were taking her husband as a hostage to the border, but a couple of hundred yards from his house, they marched him into a field and shot him dead.[484] His wife heard two bursts of automatic fire and one single shot. The attackers, taking Pte Fletcher's SLR (Self-Loading Rifle), pistol and shotgun, escaped across the border.[485] He and his wife had moved into the isolated 20-acre farm near the village of Garrison in 1969. He also had a job as a forestry worker. He had previously been a member of the B-Specials.[486] A close family friend and fellow UDR soldier, John McClure, recounts, 'They shot him 33 or 34 times. They dumped him on the river bank and strolled across the border into County Leitrim.'[487]

Two days after Pte Fletcher's funeral, John McClure left the area to live in Churchill, near the shores of Lower Lough Erne, with his wife and five children. The three other Protestant families remaining in Garrison also decided to leave.[488] According to Edward Burke, UDR Headquarters instructed a number of UDR members to move out of their homes in the border area near where Pte Fletcher was killed.[489]

WO2 (Sgt Major) Bernard Adamson (30): The UDR sergeant major and father of four was fatally wounded by a live bullet from an army-issue SLR on the firing range at Letterbreen, near Enniskillen; the incident took place during a battlefield simulation that was supposed to involve only blank cartridges.[490] He was shot by 19-year-old Pte Duncan Munro McLuckie[491] of the Royal Corps of Signals. Sgt Major Adamson died two weeks later, on 31 May, in the Royal Victoria Hospital, Belfast. No charges were ever brought against McLuckie, but he was fined £43 by a military tribunal looking into the circumstances of the incident.[492] More than thirty-five years after an initial inquest returned an open verdict, his family applied successfully to Attorney General Baroness Scotland to initiate a new inquest after raising concerns about the original hearing. The fresh inquest was held in 2011 and a jury decided that the shooting was accidental but that the decision to use mixed ammunition contributed to the soldier's death. The jury also found that that there had been inadequate medical assistance and McLuckie failed to have a blank attachment on the gun, breaching army regulations.[493] Despite these findings, the Ministry of Defence (MoD) argued that it was prevented by law from paying compensation to the family.[494]

Gunner Victor Husband (23), Gunner Brian Robertson (23): On 2 June, the two soldiers were killed instantly in a landmine explosion near Roslea, and two other soldiers were slightly injured. The device was detonated from across the border.[495]

Garda Inspector Samuel Donegan (61): Six days after Husband and Robertson were killed, on 8 June, Inspector Donegan lost his life when he took a few steps over the Cavan border into Fermanagh to examine what he believed was a hoax bomb. He and his colleagues had already come across a similar one on the Cavan side. This one, unfortunately for Inspector Donegan, was not a hoax. It had been intended for the northern security forces, but it exploded as he went to examine it. He died later in Cavan hospital.[496]

Lance Bombardier David Wynne, 4th Royal Artillery (21); Gunner Errol Leroy Gordon, 4th Royal Artillery (21): In the very early morning of 7 August, a Land Rover patrol was mined near Lisnaskea. Two members of the patrol, L/Bombardier Wynn, from Caerphilly, Wales, and Gunner Gordon, a native of Kingston, Jamaica,[497] were killed instantly. Two other soldiers were very seriously injured, both with head and facial injuries. The mine was wire-detonated – it had been placed in a culvert in the centre of the road. Between 200 and 300 lb of explosives were used, which left a crater 15 ft x 10 ft deep. The Land Rover was thrown 50 ft.[498]

L/Cpl Henry Creighton (27): The same night as the patrol was hit, L/Cpl Creighton, 4 UDR, stepped out of his car, having returned home from duty to Magheraveely, half a mile from the Monaghan border. He was ambushed by a man who fired a burst of automatic fire at him from behind a hedge. He was killed instantly. A tracker dog picked up the traces of the man, which led across the border. L/Cpl Creighton worked as a librarian.[499] His sister-in-law, Florence Creighton, recounted her experience of the night:

> I was on my own that night. Because two soldiers had been murdered in Lisnaskea the week before there was a lot of tension in the area. I was quite scared. I remember going to bed, in fact I didn't get into bed. I stayed in my trouser suit and brought the dog down to the bedroom with me. At twelve o'clock this car stopped and people got out. I was really, really scared. I went to the front door and my brother-in-law burst in and said: 'Harry's been shot.' The police made me come with them to Derrylin, because he was getting married a month later and I had to knock the door of Ethel Finlay's house and tell her that Harry, her fiancé, had been murdered. The sad thing was that his father was very protective of him, and if he was coming in at 3 or 4 o'clock, his father would have got up an hour beforehand to go around the house with an old shotgun to check no one was there. However, on that particular night they were watching the Mike Yarwood Show and it was 10.30pm in August. It was still daylight so his father hadn't gone out. Then they heard the shots.[500]

L/Cpl Alfred Johnston (32), Pte James Edward Eames (33): Later that month, on 25 August, a UDR foot patrol near Enniskillen noticed a suspicious car parked close up against a hedge. Two members of the patrol went to investigate. The car exploded and the UDR men, Johnston and Eames, were killed instantly.[501] Eleven soldiers were treated in the Erne Hospital for shock and cuts. The command wire was detonated from a nearby hill.[502] L/Cpl Johnston worked as a butcher in a local bacon factory, while Pte Eames was a post office engineer.[503] L/Cpl Johnston was married with four children; Pte Eames was married with three children.[504] John Downey, from Donegal, was extradited to answer charges for these killings in October 2019.[505]

William Trotter (57): Three days later, a mine exploded on a farm near Newtownbutler, killing Mr Trotter, a Protestant civilian, and his dog. The army report stated that 'it was apparent that the incident was a deliberate draw for the security forces but the unfortunate farmer had got there first.'[506] Mr Trotter was married and had two daughters.[507]

Pte Thomas Bullock (55), Emily Bullock (52): On the night of 21 September, at around 6 p.m., two cars, a black Hillman and a brown Ford Escort, crossed the border at Aghalane Bridge. The Escort drove to the home of Thomas and Emily Bullock. It is clear that Mrs Bullock tried bravely to obstruct the killers, as a .45 bullet was found to have entered her right hand, and lead smears were detected on a swab from the palm of her left hand. She was lying in the doorway when she was found and had been shot with a .45 revolver.[508] The attackers then moved into the house and killed her husband with a .303 or an M1 carbine.[509] Pte Bullock had been a B-Special for twenty years before joining the UDR. He was also a member of both the Black and Orange institutions. (The Royal Black Institution was formed in 1797, two years after the Orange Order was established. The members are Orangemen, and their admission to the Black Institution can be seen as a progression, although they are separate organisations.) He was caretaker for the Earl of Erne and had close ties to the Crom estate for many years, where he enjoyed fishing and attending shoots. His farm of several hundred acres was let out.[510] He was the nephew of Shan Bullock, Fermanagh's most celebrated author, and his grandfather had been a steward on the Earl of Erne's estate.[511]

Meanwhile, the Hillman, carrying five men, drove to the home of Pte John Darling, who was not at home. His wife saw the car approaching and hid the children under a bed, as well as her husband's SMG. The raiders ransacked the house, stealing his combat suit and two SMG magazines containing three rounds. They then left. Both cars then met up in the village with a third car (thought to be an old Austin A40 that was used as a scout car) and proceeded to drive back to the border. On their way, they fired a shot at Aghalane post office, which was also owned by a UDR man,[512] Mr Looney.[513]

According to South-East Fermanagh Foundation, Emily's niece said that Emily used to say, 'If anyone tries to come and get Tommy, it will be over my dead body.' That is literally what happened.[514]

Pte Robin John Bell (21): On 22 October, a UDR member, Robin Bell, the eldest of a family of five, was killed while travelling to the family's outfarm near Lough Erne in the area of Falon Bridge. He was a front-seat passenger in his father's car; two other brothers sat in the back. He was shot in the arms and head with an M1 carbine and a Garand, and he died later in the Erne Hospital.[515] Pte Bell had previously been a member of the B-Specials and joined the UDR on its formation in 1970.[516]

Michael Naan (31), Andrew Murray (23): On the following evening, 23 October, two Catholic civilians were killed by members of the Argyll and Sutherland Highlanders. This case will be dealt with in detail in Chapter 10.

Constable Joseph Calvin, RUCR (42): November 1972 saw the first police killing in Fermanagh. On 17 November, Constable Calvin was killed when his car exploded in a carpark in Enniskillen. He had just come off duty at midnight. He sat into his car along with a colleague and started the engine. He let it run for a few minutes to clear the windscreen while they chatted. His colleague then got out of the car and went to his own vehicle, which was parked nearby. Just then, there was an explosion, killing Constable Calvin instantly. His car had moved about two feet when the explosion occurred.[517] It was the first killing of the Troubles within the Enniskillen Borough boundary. Constable Calvin was married with a teenage daughter. He had worked as a health inspector[518] with Fermanagh Health Authority for over fifteen years. He was a native of Armagh.[519]

Constable Robert Keys, RUCR (55): On 28 November, a rocket attack was launched at Belleek RUC Station. Constable Keys died instantly when a rocket tore through a steel shutter in a window of the barracks. It hit him as he was mounting the stairs to come off duty. The rocket was launched from across the Erne, and this was the beginning of a sustained attack on the police station. It was believed that there were five attackers who then opened fire with rifles. Soldiers in the barracks returned fire. Gardaí and an army patrol from Finner raced to the border and immediately mounted a search through the fields on the Donegal side, but they failed to capture the attackers or the rocket launcher.[520]

Louis Leonard (26): An IRA member, he was the first loyalist casualty in the county and was killed by the UVF/UDA on 15 December. This case will be dealt with in detail in Chapter 12.

1973

Until May, 1973 was free of fatalities. During the year, seven people were killed – a marked reduction on the previous year. One UDR member was killed, as was one RUC officer and one British soldier; three Catholic civilians were also killed, and one IRA member was killed in a premature bomb explosion. Six of the deaths were caused by the IRA, while Michael Leonard, a Catholic civilian, was killed by the RUC.

Anthony Ahern (17): Mr Ahern, from Mayfield, Cork, was killed in a premature explosion on 10 May at Mullinahinch, near Roslea. He was the first IRA member from the republic to die in Northern Ireland since the deaths of Seán South and Fergal O'Hanlon on New Year's Day, 1957.[521] He was the youngest of five sons of his widowed mother [522] and was the youngest person to be killed in Fermanagh.

Michael Joseph Leonard (23): A Catholic civilian, he was shot by the RUC during a car chase near Belleek on 17 May 1973. This case will be dealt with in detail in Chapter 11.

Constable David Purvis (22): The police officer was shot while on foot patrol in Enniskillen on 5 June. Gunmen in a passing Hillman Minx with a southern registration plate fired at least twenty-five shots from a Sterling SMG at Constable Purvis and a colleague, Sgt Graham, shortly after midnight. Sgt Graham miraculously survived. Constable Purvis died in an army helicopter while being rushed to the Royal Victoria Hospital, Belfast.[523] He was a native of Maghera, County Derry.[524] The car was later found abandoned at Coa.[525]

Staff Sgt Ronald Beckett (37): On 30 August 1973, the IRA attacked the village of Tullyhommon, which is on the northern side of the border with Pettigo, County Donegal. The unit planted three bombs in the village, two of which wrecked a customs caravan and a garage, while the third, in the post office, failed to explode. The post office bomb killed Staff Sgt Beckett, a British Army ATO officer, as he attempted to defuse it. When the IRA unit placed the bomb in the garage, they tried to shoot its owner, Mervyn Johnston, a UDR soldier, who managed to escape into his home. He grabbed his Sterling SMG and began firing at the raiders, but they escaped across the border.[526]

On 28 September, what was believed to be a retaliatory attack was carried out by Fermanagh UVF members in Pettigo when they exploded a car bomb outside the home and grocery store of Plunkett Reid at 11.15 p.m. There were no injuries or fatalities, but the premises were destroyed.

Patrick Duffy (19): On 5 September, Mr Duffy, a Catholic civilian, was killed when he drove his tractor over an IRA landmine near his home in Greaghnaglera, Belcoo that was intended for the security forces. He was turning his tractor off the Belcoo to Garrison road into a field when the vehicle triggered a 100 lb device that had been placed on the roadside.[527] The Gardaí were said to be 'most co-operative during the follow-up action' and were present during 'a full clearing operation on 7 September'.[528]

Pte Matthew Lilly (54): On 7 September, the IRA took over a house at Keelogue, near Belcoo, where they lay in wait for UDR member Lilly, who was due to arrive on his milk round. On his arrival at the farm, he was shot dead while loading milk churns onto his vehicle.[529] The hijacked car used by the gunmen was later recovered by Gardaí at Blacklion, County Cavan.[530] This incident was to have repercussions for the owners of the house six months later.[531]

Raymond McAdam (20): A 23-year-old Catholic civilian was killed on 12 October while trying to save Lily Nicholl, the elderly mother of the Protestant owner of a newsagent's shop opposite his home at Annaghmore, Newtownbutler. A bomb was thrown at the newsagent's from a passing car, and as he was leading Mrs Nicholl to safety, the bomb exploded, killing him instantly and blowing Mrs Nicholl over a 10 ft wall. She suffered severe injuries to her head, hands and side, but she survived.[532] The IRA denied responsibility and refuted a number of press reports claiming that they were involved.[533] McKittrick argues that the IRA was the most likely culprit, as a number of IRA attacks on the same day appeared to represent a pattern.[534] Local nationalists and republicans deny IRA involvement, and a list drawn up by the Foreign and Commonwealth Office (FCO) after the Enniskillen bombing lends some weight to that denial. The list is headed, 'Terrorist murders in Fermanagh and south Tyrone (1971 to date)'and includes a column headed, 'Responsibility for murders'. Beside the name 'Raymond McAdam' is written 'Prot', meaning 'loyalists'.[535] Other British documents, however, state that the bomb was thrown through the shop window from a Wolseley car that had been hijacked earlier on the Clones–Cavan road, and that those responsible operated from Clonoony House, 'a well-known PIRA [Provisional IRA] safe house' located within the Drummully Salient.[536]

1974

A total of five people were killed in 1974 – two British soldiers, one Protestant civilian (a former member of the UDR) and two Catholic civilians. The IRA was responsible for three of the deaths, whereas the two Catholics were killed by loyalists.

Lt Col George Walter Saunderson (58): The highest-ranking UDR officer killed during the conflict was Lt Col Saunderson, although he was actually retired at the time of his death. He was killed on 10 April at the Earl of Erne Primary School, Teemore, where he was headmaster. He was married with seven adult children. He had a long record of service in the British armed forces, having joined the Royal Inniskilling Fusiliers when he was 18 years old, and he had served in Palestine and the Middle East.[537] He served with the Parachute Regiment throughout the Second World War.[538] When he returned to civilian life, he was appointed commander of B Company, Royal Inniskilling Fusiliers (TA), and also as sub-district commander of the B-Specials in the Derrylin area. When the B-Specials were disbanded, he helped to form the UDR.[539] He was also a member of the Ulster Special Constabulary Association (USCA).[540] He had retired as second-in-command of 4 UDR about a year before he was killed.[541]

On the morning of Mr Saunderson's killing, six gunmen hijacked a car 4 miles from the border at Gordineddan.[542] He was shot in the school kitchen while drinking a cup of coffee during the morning break. While the school's thirty-five pupils did not actually witness the shooting, as they were confined to their classrooms, they were badly frightened by the noise of the gunfire and were sent home immediately afterwards.[543] On their arrival, the gunmen had gone straight to the kitchen suggesting that they knew of both the time of the morning break and Mr Saunderson's habit of going to the kitchen.[544] The killers, on making their escape, crossed the border and smashed through a Garda checkpoint at Ballyconnell. They later hijacked another car, which was found burnt out in Cavan.[545]

Pte Norman McKenzie (25): A member of the Royal Corps of Transport, he was killed on 11 April, the day after Mr Saunderson was killed, when a landmine exploded under his Land Rover during a patrol near Lisnaskea on the road to Newtownbutler. Another soldier was seriously injured in the blast.[546] Pte McKenzie was from Bracebridge, Lincolnshire.[547]

James Edward Murphy (42): Mr Murphy was shot dead and his body was found on the forecourt of his garage at Corraveighy, Kinawley in the early hours of Sunday, 21 April 1974. He was a prominent member of NICRA. This case will be discussed in detail in Chapter 12.

Patrick (Patsy) Kelly (33): Three months later, Patsy Kelly, an independent nationalist councillor on Omagh District Council, was abducted and murdered on 24 July. Like Jim Murphy and Michael Naan, he was an active member of the civil rights campaign.[548] The Kelly case will be discussed in detail in Chapter 13.

Sgt Major John Maddocks (32): A bomb disposal officer with the Royal Army Ordnance Corps, he was killed instantly on 2 December while trying to defuse a large milk churn bomb in a field at Gortmullen on the Derrylin–Ballyconnell road. He was married with two children.[549]

1975

The murders continued at a relatively low-level between 1975 and 1979. Four people were killed in 1975 – two by the IRA, one by the British Army, and one by the UVF. Four were killed in 1976, as well as four in 1977, two in 1978 and six in 1979.

Patrick Mulroe argues that the killing of Senator Billy Fox in Monaghan in March 1974 dented IRA morale and support in Clones, and this contributed to the lull in violence along the Fermanagh border at that time.[550] An official in the Department of Foreign Affairs, however, wrote that

> At the end of January 1974 the UVF responded to an IRA request, that in return for a Provo declaration that off-duty UDR men were no longer legitimate targets, the loyalists would cease sectarian assassinations, by issuing a statement condemning sectarian executions and calling on all paramilitary bodies to ensure that such activity ceased forthwith.[551]

A cable to Washington from the American Ambassador to Britain, Walter Annenberg, also reported this development. He stated that the 'Provo campaign' against the UDR had led to reciprocal assassinations of Belfast Catholics by loyalist organisations.[552]

Although it is true to say that the IRA did not kill any UDR members in the years 1974–77 inclusive, on a couple of occasions at least, members were targeted – one of which resulted in the death of Margaret Kilfedder (see below). The sectarian murder of Catholics in other areas continued as before.

Kevin Coen (28): A member of the IRA's South Fermanagh Unit and a native of Riverstown, County Sligo,[553] he was shot dead by undercover soldiers on 20 January. There are conflicting reports of how he met his death. He was one of a group of IRA members who were attempting to hijack a Dublin–Donegal CIE bus when they were surprised by a British Army undercover mobile unit.[554] As the bus approached Cassidy's Cross, near Kinawley, a mile on the northern side of the border, the driver was signalled to stop by two armed men who told him they were taking the bus. They ordered him and his passengers onto the road.[555]

Reports from eyewitnesses said that Kevin Coen was shot dead as he ran forward to warn the driver of an oncoming car of the obstruction that the bus was causing. Unfortunately for him, it was an unmarked car containing an undercover British Army unit, and as its lights picked Coen out, the undercover soldiers opened fire and Coen was killed.[556] After he was killed, the IRA returned fire and a gun battle continued for about an hour while the bus passengers lay terrified in a nearby ditch.

The plain-clothes soldiers involved in his death claimed that as Coen approached their car, he raised a rifle to his shoulder. The soldiers fired and Coen was killed; another member of the IRA group was wounded in the exchanges that followed.[557]

Other reports claimed that Kevin Coen made no effort to fire. He was seen to be carried into the ditch by the force of the bullets, dropping the rifle. His body lay there for hours – until the following morning, when he was removed to the morgue at Enniskillen.[558] According to a report in the *Leitrim Observer*, he had previously served in the Irish Army.[559]

This killing occurred at a very sensitive time – like that of another IRA member, John Francis Green, in Monaghan ten days earlier. The IRA ceasefire, which had been brokered at Feakle, County Clare in December, had broken down on 17 January. Despite these IRA deaths, the ceasefire was renewed on 9 February.

Sgt William Robson (22): Sgt Robson of 15/19th Hussars, from Glasgow, was shot in a gun battle with the IRA at Mullan, near Kinawley, on 7 February when his border patrol was ambushed by the IRA.[560] He died later in hospital. At 22 years of age, he was the youngest sergeant in his regiment.[561] He was married just a few months previously.[562]

Patrick O'Reilly (53): A Catholic civilian from Coa, Ballinamallard, he was shot dead as he sat in the cab of his lorry on the Kilskeery–Irvinestown road on 27 May. He had been working on a road-widening scheme for several weeks. He had parked his lorry alongside an excavator when a gunman – wearing sunglasses, and with an anorak hood over his head and a scarf over his mouth – approached him. The gunman fired a burst of shots from a Sterling SMG, hitting Mr O'Reilly four times in the head and chest.[563] This case will be discussed in detail in Chapter 13.

Margaret Kilfedder (60): On 1 June, Ms Kilfedder, a Protestant civilian, was killed in her bed when a gas cylinder containing a bomb exploded and wrecked her home near Garrison in the early hours of the morning; the bedroom wall was blown in, and a part of the house collapsed.[564] Her husband Samuel escaped with minor injuries. The bungalow, which was owned by a UDR man, was rented by the Kilfedders – the IRA bomb was probably intended for the UDR man.[565] Samuel was a native of Leitrim, and they had moved from Belfast to the bungalow about a year earlier.[566] Margaret was the mother of five adult children.[567]

1976

In 1976, four men were killed – all by the IRA. Three of them were RUC officers who lost their lives in a single attack; the other man killed was a Protestant civilian.

Sgt Henry Keys, RUC (27); Constable Francis Kettyles, RUCR (39); Constable Thomas Evans, RUCR (33): The three officers died in this attack on 15 May. They were killed by a booby-trap bomb explosion at the rear of MacNean Park Housing Estate, behind the police station in the border village of Belcoo.[568] A joint army/RUC patrol was, at daybreak, investigating a shooting incident in which two UDR men were fired upon outside the local police station. The patrol was crossing a field when the police triggered the booby-trap bomb. Sgt Keys was married with a 2-year-old son, Constable Evans was married with no family, and Constable Kettyles was married with a 15-year-old son and a 7-year-old daughter.[569]

Gordon Liddle (28): The fourth death was that of a Protestant civilian, who was killed by an IRA bomb near Lisnaskea on 17 July. The bomb went off as he drove his car down the laneway from his house to collect mail from Newtownbutler post office, where he worked as a postman. He was rushed to the Erne Hospital but died despite undergoing emergency surgery.[570] It was believed that the bomb was intended for his two younger brothers, who were members of the RUCR. They were due to travel down the laneway for police duty a short time later. Mr Liddle was married and was the father of a 7-month-old baby.[571]

1977

The four people who lost their lives in 1977 – two British soldiers, one RUC officer and a Protestant civilian – were all killed by the IRA.

Sgt Martin Eamonn Walsh (28): A bomb disposal officer and a member of the Royal Army Ordnance, he was killed on 9 January while trying to dismantle a bomb near Newtownbutler – he was investigating a device in a milk churn. The bomb had been left in a shop the previous evening. Sgt

Walsh had succeeded in dragging the churn out of the shop and past the petrol pumps on the forecourt and was about to make a closer examination when it exploded, killing him instantly. He was the sixteenth ATO to be killed in Northern Ireland since 1969.[572] He was married with two children.[573]

Constable William Brown (18): A native of Strabane, County Tyrone, Constable Brown was killed on 13 March in an IRA ambush near Ballagh crossroads, about 3 miles from Lisnaskea. He had left the RUC's training depot at Enniskillen only four months earlier. He was a member of the Orange Order. Constable Brown was the driver of a patrol car when he was shot dead; a policewoman survived the incident.[574] He was the one-hundredth policeman to be killed in Northern Ireland since the start of the conflict[575] and the youngest policeman to be killed in Fermanagh.

Trooper Sean Prendergast (22): A soldier of 9/12th Lancers from Corby, Pte Prendergast died in a Belfast hospital from injuries sustained when an IRA landmine exploded under his Ferret armoured car while on patrol in the townland of Drumnasrene, just outside Belleek, on 5 April. Two other soldiers were injured in the attack.[576]

Douglas Deering (52): A Protestant civilian, Mr Deering was shot dead in his Mace shop in Roslea on 12 May. His death will be dealt with in detail in Chapter 9.

1978

Two people, a UDR member and a Catholic civilian, were killed by the IRA in 1978.

Pte Alan Ferguson (23): Henry Patterson argues that 'the exploitation of the border for attacks was clear' when this UDR member was shot dead on 25 June in a landmine and shooting attack on the Garrison–Belcoo road a few hundred yards from the Leitrim border. He was in a two-vehicle mobile patrol.[577] The mine was detonated from across the border and the IRA unit then opened fire with an M60 machine gun.[578] The attack was carried out by an eight-man unit, and because of the intensity of the shooting, no fire was returned.[579] Pte Ferguson had two brothers and was a member of the Orange Order.[580] According to Mulroe, after this attack the British Army would only patrol within 2 kilometres of the Fermanagh border in groups of twelve or more.[581]

Patrick Fee (64): The second death in 1978 occurred on 21 August when Mr Fee, a Catholic civilian, was killed. He was the front-seat passenger in a Fermanagh District Council van when it was ambushed by the IRA on the Belcoo–Garrison road. It was claimed that the intended target was the driver of the van, who was a member of the UDR.[582] However, this theory was discounted by Northern Ireland Office (NIO) official P.W.J. Buxton, who wrote a report on the shooting. He remarks that the job had been allocated only that morning and no outsider could have known in advance that a UDR man would be the driver. He surmised that it was more likely that the gunmen thought it was a security force vehicle. Local water service workers claimed that the army disguised vehicles to look like theirs for undercover work, but this was discounted by Buxton.[583]

1979

The six people killed in 1979 – one soldier, one police officer, one serving and one former member of the UDR, one Protestant civilian and one IRA member – were all victims of the IRA.

Robert Maughan, 9/12th Lancers and 14th Intelligence (described as a Field Intelligence Non-Commissioned Officer) (30); Norman Prue, RUC Special Branch Detective (29): Both men were shot outside Holy Cross Church, Lisnaskea while Mass was taking place on 6 May.[584] They both worked in intelligence.[585] Constable Prue got out of the car to buy a copy of *Republican News*, which was on sale outside the church gates. Apparently this was a weekly occurrence, thereby alerting the IRA. A gunman appeared from behind a wall and shot him. Sgt Maughan was shot by other gunmen as he sat in their unmarked Lada car.[586] The IRA grabbed the security force members' personal issue weapons before making their getaway.[587]

Jack McClenaghan (63): As he delivered bread in Garrison on 19 May, Mr McClenaghan, a Protestant civilian (and former member of the UDR), was shot in the back. He was standing at the rear of his van, about to open the doors to make a delivery to Patrick Carthy's shop.[588] His death will be discussed more fully in Chapter 9.

Michael Kearney (20): An IRA member from Belfast, he was abducted in Belfast and killed near Newtownbutler on 11 July by the IRA, who alleged he was an informer. His body was found 50 yards on the northern side of the border. He had been shot in the head. This case will be discussed more fully in Chapter 9.

Sylvia Crowe (32): A Protestant civilian, Ms Crowe was killed at a bus stop on 17 July on the Roslea–Lisnaskea road when the IRA triggered a bomb packed into milk cans on a trailer near where several civilians were standing. Four hours before the attack, gunmen forced their way into the mobile home of a local man. They held him and his family hostage while they ran wires from the mobile home to a detonation spot 50 yards from the road and waited for a UDR patrol. Four UDR members were injured – one of them, Grant Weir, very seriously[589] – as well as two other civilians, including Ms Crowe's mother. Mr Weir had previously served in the Royal Marines but had transferred to the UDR a year earlier.[590] Ms Crowe worked in the Faith Mission bookshops in Belfast and Lurgan.[591]

Cpl Herbert Kernaghan (36): A part-time corporal in the UDR, he was shot while making a regular weekly delivery of fruit and vegetables to St Tierney's Catholic Primary School, Roslea, at 9 a.m. on 15 October. Two armed men took over the school and held the staff hostage in the dining-hall. When Cpl Kernaghan arrived, the gunmen went up to the van and fired a number of shots through the driver's open window, hitting him sixteen times and killing him instantly. The gunmen escaped in the caretaker's car.[592] About twenty children were eye-witnesses to the shooting. One young boy said later that he and others had run into some trees when the shooting started, but after it stopped, they ran out and over to the place where the shooting had taken place.[593] It was a truly shocking and traumatic experience for the school children.

Cpl Kernaghan was the father of three young children, and his fourth child was born just two weeks after his death. He had joined the UDR at its formation in 1970. He was a member of Ballindarragh Orange Lodge and played the accordion in the Ballindarragh Accordion Band.[594]

Chapter 8:

THE CONFLICT IN FERMANAGH (PART 2)

CHRONOLOGY OF DEATHS (1980-94)

1980

The year 1980 saw the death toll rise to nine: three UDR members, four RUC officers and two Protestant civilians (one of them a former member of the UDR) – all attributed to the IRA.

Constable Robert Crilly, RUCR (60): On 3 January 1980, he was shot in his garage in Newtownbutler. A 12-year-old boy, Ciaran Allen, who was helping him, witnessed the shooting. Ciaran was a neighbour and a constant companion of Constable Crilly's.[595] Three men drove into the garage in a red estate car. Two of them jumped out and fired point-blank into their victim. They then drove off at high speed along the Wattlebridge road towards the Cavan border.[596] Constable Crilly was said to be a very popular Protestant in an overwhelmingly Catholic town. He had friends in both communities. He was a native of Lisburn and had established his business in the village thirty-five years earlier.[597] His garage had previously been wrecked in a bomb explosion a few minutes into the New Year of 1973.[598]

Cpl Aubrey Alexander Abercrombie (44): A part-time corporal in the UDR, he was shot on his 56-acre farm near Kinawley, 5 miles from the Cavan border, on 5 February. He was married with four children.[599] Three shots were heard in the area, and although the RUC and Garda were alerted, there was no trace of the gunmen. When Cpl Abercrombie failed to return home for his tea, a family member was sent to look for him and found him dead on his tractor.[600] He had been a member of the UDR since its inception and was also a member of Florencecourt Flute Band.[601] An IRA member, Séamus McElwain, was convicted in May 1982 of Abercrombie's murder and that of Ernest Johnston, and of conspiracy to murder members of the security forces. The judge recommended a minimum sentence of thirty years.[602]

Constables Winston Howe (35), Joseph Rose (21): Both RUC officers were killed six days after Cpl Abercrombie, on 11 February. They were members of a mobile patrol travelling from Roslea to Lisnaskea; the vehicle in which they were travelling was blown up by an 800 lb culvert bomb, killing them both instantly. A command wire was found leading from the scene of the explosion to a firing point 250 m away on a derelict farm. It is believed that two men were involved.[603] Constable Howe was married with two sons, while Constable Rose, from Dundonald, was single. Rose had been transferred from Belleek to Roslea only two days before he was killed.[604] Ernest Johnston, another member of the patrol, survived the attack, but his reprieve was to be short-lived as he lost his life seven months later, in September.

Victor Morrow (62): A founder member of the UDR and a former B-Special, he was killed on 17 April 1980 while on his way to work in a factory in Lisnaskea. He had left the UDR about a year previously.[605] He was also a member of both the Orange Order and the Black Preceptory.[606] It was first believed that he was the victim of a hit-and-run accident, until the bullet wounds were found.[607] In an article published in *Magill* magazine, the journalist Paddy Agnew described his death:

> Just after 6.00 pm he left his home on the outskirts of Newtownbutler, Co. Fermanagh to walk the mile or so into town. He worked as a machine operator at the Sir Richard Arkwright plastics [cotton] factory in nearby Lisnaskea. He was working on the night shift and was walking, lunch box under his arm, into town to get a lift with one of his workmates. The Newtownbutler–Clones road along which he walked is a typical Fermanagh country road. On one side there is open wet land of scutch-grass and rushes, whilst the other side is lined by a little wood. Morrow had gone less than three hundred yards from his home when he was shot dead, at a range of two or three yards, by a gunman who had been waiting for him, hidden in the trees at the side of the road. Morrow's killer had waited until he came alongside before hitting him

> with three bullets with such deadly accuracy that Morrow was probably dead before he hit the ground. The gunman then climbed over the ditch and onto the road. He stood over the body of Morrow who lay face down, his lunch box still firmly tucked under his arm, and fired another six bullets into the back of the prostrate man's head.[608]

According to the RUC, he was shot nine times in the back of the head.[609] Several men from around Newtownbutler were said to have been held for questioning shortly after the murder, but no charges were brought.[610] The IRA claimed that Mr Morrow had not left the security forces and had been observed operating with the UDR at a checkpoint in Fermanagh three weeks previously; that he also intended to join the RUCR.[611] However, no evidence emerged to substantiate such claims.

Pte Richard Latimer (39): On 9 June, UDR member Pte Latimer was shot in his hardware store in Newtownbutler. He was alone in the shop when a man entered, produced a handgun and fired several shots, killing him instantly. The gunmen escaped by car in the direction of the border.[612] Pte Latimer and his family had previously been intimidated out of their farmhouse near the border after gun attacks several years earlier. In 1971, shortly after he moved to the town, an attempt was made to burn down his shop – an incendiary device was thrown through the window.[613] Like Douglas Deering and Robert Crilly, his was also a Protestant business in a Catholic town. There were claims at the time that the Latimer family were 'ethnically cleansed' from their border homestead – a strategy said to be used by republicans to create buffer zones and to push the border back.[614]

Pte Latimer's brother, George, 80 years old in 2019, participated in a Methodist service for RTÉ television by providing a testimonial for the programme, which was aired on 28 July 2019:

> After I married, I worked the family farm and joined the Ulster Defence Regiment, the UDR. We were attacked by IRA gunmen on our farm on 16th March 1972 who opened fire on my brother Richard and I. We ran for cover. Richard got back to the house, found his weapon and returned a few rounds of gun fire. Then it was all over. It got worse that summer with my neighbours being murdered and blown up in bombs and shootings. Our

> farm was dominated by high ground around us and we were in a vulnerable situation. One evening in October 1972, the gunmen had another bang at us. It started at 6.30pm and lasted for four hours. After that, we were advised to leave by the army and politicians. My brother and I decided to move – our wives, my mother, sister and three year old daughter. The cattle and machinery were auctioned but we held onto the farm. My family were given Housing Executive houses in Lisnaskea but we got no compensation.[615]

Constable Ernest Johnston (34): After a lull of three months, full-time reservist Constable Johnston, who had survived an earlier attack in which his two colleagues were killed, was shot by two gunmen as he closed the garage doors at his home near Magheraveely on 23 September 1980.[616] He had worked on his father's farm since he left school and was married with two sons. He was a member of the Orange Order.[617]

In May 1982, IRA leader Séamus McElwain was convicted of his murder and also that of Alexander Abercrombie, killed on 5 February. He was sentenced to a recommended minimum thirty-year term of imprisonment.[618]

Pte Norman Donaldson (59): A full-time UDR member, Pte Donaldson was shot by the IRA on 25 November as he was leaving Derrygonnelly RUC Station, where he had been collecting money for a hospital charity. The vehicle used in the murder was a green Peugeot 504 that was hijacked by six gunmen who held ten hostages in a farmhouse near Garrison village while the shooting took place.[619] It was believed that RUC officers who normally closed the station at 7 p.m. were the targets of the gunmen. Pte Donaldson was a member of the Orange Order.[620]

John Dundas (65): Mr Dundas, a Protestant civilian and a close friend of Norman Donaldson, suffered a fatal heart attack and crashed his car after driving past the spot where Pte Donaldson had just been killed.[621]

1981

This year saw a considerable reduction in deaths – down from nine, in 1980, to four. Three of those killed were members of the UDR killed by the IRA. The fourth was a young Catholic woman who was killed by a British soldier.

L/Cpl Thomas Ronald (Ronnie) Graham (39): Mr Graham, a founder member of the UDR and an Orange Order member, was delivering coal to a house near Lisnaskea when he was shot by the IRA on 5 June. The killers had set up an ambush and were holding a woman hostage, waiting for L/Cpl Graham to arrive before gunning him down. Mr Graham lived in nearby Derryhurdian; he was survived by his wife and two children.[622] Like Victor Morrow, he had worked at the Sir Richard Arkwright cotton factory at Lisnaskea. He had worked there for twenty years, mostly on the night shift. When news of his murder reached the factory, the entire shift walked out.[623] He was a former player with Lisnaskea Rovers soccer team and a drummer in Colebrooke Pipe Band.[624] In 1986, an 18-year-old – who was 13 years old at the time of the killing – was jailed for seven years. He was convicted of moving weapons for the IRA that had been used in the murder.[625] The cases of the three Graham brothers will be discussed in Chapter 9.

Pte Cecil Graham (32): A part-time UDR member and brother of Ronnie, he was visiting his Catholic wife and five-week-old baby on 11 November. His wife was staying with her parents in Donagh because the baby was premature and required constant care. As he left his parents-in-law's house, Pte Graham was hit sixteen times by bullets from an Armalite rifle, and he died later in hospital.[626] He lived in Maguiresbridge and was a member of the Apprentice Boys of Derry.[627] After his death, a huge 'seal and search' operation was carried out in Donagh by about 500 security force members.[628]

Cpl Albert Beacom (42): A UDR member and farmer, Cpl Beacom was shot at his home in Maguiresbridge on 17 November after taking two of his young sons to a Boys' Brigade meeting in Brookeborough. He was the father of five children. He was shot five times as he crossed his farmyard. His wife ran out of the house to find him dying. His family called for no reprisals.[629] A 26-year-old Roslea man was acquitted of a charge of murdering him and of possessing two rifles.[630] The court found the man had been acting under duress when he drove the attackers to Maguiresbridge.[631]

Angela D'Arcy (24): A young, single Catholic woman had just enjoyed a visit to a friend's home in Enniskillen on the evening of 25 November 1981 when she was shot by a British soldier who was on a tour of duty with the

Royal Anglian Regiment, based in St Angelo barracks. This case will be discussed in detail in Chapter 11.

1982

Like 1981, in terms of deaths, 1982 and 1983 were relatively quiet years. Three people were killed in just two attacks in 1982 – one soldier, one RUC officer and one Protestant civilian.

Pte Colin Clifford (21): A soldier of the Royal Hampshire Regiment and a native of St Helier, Jersey, he was killed by an IRA landmine 200 yards from the border, at Meenatully, Belleek, on 30 April 1982. The device was detonated by command wire from across the border.[632] He was on an eight-man patrol when the bomb was triggered.[633]

D/Constable Garry Ewing, RUC officer (31); Helen Woodhouse (29): An IRA bomb exploded under the RUC officer's car in Enniskillen on 9 November. He had been taking an archery class in the Lakeland Forum Leisure Centre.[634] He had previously escaped death in an IRA bombing in January 1973 near Pomeroy[635] when a device exploded under a Land Rover in which he was a passenger. His colleague, the driver, was killed in that incident. Ms Helen Woodhouse, a Protestant civilian and employee at the leisure centre, was a passenger in the car on 9 November; she was critically injured and died later in hospital. She had worked as a recreation officer. She was a friend of the Ewing family, often babysitting for their two children and playing squash with Mrs Ewing.[636]

1983

In 1983, there was just a single death – that of a Protestant civilian killed by the IRA in February.

Allan Price (52): A Protestant civilian, he was shot by the IRA in a case of mistaken identity on 19 February. He was standing in for the intended target – the regular postman in the Arney area, who was a UDR member. Three armed and masked men took over the thatched cottage and waited several hours for the post office van to arrive. They held hostage the elderly man who lived there alone. After they shot Mr Price dead, they escaped in his van, which was found abandoned a mile away.[637] The IRA men were believed to have come from outside the area, as Mr Price would have been a familiar figure to locals.[638]

1984

Seven people lost their lives in Fermanagh in 1984 – four British soldiers, including an SAS member; one Protestant civilian (a former UDR member); and two IRA members.

Ronald Funston (28): A former member of the UDR, retired for six years, was killed on 13 March shortly after 8 a.m. as he worked on the family farm near Pettigo. His death will be discussed more fully in Chapter 9.

Cpl Thomas Agar (35), L/Cpl Robert Huggins (29): On 18 May, four off-duty soldiers of the Royal Regiment of Fusiliers based at Ballykelly were struck by an explosion from under their car. Two of them were killed instantly by the detonation. The other two soldiers were seriously injured; one of them died five months later. Similar to Gary Ewing, they had parked their Datsun van outside the Lakeland Forum Leisure Centre while they took part in an angling competition on the Erne.[639] They were putting away their fishing gear when the bomb exploded. Cpl Agar, from Tyne and Wear, was married with a 9-year-old son, while L/Cpl Huggins, from Manchester, was married with three young sons.[640]

L/Cpl Peter Gallimore (27): He was also a member of the Royal Regiment of Fusiliers. He died on 17 October from a heart attack brought on by the serious injuries he had received in the same explosion that killed his comrades, Agar and Huggins, on 18 May.[641] L/Cpl Gallimore was married and had a 4-year-old son. A fourth soldier survived the attack with serious injuries.[642]

Antoin MacGiolla Bhríde (27), Kieran Fleming (25): On 2 December 1984, Antoin MacGiolla Bhríde and Kieran Fleming lost their lives in disputed circumstances that also left an SAS soldier, Lance Corporal Alistair Slater, dead. These cases will be discussed in detail in Chapter 11.

L/Cpl Alistair Slater (28): He was a member of an SAS surveillance team that was secretly monitoring an IRA team on the Kesh–Pettigo road on 2 December. After the SAS shot Antoin MacGiolla Bhríde, the IRA opened fire on the soldiers, killing Alistair Slater. In his obituary in *Mars and Minerva*, the SAS internal magazine, he was described as having served in Cyprus, Berlin and Hong Kong.[643] He was posthumously awarded the Military Medal. Prior to joining the SAS, he was a member of 1 Parachute Regiment.[644]

1985

Four people lost their lives in 1985 – one UDR member and two RUC officers were killed by the IRA, and a Catholic civilian was killed in a sectarian attack by a member of the British Army.

Pte James (Jimmy) Graham (39): On 1 February 1985, a UDR member, Jimmy Graham, the brother of Ronnie and Cecil, was killed by the IRA as he sat in his school bus in Derrylin waiting to take children to a local swimming pool. As well as working as a bus driver, he also had a small farm. He was awarded the British Empire Medal in 1980 after a previous attack on his life.[645] He was found lying in the aisle of the bus with his gun beside him.[646]

Sgt Hugh McCormac (40): A Catholic RUC officer, he was shot two or three times at point-blank range in front of his wife and three children as he arrived for Mass at St Gabriel's Monastery, The Graan, Enniskillen on 3 March. The two masked gunmen ran up a hill at the side of the carpark to a waiting car, which sped away.[647] Sgt McCormac was an instructor at the RUC training centre in Enniskillen and was a native of Portadown.[648] He was a member of the Graan choir and a church collector.[649] His brother, John, had been shot dead in Belfast twelve years previously, in May 1973, by gunmen in a passing car at the junction of Raglan Street and the Falls Road. It was the first murder to be claimed by the so-called Ulster Freedom Fighters (UFF).[650]

Martin Love (24): A Catholic civilian, Mr Love was shot dead as he walked home from a hotel just after midnight on Easter Monday, 8 April 1985. A soldier from the Royal Electrical and Mechanical Engineers (REME), Mark Trotter, who was home in Enniskillen on leave, was the gunman. His accomplice, who supplied the murder weapon, a 9mm Walther pistol, was James Robert Kenny, a member of C Company, 4 UDR. Kenny's father was an RUC officer who would have been friendly with both Mr Love and his father, while Mr Love's sister lived next door to Trotter's family. The murder was claimed by the UDA using its cover name, the UFF. During the trial, there was no reference to either the UFF or UDA, as both men were members of the security forces. Subsequently, both Trotter and Kenny were sentenced to life imprisonment, which they served on UDA prison wings.[651] Kenny also received a ten-year concurrent sentence for an armed robbery of £4,525 in 1984, and three years for the unlawful collection of information.[652]

The Love family was very insulted when a wreath arrived from C Company, 4 UDR, and Mr Love's father ordered that it be thrown over a hedge in the cemetery. He was a member of the Alliance Party.[653] The officiating priest at Mr Love's funeral referred to him as having worked all his life for better community relations. He had been on the best of terms with his Protestant neighbours and was totally opposed to violence.[654]

Constable William Robert (Bob) Gilliland (39): On 18 June, RUC officer Gilliland died while undergoing emergency surgery after he was caught in a 1,000 lb IRA landmine explosion between Kinawley and Florencecourt.[655] He was a native of Lisbellaw and was married with two sons. A colleague suffered life-changing injuries.[656] Rev. Ian Paisley claimed after Constable Gilliland's murder that 'feelings among many loyalists were already running at an all-time high in areas like Fermanagh where Sinn Féin held seats in district councils'.[657] Séamus McElwain was convicted of conspiracy to murder members of the security forces.[658]

1986

Five men died in 1986. Four of them were at the hands of the IRA – a Catholic UDR member, two RUC officers and a Catholic civilian. The fifth was an IRA member killed by the SAS.

Pte John Early (22): A Catholic UDR member, he was killed on 3 February in a landmine explosion on the Belcoo–Garrison road. It was set off by remote control as he led an eight-man foot patrol. Police believed it was detonated from high ground near the village of Belcoo, close to the Leitrim border. The other seven members of the patrol received only minor injuries. [659] Pte Early had been a part-time member of the UDR since 1984 and had very recently become a full-time member.[660] There were no military honours at his funeral, and his UDR colleagues who attended wore civilian clothes.[661] The Taoiseach sent a message of condolence to the British Prime Minister, and the Minister for Foreign Affairs issued a statement on behalf of the Irish government condemning 'this latest atrocity against the UDR'.[662]

D/Constable Derek Breen, RUC officer (29); John McCabe, Catholic civilian (25): The two men were shot in a Maguiresbridge pub, Talk of the Town, on 11 February. D/Constable Breen was having an after-work drink on his way home to Lisbellaw, while John McCabe, from Ballyconnell, County Cavan, who was newly married, had been employed as a barman at the pub for six months. The IRA said his killing was an accident.[663] Three masked gunmen singled out D/Constable Breen and opened fire at close range as he sat at the bar. Mr McCabe was standing behind the bar talking to the policeman and was caught in the line of fire. As the killers departed the bar, they left behind an incendiary bomb, which exploded later, causing some damage to the building. Members of the Breen and McCabe families attended both funerals.[664] The Fermanagh Brigade of the IRA, in a statement claiming responsibility for the attack, alleged that the owners of the bar had allowed their premises to be used by the RUC as a centre for a 'spy network'. This allegation was firmly denied by the owners.[665]

Séamus Turlough McElwain (26): He was from Scotstown, County Monaghan. He was shot dead by the SAS in controversial circumstances on 26 April 1986. This case will be discussed in detail in Chapter 11.

Constable John McVitty (46): Constable McVitty, an RUC officer from Newtownbutler, was killed by the IRA on 8 July while working on his farm near Roslea, 400 yards from the Monaghan border. The IRA unit escaped across the fields and over Lackey Bridge after the shooting. Constable McVitty was cutting rushes in a field with his 12-year-old son when he was shot. He had two other children. He was a member of the Orange Order and a former member of the B-Specials.[666] Both the RUC and

Gardaí launched a massive hunt for the killers on both sides of the border, using helicopters and sniffer dogs. Shortly afterwards, Gardaí in Monaghan arrested two men and a woman near the spot where he was killed, and they were held under the Offences against the State Act in connection with Mr McVitty's murder.[667] The author is unaware of whether or not anybody was charged or convicted. Rev. Kille spoke at Constable McVitty's funeral about how Fermanagh Protestants had been driven from their border farms.[668]

1987

This was the year of the Enniskillen bombing, but three security force members were killed by the IRA prior to 8 November, bringing the death toll for that year to fourteen – the second highest number of deaths in Fermanagh for any year. Only 1972 saw a higher death toll.

Constable Ivan Crawford, RUCR (49): He was killed on 9 January when a 10 lb IRA bomb exploded outside a toy shop in Enniskillen. The device, which was hidden in a litter bin, was detonated by remote control. Constable Crawford was on foot patrol in High Street. He was a member of the Orange Order and Masonic Order. He was a native of Brookeborough and worked for the post office as a mechanic.[669] He was married with three children. At his funeral, the Bishop of Clogher, Dr Hannon, told mourners that effective security would only be achieved in a community where the people learned to live as neighbours, where no section felt alienated, where all believed they had a say and 'a stake in their country' and where all shared the same rights and responsibilities.[670]

Cpl James Oldman (39): A part-time UDR member, he was shot by the IRA as he arrived at Jones's hardware shop in Ederney on 3 April, where he worked as a manager. Three gunmen had burst into Lynch's café, close to the hardware shop, at about 1.15 a.m. and held the family hostage. The family was ordered to go to bed, having given over the keys of their car. The IRA waited all night until Cpl Oldman arrived at 8.45 a.m. A 13-year-old cousin who was with him was ordered out of the car before they opened fire. She sustained a graze to the hand and was badly shocked.[671] Cpl Oldman, previously a member of the B-Specials, had joined the UDR when it was formed in 1970 and was, at that time, one of its longest-serving members. He was also a member of the Orange Order.[672]

L/Cpl Thomas Hewitt (21): A member of the Royal Green Jackets, he was killed by the IRA on 19 July in Main Street, Belleek, when he was shot in the head by a sniper, allegedly from across the border.[673] He had arrived in the area only a few days earlier. His wife was pregnant at the time with their first child. Gardaí disputed an RUC claim that the fatal shot was fired from the republic. They had sent detectives and ballistics experts from Dublin to comb the hillside and the banks of the River Erne on the Donegal side of the border in search of evidence.[674] On 3 October 1987, Michael Joseph Heron was charged with L/Cpl Hewitt's murder in the Special Criminal Court in Dublin under the Criminal Law Jurisdiction Act.[675] In 1988, he was convicted and jailed for his involvement in the attack.[676]

William (74) and Nessie Mullan (73); Kitchener (71) and Jessie Johnston (62); Wesley (62) and Bertha Armstrong (55); Constable Edward Armstrong, RUCR (52); John Megaw (67); Alberta Quinton (72); Samuel Gault, retired RUC officer (49); Marie Wilson (20): They are the eleven people who were killed in the Remembrance Day bombing on 8 November. With the exception of Constable Armstrong, all were Protestant civilians. The Enniskillen bombing will be discussed in detail in Chapter 9.

William and Nessie Mullan: Mr Mullan was a pharmacist and a native of Limavady, County Derry. His wife came from a farming background in Armagh. She had moved to Enniskillen in the 1930s to work in Harron's Drapery Store, which was later taken over by Gordon Wilson, Marie's father.[677]

Kitchener and Jessie Johnston: An Enniskillen native, Mr Johnston had worked as an ambulance driver in the Erne Hospital, where he met his wife, formerly Jessie McKinley, from Kesh, who worked as a nurse. He retired in 1981.[678]

Wesley and Bertha Armstrong: Mr Armstrong hailed from Maguiresbridge. He met his wife, formerly Bertha Houston, when they both worked at the

Scotch Street bacon factory in Enniskillen. He later worked for Customs and Excise and British Telecom.[679]

Alberta Quinton: Mrs Quinton, a widow, was a native of Inver, County Donegal. She joined the Women's Royal Air Force nursing section during the Second World War and had served in North Africa, Italy and Yugoslavia. After the war, she obtained a post in the Erne Hospital. She had been retired for several years.[680]

Samuel Gault: Mr Gault had served as a sergeant in the RUC but had taken early retirement in 1983, having suffered a heart attack the previous year. He was a native of Larne, County Antrim. He met his future wife, Gladys Clarke, while he was training in the local RUC depot.[681]

Marie Wilson: Marie was the youngest of Gordon and Joan Wilson's children. She was about to start her third year as a student nurse in the Royal Victoria Hospital, Belfast.[682]

Constable Edward Armstrong, RUCR: Constable Armstrong was a native of Brookeborough and had served in the B-Specials before joining the RUC.[683]

John (Johnny) Megaw: Mr Megaw, a bachelor, was a native of Portglenone, County Antrim. He had moved to Enniskillen many years earlier and was a retired painter.[684]

Ronnie Hill: A native of Bray, County Wicklow, Mr Hill survived until 28 December 2000. Sixty-three people were injured, many of them very seriously. He was a former headmaster of Enniskillen High School. He was severely injured in the bombing and went into a coma two days after the attack.[685] He never emerged from the coma and died on 28 December 2000, thirteen years afterwards.

1988

Six people lost their lives in 1988 – three Protestant civilians, one UDR member, one RUC officer and one Catholic civilian, all at the hands of the IRA.

Jillian Johnston (21): On 18 March, five months after the Enniskillen bombing, Ms Johnston, a Protestant civilian, was shot by the IRA near Belleek as she sat with her fiancé in his car outside her home. He was seriously wounded.[686] This controversial case will be discussed in detail in Chapter 9.

Cpl William Burleigh (51): A part-time member of the UDR and a farmer, he was killed on 6 April when an IRA bomb exploded under his car at Derrylin as he was about to leave an agricultural machinery auction. He had served in the UDR for sixteen years and had been commended for his bravery. He was a member of the Orange Order.[687] At his funeral service, the Church of Ireland Bishop of Kilmore, Right Rev. Dr Gilbert Wilson, described his murder as part of 'a deliberate policy of genocide against Protestants'. [688] Cpl Burleigh was the last UDR member to be killed by the IRA in Fermanagh.

William Hassard (59), Frederick Love (64): Building contractor William Hassard, along with his half-brother and employee, Fred Love – both civilians – were shot by the IRA after carrying out maintenance work on Belleek RUC station on 4 August. Four masked men ambushed and shot them with 150 rounds as they drove from the RUC station. The IRA claimed to have warned Mr Hassard several times about working for the security forces. The two men were convinced they were targets and had already made their own funeral arrangements. Both men had spoken to friends of their fears after they spotted a southern-registered car following them.[689] Mr Hassard was a former member of the UDR; Mr Love was a member of the Orange Order.[690]

Constable Hugh McCrone, RUCR (20): A full-time reservist for less than a year, he was shot as he left the heavily fortified Kinawley RUC station in an unmarked car on 26 October. He and a colleague were heading towards Enniskillen when their car was sprayed with automatic gunfire. His colleague was injured in the attack. Constable McCrone had got engaged only six days before his death.[691] At his funeral, Dr Godfrey Brown, Presbyterian Moderator, hit out at the SDLP for their failure to support the security forces. He called on all the people of Northern Ireland to 'recognise their clear moral duty' to support the RUC and the armed forces.[692]

Mary Ellen Rooney: A few days later, on 31 October, Ms Rooney, a Catholic civilian in her 70s, died of a heart attack while she was being evacuated from her home during an IRA mortar attack on Roslea RUC station. Her neighbours said she had been ill for some time.[693] An ambulance was called but she was pronounced dead on arrival at the hospital.[694]

After Ms Rooney's death, there were no more deaths in Fermanagh until December 1989, when two British soldiers were killed.

1989

L/Cpl Michael Patterson (21), Pte James Houston (22): Both men were members of the Kings Own Scottish Borderers. They were killed in an audacious attack on a permanent vehicle checkpoint at Derryard on the Fermanagh–Monaghan border, near Roslea, on 13 December 1989. The IRA hadn't mounted an operation on such a large scale since losing eight men in Loughgall, County Armagh, in May 1987.

A blue Hino lorry with false number plates, stolen in Mullingar, County Westmeath on 4 December, was used in the attack. It had been reinforced by new plywood and timber. A stolen red Isuzu van with false number plates, taken in Dublin in September 1988, was also used. At least two dozen IRA men were believed to be involved in the operation; a flamethrower was used and an RPG rocket was launched, the latter seriously damaging the tower.[695] The soldier in the tower survived but was buried in the rubble and was unable to fire at the attackers.

Pte Houston was killed immediately in the gunfire, which continued for about fifteen minutes; L/Cpl Patterson was killed by the bomb in the Isuzu van, which had been driven inside the perimeter of the checkpoint.[696] There were five explosions in total. It is likely that several more soldiers would have been killed but for the timely return of four colleagues who were out on patrol. The tail fin of the rocket was found on the roadway at the checkpoint.[697] Being attacked in their own base was a demoralising event for the soldiers.[698]

In the aftermath of the attack, Gardaí in Monaghan found an arms cache about 5 miles from Roslea, near Scotstown. The find included an anti-tank rocket, a small quantity of Semtex explosive and three AK47 rifles.[699] It was reported that this attack would prove to be a nightmare for

Britain's security chiefs, as this was certainly not a soft target – the IRA had succeeded in penetrating a permanent security checkpoint.[700]

1990

In 1990, for the first time in twenty years in Fermanagh, there were no deaths as a result of the conflict.

1991

There were two murders in 1991 – a full-time RUC reservist and a former reservist were killed by the IRA.

Cullen Stephenson (63): A former RUC reservist until April 1989, Mr Stephenson was shot by the IRA as he parked his car outside his home in Brookeborough on 21 January 1991. He was returning from work at Fivemiletown Creamery, where he had been an employee for more than forty years. His wife had a narrow escape when two bullets smashed through a window close to where she was sitting.[701] The RUC and the family denied an IRA claim that Mr Stephenson had been seen on security force duties two weeks earlier. It was the second attempt on his life.[702] One of his sons was a UDR member who had survived an IRA attempt on his life the previous August.[703]

Constable Douglas Carrothers, RUCR (51): He was killed on 17 May when an IRA bomb exploded under his car near his home at Lisbellaw. He worked as a foreman in a timber merchant's. He had been a reservist for ten years and was believed to have been an IRA target for some time. He had recently moved house from Brookeborough on security force advice due to the murder of his neighbour, Cullen Stephenson.[704] His widow, Phyllis, recalled:

> That is a day I will never forget – the day my husband was so brutally taken from me and I was catapulted into the role of provider and head of our family. I had to fulfil those roles for our three children who were deprived of a father. I will never forget the afternoon I had to break the news to my children that their father was dead.[705]

The IRA attackers were guided to the house by a local man who was jailed for life in 1993.[706]

1992

Two people were killed in 1992 – an RUC reservist, by the IRA, and an IRA member, by the UDR.

Joseph McManus, IRA (21): On 6 February 1992, Mr McManus, from Sligo town, was killed during an attack on a UDR member at Belleek. The UDR man was employed by Fermanagh District Council as a dog warden and went to an isolated farmhouse to investigate a report that a dog was worrying sheep. The call was bogus, and a four-man IRA unit had taken over the house the previous night, holding the elderly owner captive as they lay in wait. A number of shots were fired at the UDR man's van as it approached the house, hitting him in the legs, but he fired back with his personal weapon, killing Joseph McManus, who came from a well-known republican family. His father, Seán McManus, was a member of the Sinn Féin delegation, headed by Martin McGuinness, that later travelled to Stormont for the first-ever open contact between Sinn Féin and the British government in December 1994. Gerry Adams, who was a personal friend of the family and had stayed in the McManus home many times over the years, gave his funeral oration.[707]

Constable Alan Corbett, RUCR (25): A full-time reservist and a native of Banbridge, County Down, he lost his life on 15 November when he was shot by a sniper at a joint RUC/army cross-border checkpoint in Main Street, Belcoo. The shooting, which had occurred late the previous night, was believed to have come from high ground, 300 yards away, on the Blacklion, County Cavan side of the border.[708] Constable Corbett died in hospital four hours after the attack. He had joined the UDR in 1986 and became a full-time member in 1990.[709]

1993

As in 1990, 1993 was death-free.

1994

The final victim of the conflict in Fermanagh was killed in 1994.

Caroline Moreland (34): A Catholic civilian from Belfast, she was shot by the IRA on 17 July 1994, shortly before the IRA announced its ceasefire. They alleged she was an informer, and her body was dumped on the border near Roslea. The case will be discussed more fully in Chapter 9.

After the IRA called its first ceasefire on 31 August 1994, there were no more conflict-related deaths in Fermanagh.

Chapter 9

KILLINGS AT THE HANDS OF THE IRA – CASE STUDIES

It is undoubtedly true that all conflict-related deaths were controversial and all IRA killings in Fermanagh, as elsewhere, were contentious. The controversial nature of killings carried out in schools has already been highlighted, but there were other highly contentious killings elsewhere. The case studies in the following two chapters include: those Protestant civilians who were deliberately targeted; those former members of the UDR who had left the organisation several years previously; those killed in the Enniskillen bombing and those who were alleged informers. Also examined are the deaths of three UDR brothers.

DOUGLAS DEERING

Mr Deering, a married man with three adult children, was shot dead in his shop on 12 May 1977. Three young men pulled up at his petrol pumps. As his young shop assistant went out to serve them with petrol, two of them got out of the car and entered the shop. They were unmasked. The assistant, Mary McGeough, was just about to serve the petrol when she heard shots. The two men rushed out of the shop, got into the car and drove away towards the border. Mary found her employer lying on the shop floor. She immediately rang the local doctor, who rushed to the shop only to pronounce that life was extinct. Mr Deering had been shot in the chest and head.[710] The Gardaí set up a number of checkpoints but failed to capture the gunmen.[711]

Mr Deering was the last Protestant shopkeeper in Roslea with a very successful cross-border trade. Indeed, the *Evening Herald* claimed that he was the last Protestant male in the village.[712] He was well-known and highly respected – his murder shocked the entire community and was unreservedly condemned.[713] He was a member of the pacifist Plymouth Brethren congregation and had no connection with the security forces. In fact, the Brethren forbade its members to get involved in politics. He was also a lay preacher who ran a Sunday school service for children.[714]

His role as a justice of the peace, however, may have marked him out as a so-called 'legitimate target' in the eyes of the IRA.[715] He also served soldiers in his shop.[716] Four months earlier, the IRA had killed another justice of the peace, Robert Mitchell, near Newry. Mr Deering's murder certainly suggests a sectarian motive, which might explain why the IRA denied responsibility for it. They pointed the finger at loyalists, claiming Mr Deering had been killed because he had kept his shop open during the loyalist strike, which continued from 3–13 May. It is generally accepted, however, that the IRA was responsible, as his shop had been bombed four times in the months prior to his murder.[717]

JACK MCCLENAGHAN

Mr McClenaghan was killed as he delivered bread in Garrison on 19 May 1979.

He had been employed by the Enniskillen Co-operative bakery and, more recently, by Mother's Pride bakery. He arrived in Garrison every day of the week, except Sundays and Mondays, at approximately the same time. Two men drove up beside him on a motorcycle at around midday. The pillion passenger opened fire with an Armalite rifle, firing seven shots. The killers escaped across the border and the motorcycle used in the murder was found about a mile from the border on the southern side. It had been stolen from Kinlough about three weeks earlier.[718] A man from Belleek was convicted of scouting for the IRA in this case and was jailed for life.[719] Mr McClenaghan had retired from the UDR four years previously and lived in Edenmore, Florencecourt.[720] He was a member of the Masonic lodge in Pettigo.[721]

RONALD FUNSTON

Mr Funston was killed on 13 March 1984 as he worked on the family farm near Pettigo. He was found by his mother, Florence, and died in her arms.[722]

He had lived on the farm with his parents. His mother heard the automatic gunfire and saw two men running across a field towards the border.[723] He had retired from the UDR six years previously. The IRA claimed that Mr Funston was a serving member of the UDR and that he had been observed in uniform eight weeks previously – a claim that was denied by both the UDR and the RUC.[724]

What was the IRA's motive in killing Jack McClenaghan, who had retired from the UDR four years previously, and Ronald Funston, who had retired six years previously? Even from their perspective, it is difficult to understand the logic in killing former members of the security forces. One reason suggested to the author was that the IRA believed retired UDR men were continuing to provide intelligence to serving members of the regiment. Another possibility that was suggested was that the IRA may not always have been aware that UDR members were no longer serving. While that might be the case for members who had recently left the regiment, it is far less likely for those who had resigned several years previously. Those who decided to retire from the regiment were discouraged from announcing their decision in case it would demoralise serving soldiers or be seen by the IRA as a sign of defeat. As has been noted, the IRA claimed in some of these cases that the retired person was still serving – claims that were strenuously denied and caused great hurt to their families.

THE THREE GRAHAM BROTHERS – RONNIE, CECIL AND JIMMY

Although all three brothers were serving members of the UDR, they also deserve special recognition. Their father had served in the B-Specials for many years. When the UDR was formed in 1970, he joined, along with three of his sons. Hilary, one of his daughters, joined in March 1974. She sustained severe injuries when a car crashed through a UDR checkpoint. She never recovered and died some weeks later, in November 1979.[725] The IRA killed Ronnie, aged 39, in June 1981 as he delivered coal to a house near Lisnaskea. Cecil, aged 32, was killed five months later while he was visiting his Catholic wife and five-week-old baby. They were staying with her parents in the nationalist village of Donagh because the baby was premature and required constant care. They attempted to kill Jimmy, aged 39, on two or three occasions, for which he was awarded a British Empire Medal (BEM). The IRA finally succeeded in February 1985, when they shot him as he sat in his school bus in Derrylin.

Journalist, author and former priest Michael Harding, who, at the time of the attack on Jimmy, was the curate in Derrylin, describes what happened:

> One morning in February, I was having porridge in the kitchen when I heard gunshots outside. I went to the front door and saw a van drive away from the school bus on the other side of the street. Masked men with guns were in the back of the van, and they shot and cheered and yahoo-ed as they drove away from the bus. The bus driver was lying dead on the floor of the bus in a pool of his own blood. By mid-afternoon journalists had arrived. When they asked me questions, I told them what I had seen. I described the men roaring in the back of the van. That night on the news it was the main headline [...] the story was personal. It revealed something about the killers. They weren't disciplined. They were full of vengeful, sweaty lust and, as they went away, were as delighted as football fans when a goal had been scored.[726]

Were the Grahams singled out for special treatment? The dreadful losses endured by this family are often cited as proof that the IRA's aim was to wipe out whole Protestant families, or at least the male members of families, in border areas. Ken Maginnis commented after Jimmy was killed, 'It underlines the point I have made repeatedly that this is genocide – a conscious effort by the IRA to systematically wipe out Protestant families in the community.'[727] The shocking toll exacted on this family, though in fact exceptional, is frequently referenced in discussions on the impact of IRA killings in the county.

The Grahams were described by a Church of Ireland clergyman as 'traditional border Protestants, typical of the rank-and-file members of the UDR'. He went on say that

> Such rank-and-file [members] were strongly loyalist; lived in isolated rural areas, worked as labourers, factory workers and drivers, playing in local football and tug-o'-war teams, occasionally still went out with Catholic girls, and died because they lived – not as soldiers under siege – but as not particularly bright, and sometimes indiscreet, young men in a bitterly divided community.[728]

Nationalists in Fermanagh, interviewed by the author, denied that there was any grand plan to kill the Grahams – they were simply very soft security force targets, very visible in the community, who stuck doggedly to regular routines despite the obvious danger.[729] There may also have been an element of envy, as the brothers each had multiple jobs. As well as being UDR members, they were all employed in the Sir Richard Arkwright cotton factory in Lisnaskea. Jimmy was also a school bus driver and owned a small farm, while Cecil had just bought a farm in Maguiresbridge. Ronnie also worked as a coal delivery man.

Michael Harding explains that he attended Jimmy Graham's funeral to express his sympathy with the victim's family. He describes how he walked past lines of uniformed UDR soldiers in the cemetery while wearing his Roman collar and black suit and stood beside the Church of Ireland clergy at the graveside. This act, he comments, offended members of the Unionist community, 'who tended to see priests as fellow travellers with the terrorists'.[730]

The following month, the *Impartial Reporter* carried a report of a debate on security in the Northern Ireland Assembly during which Rev. Ivan Foster, an elected representative from Fermanagh and a member of the Democratic Unionist Party (DUP), claimed that the unionist population along the border had two enemies – the IRA, who were killing their people, and the priests, who tacitly supported them. In a pointed reference to Harding, Foster commented that he found it offensive to see a Catholic priest at the graves of dead unionists. To illustrate his point, he spoke about having a photograph of the priest from Derrylin 'who not so long ago was shedding crocodile tears at the graveside of a UDR man'. The photograph showed, he claimed, the priest presenting medals to IRA men.[731]

Harding explains that the men to whom he had presented medals were in their nineties and had fought in the War of Independence, and the medals had been presented to commemorate the centenary of the GAA the previous year. Harding was horrified and terrified by Foster's comments. He states that there was a pattern whereby certain politicians demonised individuals in public speeches over a sustained period of time until eventually some loyalist decided to execute the person in question. The teacher outside whose school Jimmy Graham was killed received a death threat about a month after the shooting. The RUC verified that the threat was genuine, and armed police kept a close eye on both Harding and the teacher for a few weeks. Eventually, Harding wrote an open letter to Rev. Foster, which was published in the *Impartial Reporter*, and that was the end of the matter.[732]

In a poignant recent interview with the only surviving Graham sibling, Pam Morrison, she told a BBC reporter that she felt she should speak about the loss of her three brothers and her sister, remarking plaintively, 'Who else is going to remember them unless I say something about it'.[733]

MICHAEL KEARNEY

The 20-year-old IRA member was brought from Belfast and shot dead on the border on 11 July 1979. He was from Lenadoon, and the IRA described him as 'a former Irish Republican Volunteer'. He had been missing from his home for two weeks. His body was found 50 yards on the northern side of the border, near Newtownbutler.[734]

Ciarán de Baróid wrote that, in March 1979, Ballymurphy volunteers were involved in one of the biggest operations ever planned by the IRA:

> Forty-two bombs were prepared and stored in a warehouse in Short Strand for what a senior IRA Volunteer would later describe as 'the one that if it had come off, would have ended the war'. However, the British were tipped off about the location of the bombs and a large contingent of SAS was moved into Short Strand in a joint RUC/army manoeuvre. Upwards to 30 Volunteers were to have taken part in the operation, and the heavy deployment of the SAS [...] would suggest a British intention of devastating the Belfast Brigade with a major killing of Volunteers.[735]

The IRA, however, became aware of strange activities around the area, and all the members involved got away. Michael Kearney was blamed for tipping off the security forces about the location of the bombs. In his book *Ballymurphy and the Irish War*, published in 1990, Ciarán de Baróid quotes a Ballymurphy IRA member naming Kearney as having tipped off 'the Brits'.[736]

According to McKittrick and others, new information emerged in 2003. De Baróid apologised publicly to the Kearney family, saying that the information provided to him by the Ballymurphy IRA member had since proved inaccurate. De Baróid said the IRA had acknowledged that Michael had no part in providing the information about the Short Strand operation and had also acknowledged that at no time was Mr Kearney an informer.[737]

THE ENNISKILLEN BOMBING

The bombing of the Remembrance Day ceremony on 8 November 1987 was one of the worst atrocities of the Troubles. Eleven people, including one serving and one retired member of the RUC, were killed, and one survivor, Ronnie Hill, died in 2000, having remained in a coma for thirteen years. The no-warning bomb exploded as people were gathering for the ceremony. If the bomb had gone off eight minutes later, most of the 114-strong contingent of UDR soldiers would have been formed up at the site of the explosion and would likely have suffered heavy casualties, but the device was triggered prematurely by an incorrectly set timing device.[738]

In terms of civilian casualties, it was a high-risk strategy. Even if the IRA had been successful – from their perspective – and killed a number of UDR members, it would have been impossible to avoid civilian deaths as well. Denzil McDaniel, a former editor of the *Impartial Reporter* (a Fermanagh newspaper) and the author of *Enniskillen: The Remembrance Sunday Bombing*, told a journalist in 2007 that he didn't believe the IRA had set out specifically to kill civilians. He said he believed they had made a mistake with their intelligence on the timetable for the service, but that they were reckless about civilian lives.[739]

At the top of Belmore Street, where the War Memorial stands, there was a building that was known locally as the Reading Rooms and which belonged to St Michael's parish. It had originally housed the town's Catholic schools, but as new schools were built, it had fallen into disrepair and was, in 1987, being used as a community centre.[740] In this building, on the first floor, beside the gable wall that faced onto the War Memorial, the 40 lb bomb was placed, contained in an old sports bag.[741] By 10.43 a.m. on Remembrance Sunday, almost forty people were gathered by the gable wall. At that moment, the bomb exploded and the wall disintegrated, crashing down on the group of people gathered in front of it. They were immediately buried in rubble. Heroic efforts were made by civilians, members of the security forces and emergency services to dig them out.[742]

Julian Armstrong, the 16-year-old son of victims Wesley and Bertha Armstrong, who was standing between them, miraculously survived.[743] In 1998, Wesley's brother, a retired Methodist minister, publicly backed the campaign for a 'yes' vote in the referendum on the Good Friday Agreement.[744] Edward Armstrong, another victim, was a member of the Chosen Few Orange Lodge.[745] His son, Clive, also aged 16, had been standing beside his father but moved over a little to talk to a group of teenagers. He, too, survived.[746] Stephen Gault, aged 18, was standing beside his father, Sammy, who was killed. Stephen was thrown over the railing but survived.[747]

Alberta Quinton was originally from Donegal. During the Second World War, she had served in the nursing section of the Women's Royal Air Force in Italy, Yugoslavia and North Africa. After the war, she took a job in the Erne Hospital and attended the Remembrance service each year wearing her service medals.[748] She lost her life.

Marie Wilson, who survived the blast, was taken to the Erne Hospital. Surgeons struggled for four hours to save her life, but in the end she passed away.[749] She was 20 years old. Her father, Gordon Wilson, gave an interview to the BBC that evening in which he said he forgave those who had planted the bomb and killed his beloved daughter. The interview had a huge impact and was viewed around the world.[750]

Six of the dead were members of the Presbyterian Church. Three were Methodists and two were Church of Ireland. Among the dead were three married couples.[751]

McDaniel, who interviewed security and IRA sources, put together the movements of the teams and the bomb in the hours preceding the attack. He claims that the bomb was manufactured in the Ballinamore area of Leitrim by the IRA's South Fermanagh Brigade.[752] The help of other units was required to bring it across the border and plant it in the community building. Two Enniskillen men provided details of the ceremony's running order. A member of the IRA team due to plant the bomb visited Enniskillen and was shown around the area by one of the locals. He was given a rundown of how to get in and out of the building quickly.[753]

The journey from Leitrim to Enniskillen began late on Friday night, 6 November. Members of the West Fermanagh Brigade, based in the Ballyshannon–Bundoran area, came in to assist. It was deemed too risky to drive directly from Ballinamore to Enniskillen, so the journey was undertaken in relays with scouts in front to ensure the way was clear for the vehicle containing the bomb to proceed. McDaniel estimates that about thirty IRA members in total were involved. By early Saturday, the bomb was on the outskirts of Enniskillen, and by late Saturday night or early Sunday morning, it was in place inside the Reading Rooms. The two Enniskillen men who had provided the vital information guided the four-man bomb team in. The device was left primed and ready.[754]

Although the Reading Rooms was a dilapidated building, it was used as a community centre for a number of activities, including bingo sessions. On Saturday, a bingo session began at 9 p.m. and ended at about 10.30p.m. The bingo hall was on the middle floor (at ground floor level), and its entrance door was near to where the bomb was planted. At the end of the bingo session, the building's caretaker and three other men went down to the basement to play cards. Around midnight, two of the men thought they heard noises coming from the bingo hall upstairs. They went quiet but the noise stopped. Ten minutes later, they heard a sound like footsteps. One of the men went to the foot of the stairs but didn't see or hear anything further. The men finished their card game at 12.40 a.m. and walked out together – the caretaker locking the door that had been left open all evening, as was customary.[755]

With regard to the bomb's detonation method, the initial IRA statement claimed that a remote control device had been used and that the bomb had been triggered early by electronic equipment belonging to the British Army, which was scanning the area.[756] Following forensic sifting of material, this claim was found to be false, proving that the bomb had been detonated by a timing device.

A total of ten people were arrested and questioned – eight of them soon after the attack, and two more in 1990 and 1991.[757] No charges, let alone convictions, were ever brought against any individual for this appalling attack.

On the same day as the Enniskillen bombing, a 130–150 lb beer keg bomb was reported at Tullyhommon, 18 miles north-west of Enniskillen, on the border with Pettigo, County Donegal. It had been placed at the assembly point for a parade involving children of the Boys' and Girls' Brigade to mark Remembrance Day. A timer was not used, but the bomb was attached to a command wire that led about 250 m to a detonation point on high ground in Donegal.[758] On Sunday evening, an IRA caller notified a Belfast radio station of the bomb's location. For fear of booby-traps, it wasn't until

Tuesday that army explosive experts were able to defuse the bomb. The caller had said that three soldiers were 'unwittingly standing beside the device' when IRA members tried but failed to detonate it.[759] The time of the attempted detonation is not known. The bomb was planted behind a hedge 25 m from the assembly point, which showed a shocking disregard for civilians, particularly the children of the Boys' and Girls' Brigade.

On the day following the Enniskillen bombing, James Molyneaux MP, Ken Maginnis MP and four representatives from Fermanagh met with Prime Minister Margaret Thatcher. The representatives were James Cooper, a solicitor; Sammy Foster, a former B-Special and a former UDR Major who was elected to Fermanagh District Council in 1981; Walter Parke, a justice of the peace; and Rev. Edwy Kille. Maginnis stressed that the basic responsibility for providing security 'lay with HMG [Her Majesty's Government]'.[760] He was concerned on behalf of local unionist councillors who had to work with Sinn Féin representatives on district councils. He complained that the failure of the SDLP to support the security forces was also very discouraging. He suggested that the government should consider selective internment. Cooper suggested 'relaxing constraints on the security forces' and wanted an end to the right to silence; he also sought the introduction of selective internment. Foster gave an account of the harrowing experience of Enniskillen. He wanted Sinn Féin proscribed, and he also favoured internment. Both Parke and Rev. Kille complained about inadequate security on the border.[761] Margaret Thatcher seemed to be in listening mode and didn't suggest any new initiatives.

So why was the Remembrance Day ceremony targeted? A number of possibilities have been put forward which centre around the fact that the previous couple of years had been difficult for the IRA. In November 1985, the Anglo-Irish Agreement was implemented, to which the republican movement was bitterly opposed. Exactly six months before the bombing, on 8 May 1987, the IRA had suffered its greatest loss when eight members of its East Tyrone Brigade were shot dead by the SAS at Loughgall, County Armagh. On 1 November, just a week before the attack, the *Eksund*, a ship containing 150 tons of arms, ammunition, rocket launchers, mortars, grenades, explosives and detonators from Libya, intended for the IRA, was intercepted and seized by the French authorities.[762] Some people believed that the attack at Enniskillen was 'a measure of the frustration of the terrorists' in light of recent successes by the security forces.[763]

Another possible explanation for the unprecedented bombing is that it was a retaliatory attack for the harassment of republican funerals by the security forces. At that time, the security forces – and also the Catholic Church – were trying to prevent paramilitary displays at the funerals of IRA members. There had been a number of contentious funerals during the year where the security forces were perceived as being heavy-handed, and where violence had flared. Just six days earlier in Derry, on Monday, 2 November, thousands of people were attending the funerals of Paddy Deery and Eddie McSheffrey, IRA members who had been killed by their own bomb in a premature explosion. More than forty British and RUC armoured vehicles placed a cordon around the Bogside, and a helicopter overhead shined its searchlight on the funeral cortege. After four hours of protracted negotiations between the families, local Catholic priests, politicians and the RUC, the funeral was allowed to proceed. Bishop Edward Daly of Derry was very outspoken in his opposition to violence from all sides. In 1976, he introduced a ban on paramilitary trappings at Catholic funerals in his diocese.[764]

A hooded IRA man fired eight shots into the air when the funeral procession was 200 yards from the cemetery. The police rushed forward through the crowd in an attempt to grab him, but in doing so they caused injuries to several civilians. An *Irish Times* reporter described it as one of the worst outbreaks of violence seen at any of the 'controversial IRA funerals' in recent years.[765] The worst of the violence occurred close to the pall-bearers carrying the Tricolour-draped coffins of the two men.[766] A woman fainted during the attacks on the crowd, and the pall-bearers were beaten and shoved – one of the coffins was twice knocked to the ground in the melee. It was claimed that plastic bullets were fired at point-blank range. The crowd was incensed at the aggression and disrespect shown by the police. Their actions were said to have infuriated many units of the IRA in west Ulster.[767] This may have led to a decision to retaliate by attacking a remembrance ceremony dear to the hearts of the security forces.

Regardless of the reasons for the attack, the Enniskillen bombing was a catastrophe for the IRA and Sinn Féin. It provoked outrage and condemnation throughout Ireland and, indeed, throughout the world. Even the Gaddafi regime in Libya withdrew its support – and with it the supply of weapons and explosives intended to sustain the 'Long War'. [768] It must have been obvious to the attackers that their actions – placing a bomb near where Protestant civilians, as well as security forces, would congregate for a ceremony – were potentially murderous and sectarian.

From an IRA perspective, another negative result of the attack was that it eased the passage of the Extradition Act, which, up to that point, the Irish government had been very reluctant to pass.[769] The case against extradition had always been that Britain's and Northern Ireland's systems of justice could not be relied upon in cases involving Irish republicans, and this proved particularly divisive within Fianna Fáil.[770] The SDLP also reacted to the bombing by switching their support from Sinn Féin to Ulster Unionist candidates for the chairperson positions on Fermanagh District Council.[771]

JILLIAN JOHNSTON

On 18 March 1988, five months after the Enniskillen bombing, the IRA shot 21-year-old Ms Johnston. She was with her fiancé, in his car, having just arrived back at her home in Tonaghgorm, Belleek after an evening out. She died instantly, while he was seriously injured. She was the second youngest of a family of six.[772] There was widespread condemnation of the killing from church leaders, politicians and others on both sides of the community. At first, the IRA claimed that the target, her brother, was a member of the UDR. In a later statement, however, the IRA admitted that Ms Johnston's murder 'was a mistake' and that the intended target, her brother, was not a member of the UDR.[773] Her post mortem revealed that there were twenty-seven bullets in her body.[774]

Her mother painfully recalled the night of her daughter's murder:

> I was on my own at the time – my husband had gone out to visit neighbours – and I had heard awful automatic gunfire. I was terrified. I rang my sister-in-law [...] and she came up. Just as she came up, I heard Jillian's fiancé calling out – lamenting. I ran out and the minute I saw her I knew Jillian was dead. I lifted up her head and it fell down again. I will never forget that night.[775]

At the inquest in October 1988, the coroner described her murder as 'an obscene and senseless waste of life'. Her fiancé, Stanley Liggett from Drumquin, County Tyrone, told the inquest that he had never been a member of the security forces.[776]

After Enniskillen, the controversial murders of Jillian Johnston in 1988 and Harry Keys in 1989, and injuries to school children, the IRA Army Council allegedly took the decision to stand down the West Fermanagh Brigade.

Harry Keys

Mr Keys was not killed in Fermanagh and is, therefore, not included in the total figure, but it is important to reference him, as he was killed by the same IRA unit. He was a native of Ballycassidy, County Fermanagh who was killed in Ballintra, County Donegal on 15 January 1989. He was visiting with his girlfriend's family at the time. He was a former RUCR officer, having retired about two years previously. The West Fermanagh Brigade of the IRA claimed responsibility for his murder, alleging that he was working covertly for the RUC in Donegal by observing local republicans. According to the *Irish Times* security correspondent, the West Fermanagh Brigade was considered to be one of the organisation's most active and ruthless; it was linked to the Enniskillen bombing and the death of Jillian Johnston.[777] It seems Mr Keys did not take seriously the warnings of police on both sides of the border that his life was at risk.[778]

Two days later, the *Irish Times* claimed that the Gardaí knew the identity of the killers, some of whom were said to be 'On the Runs' (OTRs) from Northern Ireland while others were from the Republic. A Limerick man in his early 20s and a woman, also from Limerick – a former bank official – were said to be involved. The report continued that, for the previous two years, this unit had been 'a footloose grouping of young IRA activists with no real internal hierarchy and sometimes strained relationships with the IRA leadership'. The report quoted a 'senior security source' in Dublin who stated that 'this unit has learned the lesson of Loughgall and will not place themselves on the front line' but rather 'seek the softest of soft targets'. It was claimed that the killers cheered as they drove away from Harry Keys' murder scene. A senior RUC officer told the *Irish Times* reporter that 'every morsel of Garda intelligence in Donegal is passed to us and vice versa – one could not wish to deal with more dedicated professional policemen'.[779]

The IRA leadership allegedly made the unprecedented decision to disband the West Fermanagh unit after an internal inquiry into the murder of Harry Keys. They did not accept the explanation that he had worked covertly for the RUC. It was claimed that firearms and explosives were taken from seven men and one woman, who largely comprised the unit. However, the security forces were said to be treating the claim with some suspicion.[780] In his obituary, Kevin McKenna, described as the longest-serving IRA chief of staff, was pinpointed as the person who had 'purged the IRA's West Fermanagh Brigade in the late 1980s after it carried out a series of blatantly sectarian killings'.[781] Martin McGuinness told the Sinn Féin Árd Fheis in 1989 that the unit had been disbanded because the organisation believed that the killing of civilians was 'wrong, full-stop'.[782]

The West Fermanagh Brigade was believed to be responsible for the Tullyhommon bomb as well as the murders of Jillian Johnston and Harry Keys, and William Hassard and Frederick Love in August 1988,[783] and for placing a bomb under a school bus in June 1988, injuring a 14-year-old girl.[784]

The wider context of the brigade's disbandment was that Gerry Adams had begun secret talks with John Hume about ending the armed campaign and seeking an alternative way forward, which meant that civilian deaths were a particular embarrassment at that time.

CAROLINE MORELAND

A 34-year-old mother of three children aged 14, 12 and 11, Ms Moreland was killed on 17 July 1994. Her body was dumped at Clough, Roslea. She was the third of three women killed by the IRA as alleged informers during the conflict. She had been held and interrogated for ten days before she was killed. The IRA claimed that she had admitted to working for RUC Special Branch as an informant for two years; that she was initially recruited in September 1992 at Castlereagh Holding Centre, where she had been taken for questioning for her part in various small-scale IRA activities.[785] Special Branch had paid her paltry sums of money for information and she was asked to monitor the movements and activities of two particular women.[786]

Ms Moreland was described as a loving mother and a dutiful daughter, visiting her sick mother every day. Her brother Martin had suffered from muscular dystrophy and had eventually died of the disease. As a result, she became involved in the Muscular Dystrophy Association and raised thousands of pounds for the charity.[787]

It is alleged that she was the last victim of the so-called 'nutting squad' under Freddy Scappaticci.[788] Her daughter Shauna told BBC's *Spotlight*, on a programme that was broadcast on 10 June 2015, that she blamed both the IRA and the British Intelligence Services, who had recruited her mother as an informant, for her mother's death. The programme raised questions as to why, if Scappaticci was involved in her murder, his British Army handlers did not act to prevent Ms Moreland's death. *Spotlight* recounted how, as a lone parent, she had felt obliged to become an informer because those who recruited her warned that she could face twenty-five years in prison for IRA activity and that her three children would be taken into care. A recording was played on the programme in which she admitted she was an informant.[789]

Ms Moreland was the last person to be killed in Fermanagh as a result of the conflict.

Chapter 10

KILLINGS AT THE HANDS OF THE SECURITY FORCES – CASE STUDIES (PART 1)

MICHAEL NAAN AND ANDREW MURRAY

The first Catholics to be killed in Fermanagh during the conflict were the victims of what were mistakenly, or perhaps disingenuously, called the 'Pitchfork murders'. It was one of the most notorious crimes of the Troubles.

New information on the circumstances of these murders came to light with the publication in 2018 of *An Army of Tribes*. The book's author, Edward Burke, Assistant Professor in International Relations at the University of Nottingham, gained access to a file from a legal professional who was centrally involved in the trial of three members of the Argyll and Sutherland Highlanders for the murders in January 1981. This file is pivotal and contains many documents that had been removed or redacted from the relevant Public Records of Northern Ireland (PRONI) file. A draft report from the Historical Enquiries Team (HET), available to this book's author, also provides important new information on the case but reaches no conclusions, as it was never completed.

Michael Naan was a 31-year-old bachelor farmer who lived at Aughnahinch, Newtownbutler; Andrew Murray, 23 years old, from nearby Derrykenny, was a labourer who had been employed by Mr Naan for only two months when he was killed.[790] The two men were attacked at Naan's home on the evening of 23 October 1972. At the time, the deaths were believed to be a reprisal for the killing of Robin John Bell, a local UDR private, by the IRA the previous day.

Mr Naan was a prominent local member of NICRA who had taken part in a number of protest marches. According to a friend, shortly before his death he had been subjected to aggressive 'stop and search' incidents involving local UDR personnel.[791] As a Catholic occupying a large farm once owned by a Protestant, Naan was challenging a finely balanced local symmetry.

The inquests into their deaths concluded that Michael Naan had been stabbed seventeen times in the upper chest, neck and back, and he had also been struck on the right side of the face, leaving an abrasion. Andrew Murray was stabbed fourteen times with the same knife on both chest and back.[792] The coroner described the murder weapon as being double-edged and at least 5–6 inches long.[793] It was never recovered.

Police investigators received significant information from Oliver Melarkey and Dympna Brady, who saw soldiers outside the Naan farm on the evening of the murders. At 6.45 p.m., Melarkey, a lorry driver, was driving past the farm entrance with his side lights on when he spotted four men in military uniform. It was dusk at the time, and he switched his headlights on to see more clearly. One of the men had a walkie talkie radio set with an aerial. Melarkey described their headgear as 'black berets of the Glengarry type' (as worn by Scottish regiments). He expressed surprise at the behaviour of the soldiers in keeping their backs turned to him and remarked that he had never previously seen soldiers on foot on that road.[794]

Dympna Brady drove past forty-five minutes later, at 7.30 p.m. By now darkness had fallen. She described seeing a black Morris Minor stopped on the right-hand-side of the road with a number of soldiers around it talking to the driver. She believed that there were two people in the front of the car. She slowed down, expecting to be stopped, but the parked car moved off slowly ahead of her. The soldiers shouted at her to move on in an accent that she described as 'not English', but she was unsure as to what accent it was. She said she drove behind the car and it turned left at the chapel, 'out the Galloon Island Road'.[795]

Following receipt of this information, Detective Inspector Patrick Gilligan, RUC Enniskillen, made enquiries with an Army Intelligence Officer, Captain Vernon Humphrey Rees, Royal Horse Artillery,[796] at St Angelo camp near Enniskillen, requesting information about the deployment of soldiers in the area at the time of the murders, but he received no response.[797]

He then contacted the army in Kinawley and Roslea, again without result. He eventually met with Captain Rees on 15 November, who claimed there were no military patrols at or near the scene of the murders. Not satisfied with this information, Gilligan made further enquiries with the Special Investigation Branch (SIB) of the Royal Military Police (RMP). He was told that there were four Army Saracens performing Vehicle Checkpoints (VCPs) at various locations in the Newtownbutler area on the day of the murders but that no foot patrols had been deployed near the farm.[798]

In a report to police headquarters, dated 24 November, D/Inspector Gilligan noted that a considerable amount of opinion in the Newtownbutler area was that the army was responsible for the murders.

On 18 January 1973, personnel from the RMP SIB visited the Argylls' camp at Kirknewton in Scotland and interviewed Major Mackenzie. Mackenzie was the officer in charge of D Company; he was on attachment from the Queen's Own Highlanders during their short deployment in Fermanagh.[799] Mackenzie was of colonial stock and had served in Borneo with General Harry Tuzo, the General Officer Commanding of Northern Ireland at the time.

In his statement, Major Mackenzie provided grid references for their base locations and gave details of 13 Platoon's activities (the platoon based in that particular area) on the day of the murders, but he insisted he had no troops within 2 miles of the Naan farm until 2 p.m. on 24 October, when he provided roadblocks to cover Private Bell's funeral. D/Inspector Gilligan submitted a report to the Chief Constable in September 1973 in which he pointed out that, in this case, the army was very slow in assisting the police.

There the matter rested, and it is doubtful that the investigation would have been advanced but for pure chance. On 4 May 1978, nearly six years later, West Yorkshire police investigating the notorious Yorkshire Ripper murders received an anonymous telephone call at their incident room in Huddersfield. The caller said he had served with the army in Northern Ireland.[800] He claimed that the Ripper murders were linked to two similar cases in Fermanagh in 1972 and named two soldiers as being responsible.[801] In reality, there was no link, but the information provided led to the reopening of the Naan-Murray investigation.

The information was passed to the RUC's Detective Chief Inspector, William Scott, who contacted RMP SIB, Lisburn, requesting details of soldiers in the Newtownbutler area at the time; he asked for particular attention to be given to the names provided by the anonymous caller.[802]

Inquiries were carried out throughout 1978 and Major Mackenzie was interviewed on two occasions.

In December 1978, the same caller – who was an ex-member of the Argyll and Sutherland Highlanders – contacted Edinburgh police. RUC D/Superintendent Ernest Drew, D/Chief Inspector Scott and Staff Sgt Malcolm Denton (SIB) travelled to Scotland to interview him. He told them that on the evening of 23 October 1972 – the evening of the murders – he and other soldiers had been briefed by Major Mackenzie at 15 Platoon's camp north of Newtownbutler. Major Mackenzie indicated that a planned search of the Naan farm was to take place the following morning. The caller said that at about 7 p.m., Major Mackenzie and Company Sergeant Major (CSM) John Campbell Higgins left company headquarters in a Q van (an unmarked vehicle), taking a Night Observation Device (NOD) with them. When they returned about an hour or two later, both men were in an agitated, almost shocked condition.[803]

Iain Fletcher Chestnut, one of the soldiers eventually convicted, claimed that, in January 1979, the Argylls were forewarned of the police investigation by an RUC officer. In a statement dated 12 June 1979, Chestnut related how a former army friend, now an RUC officer, had revealed to him the identity of the Argyll 'grass' (police informer). This statement was provided to Edward Burke and is missing from the PRONI file.[804]

According to the regiment log book, D Company of the Argylls was sent to Fermanagh from Bessbrook on 21 October in their role as Brigade Reserve. The aim was for the Argylls, an efficient infantry unit, to support the artillery troop. 13, 14 and 15 Platoon were deployed. 14 Platoon was stationed at Belleek RUC station throughout the deployment, while 15 Platoon was located at Lisnaskea. 13 Platoon, under 2nd Lt. Andrew Malcolm Burlton Snowball, was based near the Earl of Erne's[805] estate at Crom Castle, about 4 miles west of Newtownbutler, for the duration of their deployment.[806] According to Major Mackenzie, 13 and 15 Platoon had the specific task of providing a presence in the area and reassuring the local population.[807]

The army was coming under pressure from local politicians because of the number of killings that had taken place in the county during the year. This is borne out by the fact that John Brooke MP, the Chairman of Fermanagh County Council and the future 2nd Viscount Brookeborough,[808] led a delegation of UDR families to the House of Commons two weeks after the murders of Naan and Murray to complain about the lack of security.[809] Also, the Earl of Enniskillen and the Duke of Westminster made representations to Secretary of State for Northern Ireland, William Whitelaw, and Prime Minister Edward Heath, respectively.[810]

Burke discovered that a very significant event occurred on 23 October which made it distinct from the other days of D Company's sojourn in Fermanagh. Private Owens of 15 Platoon was declared missing at 2 p.m. His patrol had inadvertently left him behind at a Vehicle Checkpoint (VCP) near Lisnaskea. This caused consternation and dictated events for the rest of the day. Owens wandered around the countryside for over seven hours before finally turning up, unharmed but exhausted, at Lisnaskea RUC Station, where D Company Headquarters was based, at 9.25 p.m.[811] During his hours of absence, there was widespread concern and fear that he had been captured by the IRA.

Around mid-afternoon, 13 Platoon moved camp from the Crom estate to within a few hundred yards of Naan's house. Brian MacDonald identified the location as being 'an extensive level area on top of a drumlin in Sandholes townland'.[812] Burke interviewed a former soldier who recalled a verbal confrontation between his section commander and Michael Naan at some point during the day – Naan was demanding that the soldiers leave his property.[813]

During the trial at Belfast Crown Court on 15 January 1981, Higgins recalled that he and Snowball then travelled to 13 Platoon's camp, close to Naan's farm, where Snowball briefed his men.[814] Sgt Stanley Alexander Hathaway and another non-commissioned officer in 13 Platoon, Lance Corporal James Healey, also recalled that Lt Snowball briefed 13 Platoon – his platoon – in the early evening of 23 October, informing them that Naan was a quartermaster for the IRA.[815]

Shortly after the briefing, at least four soldiers went out on patrol, led by platoon commander Sgt Hathaway. He was accompanied by Corporal John McFadyen Byrne, L/Cpl Iain Fletcher Chestnut and Private John Brennan Mcguire.

CSM Higgins, as affirmed by his own testimony, was observing the patrol in an Observation Post (OP) overlooking the farm with the aid of a NOD. He was there for the duration of the patrol's time at the farm.[816] Hathaway revealed to SIB Staff Sgt Malcolm Denton that when they returned to Bessbrook, Higgins told him that he *and the major* had seen what had happened – that they had both been in an OP overlooking the farm.[817] This is borne out by the statement of the whistle-blower.

Mackenzie certainly appears to have been nearby, as Hathaway told investigators that he had arrived at 13 Platoon's camp immediately after the murders and ordered them to move back to the Crom estate, which they did before daybreak.[818]

Hathaway, Byrne and Chestnut were tough men. They had all served in Aden, and Chestnut, at least, had also served in Borneo. They may have been chosen specially to confront Michael Naan, as, atypically for a patrol, they were selected from different sections of the platoon.[819]

When the soldiers entered Naan's farmyard, Hathaway and Byrne headed for the byre, where they found Michael. After some sort of altercation, Hathaway, clearly with assistance from Byrne, stabbed Michael to death. Meanwhile, Chestnut and Mcguire had stopped and questioned Andrew Murray at the farmyard gate. Chestnut ordered him to lie down on the ground (Aden-style).[820] When Hathaway and Byrne re-joined them, they decided that Andrew would also have to be killed to prevent him reporting Michael's murder. He was held down, stabbed front and back, and thrown into a nearby area of marshy land. The knife was never recovered, and varying accounts of its disposal were given.

Private Mcguire, in his statement, said that as the soldiers left the farm after killing the two men, he had seen Dympna Brady and that either he or another soldier told her to move on.[821] He explained that they had all started to run back to 'the bivvy' (the camp site) when a car appeared that was being driven by 'a young girl'.[822] However, he made no mention of the Morris Minor, nor does he appear to have been questioned about it. Shortly after the murders took place, police conducted enquiries to trace the car. The owners of all Morris Minors bearing the registration letters provided by Dympna Brady were interviewed, but the owner was never traced. Was the Morris Minor a Q car containing soldiers? It turned left onto the Galoon Road, which would have led to the army camp.

The patrol later claimed in their statements that when they arrived back at the camp they informed Snowball of what had happened. Chestnut said he believed the order had been given from 'higher up', because Hathaway had gone back to the camp and 'washed himself openly' in front of Snowball under the light of a torch.[823] He also suggested that it was part of the plan to camp so near to Naan's farm, 'as it was known that he was a PIRA man'. Mcguire, in his statement, said that they were going to the farm to talk to the person who lived there.[824]

During the course of that evening, Lt Snowball and Sgt Hathaway ordered that the entrance to the farm be sealed off and sentries be put in place to guard it. One of the sentries, L/Cpl Joe Burke, recalled in his witness statement that the cordon was set up, with the knowledge of D Company Headquarters, to preserve a murder scene. This is remarkable, since Major Mackenzie, CSM Higgins and the RUC gave evidence that they were unaware that any crime had taken place until John Hanna, the man who discovered Andrew Murray's body, called to Newtownbutler RUC Station the following evening.[825]

In their statements, the two sentries ordered to guard the farm described a very strange occurrence during the night. One of the sentries referred to four male occupants of 'a shooting brake'[826] (estate car) dressed in white plasterers' overalls making their way up the lane towards the farm. One sentry claimed that when he stopped the vehicle, the men told him they were from Clones. The details were passed to company headquarters, which cleared them to proceed to the farm.[827] They returned about ten to fifteen minutes later; the vehicle was then searched before they were allowed to leave the area. One sentry implausibly told the RMP SIB and RUC that he recognised the men, and later told the trial that they were 'IRA terrorists'; he then went on to withdraw most of his testimony under cross-examination because, he claimed, his memory had become hazy.[828]

It seems highly unlikely that the sentry would have recognised 'IRA terrorists', as the Argylls had been in Fermanagh for only two to three days at that stage. It is much more likely that the men in overalls were soldiers tasked with carrying out a clean-up job at the farm. Another possibility is that this event never happened but was concocted by the soldiers in order to impugn Michael Naan, suggesting that IRA men had called to his house during the night.

The missing Private Owens was almost certainly the cause of the patrol being sent to confront Michael Naan on that particular evening. Because of false information received from the local UDR, the Argylls believed Michael to be either a quartermaster or a recruiter for the IRA who might be expected to have knowledge of whether or not the missing soldier had fallen into IRA hands.[829] This belief is reinforced by the line of questioning adopted by Hathaway, who, according to his statement, asked Naan about his movements during the previous two or three hours.[830] In an early version of Major Mackenzie's statement, he acknowledged that the failure to find Owens was a cause of considerable concern. However, this sentence was omitted from later versions prepared for the trial in which he recalls 23 October as being relatively uneventful.[831] Chestnut, before the trial, alleged that Major Mackenzie's orders were to intimidate Naan – to get information through rough methods or to provoke him into a panicked response. He said they had done this elsewhere under Mackenzie.[832] The RUC failed to grasp the relevance of the missing soldier and should have realised that this was a significant event.

The victims had been dead for almost twenty-four hours when the body of Andrew Murray was discovered by John Hanna, a local oil company representative, who had called to collect a cheque just after 6 p.m. on 24 October. He immediately alerted the RUC. Were the police really not aware of the deaths until then, considering they were side by side with D Company Headquarters in Lisnaskea RUC Station?

When CSM Higgins was interviewed, he recalled intelligence about Michael Naan's alleged IRA associations being received from Commander Albert Liddle of C Company, 4 UDR[833] and a local doctor. He also concurred with the whistle-blower that there was a plan to search Naan's farm on the following day, 24 October. He remarked that 'sometime during the night', Major Mackenzie informed him the search was called off but gave no reason.[834] Snowball, in his statement, said of Naan, 'it was known that he was involved in everything that went on down there.'[835]

Burke argues convincingly that the RUC investigation was kept very narrowly focused and had a ceiling put on it. The officers concerned, Mackenzie and Snowball, were absolved of all responsibility for the murders.

THE PROBABLE SEQUENCE OF EVENTS:

- In the hours beforehand, D Company received false intelligence from the officer commanding C Company, 4 UDR that Michael Naan was a senior IRA figure.

- At 2 p.m. on 23 October 1972, Private Owens was declared missing. This information was conveyed up as far as the GOC, Harry Tuzo. Owens was not located until 9.25 p.m.
- 13 Platoon was moved to within a few hundred yards of Naan's house in mid-afternoon.
- An atypical patrol was selected to go to the farm and ordered to question Michael Naan, particularly as to his movements over the previous few hours. It is not clear whether or not they were instructed to kill him.
- A planned search of the farm was scheduled for the following morning with Major Mackenzie pointing out the location on a map at an O Group meeting.[836]
- An OP occupied by Major Mackenzie and CSM Higgins was set up overlooking the farm.
- Hathaway's patrol entered the farmyard, questioned Naan and – either by order or otherwise – killed him. Murray was killed because he was a witness.
- Mackenzie and Higgins returned to D Company HQ at Lisnaskea RUC Station in 'an agitated, almost shocked condition'.
- Lt Snowball was made aware of the murders and had a discussion with Hathaway and Byrne in the immediate aftermath.
- A cordon was placed around the farm with two soldiers acting as sentries.
- Mackenzie ordered 13 Platoon to move back to the Crom estate almost immediately after the incident.

On the evening of the murders, a member of the Garda Síochána encountered three armed British soldiers at Rathkeelan, near Ballyconnell, County Cavan.[837] He informed them that they were almost a mile inside the Republic. They claimed they had made a mistake.[838] Later, as he returned from Ballyconnell Garda Station with a colleague, the soldiers were still more than half a mile inside the Republic.[839] When challenged by the Gardaí, they levelled their guns on them and became abusive, insisting they were in Northern Ireland. They could not have mistaken the road sign that read 'Welcome to Co. Cavan' at a point 45 yards inside the Republic.[840] Burke was told by an Argyll officer that these soldiers were sent across the border to observe an alleged IRA member's house in Ballyconnell while Private Owens was still missing.[841]

In January 1981, Staff Sgt Hathaway, serving with the Royal Electrical and Mechanical Engineers (REME) in West Germany at the time of his trial and Sgt Byrne, serving as a sergeant in the Military Provost Staff Corps at HM Prison Maze, were convicted of the murders of Michael Naan and Andrew Murray. These convictions came after Hathaway and Byrne changed their original plea to guilty on the fourth day of the trial.[842] Iain Fletcher Chestnut pleaded guilty to the manslaughter of Andrew Murray and was sentenced to four years in prison. (He actually walked free from the court, as he had already spent two years in custody). Captain Andrew Malcolm Burlton Snowball pleaded guilty to withholding information about the murders and received a one-year suspended sentence.[843] Major Mackenzie, although he had been interviewed under caution, was never charged with any offence.

Captain Snowball was 20 years old at the time of the incident; he was one of the youngest officers in the British Army. He had an impressive military pedigree in that his Scottish father, Brigadier Edward Snowball, was a former army and NATO general who had been awarded an OBE in 1946. His maternal grandfather had been an army colonel.

Controversy arose when it emerged after the trial that Snowball had returned to his regiment and was serving as aide-de-camp to the GOC of Scotland. In April 1981, he announced his decision to resign his commission after a request from the Army Board. Nevertheless, his resignation was against the wishes of his colonel, who described him as an exemplary officer.[844]

Certain elements of the trial were also controversial. It was repeatedly delayed because of Hathaway's 'hysteria'. While the trial continued, there were negative references to Michael Naan's refusal to co-operate, and there was a disclosure that the patrol had been shown an army intelligence assessment in which Michael Naan was described as 'suspect'. There was the dramatic change to a guilty plea on the fourth day of the trial – a development that possibly prevented embarrassing details from emerging. Justice MacDermott caused a commotion when he seemed to equate the victims with the perpetrators, describing the day of the double murder as 'a sad and tragic day, not only for the unfortunate victims and their families but also for the accused men, their families and their regiment.' MacDermott also declined to recommend a minimum sentence having heard 'the circumstances in which the unit was serving at the time' and the medical evidence regarding Hathaway.[845]

It is clear that a particular narrative of events was constructed to assist in the cover-up, and to prevent more senior officers being charged. Hathaway, Byrne and Chestnut could be depicted as the proverbial 'bad apples' by the higher echelons of the British Army and government. The investigation was flawed because the RUC acted in a manner that was protective of, and deferential towards, British Army officers.

Chapter 11

KILLINGS AT THE HANDS OF THE SECURITY FORCES – CASE STUDIES (PART 2)

The deaths included in this chapter are shootings carried out by the security forces in which excessive force is suspected, and where a young woman was deliberately shot dead.

MICHAEL JOSEPH LEONARD

Mr Leonard was the only person killed by the RUC in Fermanagh during the conflict. He lived at Tievemore, Pettigo, across the border in Donegal. He was killed on 17 May 1973 during a car chase in the townland of Letter, on the Pettigo-Belleek road on the northern side of the border with Donegal. At the time of his death he was engaged to be married to Mena Gallagher, who lived near Ederney, County Fermanagh.[846]

A number of different versions of how Michael came to be shot emerged in the immediate aftermath, as is clear from army logs. At first it was claimed he had tried to break through an RUC VCP near St Angelo.[847] This report stated that he was wounded and that 'the occupants have been apprehended'.[848] In a log entry three hours later, it was stated that Michael died after the incident; that he was driving into Northern Ireland while disqualified from driving, and it was thought that this was the reason he failed to stop. This report noted that 'there was no other occupant in the car'. In the right-hand column, it was noted, 'B2 report[849] says he is PIRA.'[850]

Two hours after that, in a log entry headed 'New Story', it was reported that the RUC, on a routine patrol, entered a shop and, recognising Leonard, went to question him. It was claimed that he ran off despite the fact that he was told to halt. It was noted that as he drove off, the police fired two shots at his car, which did not stop. They gave chase in a Land Rover and fired another shot that hit and fatally wounded him.[851]

In a telegram to the FCO in July, the British Ambassador in Dublin, Arthur Galsworthy, reported that Neil Blaney, a Donegal TD, had raised the subject of the shooting in the Dáil the previous day.[852] In reply, the Minister for Foreign Affairs, Dr Garret FitzGerald, said that he had sought a report from the British authorities about the circumstances in which Michael had lost his life but was told that investigations were incomplete at that stage.[853]

A report prepared for the NIO by the RUC was sent to the FCO in August. It contained the following information, which, again, varies from previous accounts:

> Police had observed the deceased running from a shop towards an old and decrepit car bearing an English registration plate and, as a result, their suspicions were aroused. Leonard was called upon to stop but ignored the call and drove off towards the border. The police vehicle gave chase along a narrow twisting road. The RUC's version of events was that they were unable to overtake Leonard's car but availed of every possible means of stopping it, without success. The police landrover bumped into the rear of the car eight or nine times but Leonard's car held the centre of the road and would not stop. The police, as a last resort, intended to fire a warning shot over the vehicle and a member of the crew was detailed to do this. The officer took aim by placing his rifle out through the window and was about to fire a shot when the landrover lurched and he involuntarily discharged a shot which entered the rear of the vehicle through the boot, passed through the rear and front seats and struck Michael on the side. He died later as a result of this wound.[854]

In this version of events, there is no mention of two shots being fired as Mr Leonard drove off. The RUC claimed that the entire incident was receiving the fullest possible investigation, and, when completed, a file would be sent to the Director of Public Prosecutions (DPP) for his direction as to whether criminal proceedings should follow.[855] In her accompanying memo, Wendy Clements, an official, noted that the report, 'although factual', was not really intended for public consumption.[856]

In a memo to David Blatherwick at the British Embassy in Dublin, another official remarked, 'It is a rather peculiar story and it would be best to restrict yourselves to saying it is being investigated very fully.'[857]

In his pamphlet on the death of Mr Leonard, Fr McVeigh, a cousin of the deceased, refers to a report prepared by Brigadier Commander C.S. Wallis-King of 3 Brigade, dated 8 September 1973, in which he included a reference to Mr Leonard's death. Wallis-King wrote, 'On 17 May 73 at 1740 hrs Michael Joseph Leonard (25) was shot dead by the RUC after refusing a call to halt in a car. He was known son IRA man *(sic)*.'[858] This was totally untrue and clearly designed to blacken the name of Mr Leonard's father and family. As noted above, in the hours after his death it was suggested, falsely, that Mr Leonard was a member of 'PIRA'.

When the inquest into Mr Leonard's death was held in Enniskillen on 31 October 1973, yet another version of events was presented. None of the three police officers involved in the incident was present in the coroner's court. [859] The coroner made the decision not to call these officers, stating that he felt 'it was proper that they should not be present at the Inquest.'[860]

Inspector Darrell Beaney of Kesh RUC station relayed information from the three officers to the coroner. Again, in his rendering of events, there was no mention of two shots being fired before the car chase began, but there was a new claim that the officer driving the police Land Rover 'saw Leonard turn half-way around in his seat and raise his right arm'. Inspector Beaney told the coroner that the driver, 'unsure of Leonard's intention, swung hard immediately to his right to try and get out from behind Leonard's car.' This action, he claimed, caused the constable with the rifle to 'accidentally pull the trigger and discharge a round'. This bullet struck and fatally wounded Mr Leonard. He died shortly after his arrival in the Erne Hospital, Enniskillen. When questioned by Patrick Fahy, the family's solicitor, about the significance of Mr Leonard having raised his right arm, Inspector Beaney replied, 'I would imagine that anyone turning round in such a fashion in a car would give rise to concern to the security forces.'[861]

When asked if that was an allegation that indicated Mr Leonard might have had a weapon, Inspector Beaney said it was. There was, however, absolutely no allusion to any weapon being found subsequently in Mr Leonard's car. Beaney noted that Mr Leonard had a number of convictions, which Fahy sought to clarify as being motoring offences. He responded to a further question from Fahy, saying he had no knowledge of Mr Leonard being a member of the IRA.[862] A verdict of misadventure was returned.

The late Patrick Fahy told Fr Joe McVeigh some months before his death that, in his view, the inquest was 'highly unusual even by the standard of the times'. He observed that there were no statements from the police officers involved. In his opinion, this was 'highly irregular'.[863]

After the DPP took the decision not to prosecute in the case, a sceptical NIO wrote to the Royal Courts of Justice in April 1975 requesting information on the circumstances of the case.[864] An official, P. Coulson, noted that they had approached the RUC on the matter without much success. He further observed that the Chief Constable of Northern Ireland had refused to disclose any of the findings of his investigation to the Republic, and, so far, the NIO had supported that line in all communications with the Republic. Nevertheless, he said he was finding the RUC's version of events and the failure of the Chief Constable to disclose the findings of his investigation a most unsatisfactory position to defend for the following reasons:

1. The sole investigators of this tragic occurrence have been RUC and, as one of the principals is an RUC officer, doubt can be thrown on the impartiality of the investigation. For instance, there is no satisfactory explanation of why, when the road was of such poor quality, that one bump caused the accidental discharge of a weapon. Leonard was able to control his vehicle with one hand whilst having the other nonchalantly stuck out of [the] car window. This and other anomalies weaken our ability to defend our position without full and detailed knowledge of the facts of the matter.

2. The DPP based his decision not to direct a prosecution on papers which, presumably, were laid before him by the RUC. Without in any way imputing partiality to the DPP, it could be argued that his decision had to be based on evidence and material which could well be partial.[865]

Coulson sought advice on what line he should take in any further dealings with the Republic. He advised that, as the subject of compensation had been brought up, they must be careful to avoid any statement that could be construed as an admission of liability. He did, however, wish to be as open as possible so as to avoid any misunderstanding with the Republic.[866]

The author is unaware as to what reply the Royal Courts of Justice sent to the NIO, or what the outcome of these enquiries was. The fresh claim made at the inquest – that Mr Leonard raised his right arm, causing the police driver to swerve hard – was clearly intended to suggest that the officers feared for their lives and, as a result, the officer with the rifle discharged it accidentally. It is apparent that Coulson, the NIO official, did not believe the RUC version, or versions, of events. The early assertion that shots were fired by the police officers just before the car chase began was not repeated at the inquest or subsequently. What is abundantly clear, from the army and NIO documents, is that a false narrative was concocted by the RUC.

ANGELA D'ARCY

Angela, 24 years old, had been made redundant from her job at a local factory in her hometown of Enniskillen just a month before she met her untimely death. She had gone to visit a friend, Carole Williams, on the evening of 25 November 1981. At the end of the visit, Carole, who was carrying her baby, was accompanying Angela part of her way home when they were confronted by a young man who produced a gun and demanded money from them. Angela told him to 'go to hell', that they had no money. Incredibly, his response was to shoot Angela in the head, killing her instantly, before running away from the scene. It transpired that the killer was 25-year-old Pte Rodney Birkett, a soldier serving a tour of duty with the Royal Anglian Regiment based at St Angelo Barracks, about 5 miles from Enniskillen. He was a native of Scunthorpe, Lincolnshire.[867]

That evening, Birkett, along with two other soldiers, had been dropped off in the town. Being off-duty, they were attired in civilian clothing but were all armed with 9mm Browning pistols. They made their way to the Vintage pub in Townhall Street, where they consumed a couple of drinks. They then moved on to the Harp and Crown in Head Street, where there was an exchange of words that caused them to leave and return to the Vintage, which they left for a second time at about 11.40 p.m. They made their way down High Street, kicking a sign outside the Crow's Nest pub as they passed and creating a lot of noise. Birkett then ran down a side street – Middleton Street – telling his companions he needed to 'relieve himself'. That was when he confronted the unfortunate Angela and Carole. [868]

After the shooting, he ran back to High Street and re-joined his friends. The three of them ducked down a laneway called Peg O' the Bulls Lane to avoid being seen. They were observed in Castle Street by an RUC sergeant who would later testify in court to the effect that the three men were walking 'in an orderly and civil fashion' up the street – in other words, there were no obvious signs of drunkenness. Army bullets were later found in Castle Street as a result of the sergeant's evidence.[869]

Birkett was quickly charged, and he admitted the killing but claimed to have been drunk at the time. An RUC inspector told the court that the killing did not have a political or religious motive.[870] On the morning following Angela's brutal slaying, it was announced on the news that she had been in the company of drunken soldiers and had been involved in a pub brawl before being shot. The RUC Press Office had issued the statement, but the source of the malicious story was more likely the British Army. It was several hours before the true version of how Angela met her death was broadcast.[871]

Enniskillen RUC made a genuine effort to press a charge of murder and assured the family that it was 'a clear cut case of murder'. However, when the trial was held in Belfast Crown Court on 24–25 June 1982, it lasted just four and a half hours. The judge refused to accept a manslaughter plea, and the trial proceeded. A doctor who had examined Birkett three hours after the shooting was the crucial witness in the case. He declared that the defendant showed an alcohol content of 275 milligrams per 100 millilitres of blood at that time, and, in his opinion, the reading at the time of the shooting would have been in excess of 300 mgs, which was an abnormally high level of intoxication and could prove fatal. In his opinion, Birkett would not have been capable of making a rational judgement.[872]

The prosecution called no other expert witnesses, and no questions were raised as to the possibility that the soldier might have deliberately consumed more alcohol when he returned to barracks. Other soldiers claimed he was very drunk and incoherent. Birkett claimed to remember only that his gun went off and that he ran down a side street afterwards. In the end, Lord

Justice Gibson, describing Birkett's actions as 'a lunatic performance',[873] acquitted him of murder and sentenced him to seven years' imprisonment for manslaughter.

Faul and Murray express the view that, in the eyes of her family, Angela died three times – first when she was shot in the head, secondly when her character was taken away by statements issued by the RUC Press Office and thirdly when her death was trivialised, distorted and misrepresented at the trial of her assailant.[874] Fr Faul later questioned the impartiality of two particular judges, Gibson and McDermott, who appeared to hear almost all cases involving security force members on murder charges. Gibson was the judge in the Birkett trial.[875] Angela's mother, in her statement, noted that the judge had said 'he was worried about this man's job and his livelihood.' Josephine D'Arcy was so shocked at these remarks that she stood up in the court.

It is a further injustice to the memory of Angela D'Arcy that she is omitted from the official narrative of the conflict – the details of her death are not included in *Lost Lives: The Stories of the Men, Women and Children Who Died as a Result of the Northern Ireland Troubles.* The authors of *Lost Lives* appear to have taken the view that the shooting of Angela D'Arcy was not directly connected to the conflict – that it was not political. It is the author's belief that her death should have been included for the reasons given below.

A young British soldier legally permitted to carry a gun while off-duty and consuming alcohol shot Angela gratuitously. He is unlikely to have been aware of the religion of his victim, but perhaps he was possessed of the colonial mindset that he had *carte blanche* to run riot on the streets of an Irish town. The statement issued to the media after Angela's death was an established form of British Army black propaganda – to try to besmirch the good name of the victim and protect the reputation of the army. Birkett's subsequent trial was undeniably political in that the aim of both the prosecution and defence, rather than seeking justice for Angela, was to minimise Birkett's role by claiming he was in a drunken state – again, in order to protect the reputation of the army. Carole Williams's testimony proved he was perfectly coherent when he demanded money from the two young women, and the RUC officer who observed him in Castle Street a few minutes later noted that he and his companions were walking in an 'orderly and civil fashion'.

ANTOIN MACGIOLLA BHRÍDE AND KIERAN FLEMING

Around midnight on 1–2 December 1984, a five-strong IRA unit was placing a bomb on a link road between the Kesh–Pettigo road and the Kesh–Belleek road at the entrance to Drumrush Lodge Restaurant; the bomb was intended to catch an RUC patrol.[876] Antoin MacGiolla Bhríde (McBride) was called in at the last minute to drive a van used in the operation. The unit was, however, being secretly monitored by an SAS patrol, which arrived at the scene in two cars. For some unknown reason, MacGiolla Bhríde, wearing civilian clothes, approached one of the SAS cars in foggy weather conditions. At the inquest hearing into the deaths of IRA members Antoin MacGiolla Bhríde and Kieran Fleming and SAS L/Cpl Alastair Slater, statements made by 'Soldier A' and 'Soldier B' were submitted by the RUC. The soldiers in question were not present at the inquest.[877]

Soldier A deposed that his colleague, Soldier B, shouted a warning and instructed MacGiolla Bhríde to put up his hands. Instead, he ran back up the road and jumped over a wire fence into a field. Soldier A contended that he continued to call on him to stop and then fired 'a warning burst' with his HK53 rifle, and Soldier B also fired. Soldier B, in his statement, said that after the warning shots, MacGiolla Bhríde did put his hands up and began to walk back towards them. He came back over the wire fence, and they assisted him onto the road. He was then placed on the road, face down. Soldier B searched him but found no firearms or explosives on him. He was told he was being arrested and detained until the RUC arrived. At this point, two IRA men opened up from the nearby ditch – one was armed with a rifle and the other with a shotgun. This firing hit a third soldier, L/Cpl Alistair Slater.[878]

Soldier A shouted for Slater to bring forward the plasticuffs (handcuffs), but Slater did not respond. Soldier A claimed that Soldier B then handed him his HK53 rifle and began looking for the plasticuffs. Soldier A then noticed that Slater was lying injured on the road. At that stage, both Soldiers A and B claimed that MacGiolla Bhríde 'made a surge forward' and attempted to get hold of Soldier A's rifle. Soldier A said he dropped one rifle – he was holding both – so that he could push 'the terrorist' back. MacGiolla Bhríde, he claimed, ran off, and 'thinking he had picked up the rifle I had dropped', both he and Soldier B ran up the road in pursuit.

Soldier B, who was still in possession of a firearm, fired several rounds, and MacGiolla Bhríde fell to the ground. Soldier B returned to their vehicle and gave first-aid to Slater. According to Soldier A, MacGiolla Bhríde 'made a movement' to try and get up off the ground. Soldier A then fired several shots at him, as he claimed to believe he was going to open fire on him. Soldier A then checked his condition and found that he was dead. He checked the body for firearms but found none. When he went back to the ditch, he found the HK53 where he had dropped it.[879]

MacGiolla Bhríde's brother, Damien, requested the coroner's permission to make some observations on the soldiers' statements. He suggested that only one bullet wound had been inflicted prior to his brother's arrest, when he was hit by one of the warning shots – he claimed it was the only entrance wound on the front of the body, and that all the other injuries were caused when he was shot in the back while lying on the ground. The coroner rejected this claim and remarked that there were 'some four entrance wounds to the front of the body'.[880]

The interesting question is: if the soldiers' statements are true, all of the shots would have been fired from his rear, so how could there have been four entrance wounds in the front of the body? Soldier B fired at him as he was running away and MacGiolla Bhríde fell to the ground; Soldier A fired at him as he lay on the ground and 'he slumped forward'.[881]

Raymond Murray states that the McBride family also believed that injuries on the body showed he had been mistreated. He had bruising and a gaping laceration on his face.[882] This submission, also made by Damien McBride, was likewise rejected by the coroner, Dr Hanna.[883]

Three other members of the IRA unit escaped over the border, but Kieran Fleming drowned as he attempted to swim across the Bannagh River. His body wasn't recovered until 21 December. He had escaped from Long Kesh in the mass escape of 1983.

Loyalists had previously shot MacGiolla Bhríde at his former home in east Belfast, in 1972, when he was 14 years old. His father was seriously wounded in the attack and died as a result of his injuries fourteen months later. Similar to Kevin Coen, MacGiolla Bhríde had joined the Irish Army and served from 1975 until he deserted in 1979 to join the IRA. He lived in Desertmartin, County Derry; Kieran Fleming came from the Waterside area of Derry city.[884]

SÉAMUS MCELWAIN

Like Kieran Fleming, McElwain had been on the run since the mass prison escape in September 1983. A couple of days before he was killed, an 800 lb IRA landmine, most likely laid by McElwain's unit, had been placed in a culvert but had failed to detonate. A member of a regular army patrol had spotted the command wire and reported back to his superiors. A covert inspection confirmed that it was indeed a command wire. An SAS unit took up position on 25 April 1986 and waited.

At dawn on the following morning, Séamus McElwain and Seán Lynch, both carrying rifles, approached the firing point.[885] As they did so, the SAS opened fire. According to Lynch, McElwain was felled by the first shot; Lynch, although injured, escaped across a field, rolled into a hedgerow for cover and hid. He was captured several hours later by the regular army and RUC, and he was flown by helicopter to Enniskillen, where he underwent surgery for his gunshot wounds. He was then transferred to intensive care in the Royal Victoria Hospital, Belfast; after that, he was moved to Musgrave Park Hospital, where he remained for two months, recovering from his injuries.[886] He was then arrested and charged with possession of explosives and a rifle, and was subsequently sentenced to twenty-five years' imprisonment. At his trial, the army testified that there had been four soldiers in two OPs overlooking the firing point when the shooting happened.[887]

In January 1993, McElwain's inquest returned a verdict of unlawful killing. Seán Lynch testified that McElwain had been wounded and incapacitated, then questioned by the soldiers and – within five minutes – shot dead. His testimony was accepted by the jury and the coroner.[888]

The jury's initial findings – that the two IRA men could have been arrested – were met with applause from the courtroom in Enniskillen, but after legal submissions from the MoD and RUC, it was agreed that this opinion was beyond the powers of the coroner's court, and the jury agreed to delete that part of their findings.[889] The DPP requested a full report on the inquest from the RUC, but nobody was ever prosecuted. Unionist politicians were incensed by the verdict, with Ken Maginnis and David Trimble claiming that the soldiers did not have to give a warning 'once engaged by armed terrorists'.[890]

An RUC detective inspector testified that ballistic tests on the two weapons recovered from the scene showed incriminating results – the Ruger M14 was involved in the attempted murder of a policeman in Newtownbutler, and the FNC rifle was connected with two attempted murders in 1985 and the double murder of D/Constable Derek Breen and John McCabe, a barman, in Maguiresbridge in 1986.[891]

The loss of McElwain was a huge blow to the IRA in Fermanagh. Over 3,000 people attended his funeral in his native Monaghan. Nonetheless, he was a hugely contentious figure for the local unionist community. Mark Urban claims that when he visited the area some years later, a British intelligence officer said of McElwain, 'He was an extraordinary bloke who would have been in the SAS if he was in the Army – it is just as well he is dead.'[892]

Chapter 12

KILLINGS AT THE HANDS OF LOYALISTS – CASE STUDIES (PART 1)

The four killings carried out by loyalists are included in the following two chapters because of strong suspicions of collusion in each case. In January 1973, Brigadier Peter Bush, commander of the 3 Brigade area – which included Fermanagh – estimated that up to 300 (approximately 10 per cent) of the part-time soldiers (i.e. the UDR) in the 3 Brigade area of operations were members of militant Protestant organisations.[893]

During the early 1970s, a gang of UVF/UDA members – several of them serving members of the UDR, former members of the B-Specials, and with possible links to the British Army – were responsible for most of the loyalist violence. Some of these men were named by one of their members, George Farrell, a serving member of the UDR, when he was arrested and interviewed by Gardaí in Ballyshannon, County Donegal in May 1976.[894] The names Farrell provided were published in the *Irish Times* during Farrell's trial for the bomb attack at Plunkett Reid's shop in Pettigo on 28 September 1973.[895] He named Robert Bridge as the leader of the gang while admitting that he himself was a member of both the UDA and the UVF, as well as the UDR.[896] He was convicted on 4 November 1976 and sentenced to fifteen years' imprisonment. On appeal, however, his conviction was overturned on a technicality. [897]

The gang carried out at least one attempted murder in Fermanagh: on 17 September 1973, they set out to kill Frank McManus, an MP and a member of NICRA. They also carried out numerous non-fatal attacks, both north and south of the border, during these years. It was reported that Bridge had been arrested on 27 September, the day preceding the Pettigo bombing. Following a search of his home at Woaghternerry (a townland near Enniskillen), a revolver

Enniskillen bombing, 8 November 1987.
(Courtesy of Pacemaker Press International Ltd)

Funeral cortege of Séamus McElwain, April 1986.
(Courtesy of Pacemaker Press International Ltd)

Ardess Famine Pit, restored and memorial unveiled in 2000.
(Courtesy of John McVitty, *Impartial Reporter*, Enniskillen)

Patsy and Teresa Kelly on their wedding day. Patsy was killed on 24 July 1974.
(Courtesy of John McVitty, *Impartial Reporter*, Enniskillen)

RIGHT: Douglas Deering, killed on 12 May 1977.
(Courtesy of John McVitty, *Impartial Reporter*, Enniskillen)

BELOW: Crom Castle, home of the Earls of Erne.
(Courtesy of John McVitty, *Impartial Reporter*, Enniskillen)

ABOVE: Scene of shooting of UDR Corporal, Herbert Kernaghan, at St. Tierney's Primary School, Roslea, on 15 October 1979.
(Courtesy of John McVitty, *Impartial Reporter*, Enniskillen)

BELOW: Funeral cortege of Louis Leonard, December 1972.
(Courtesy of John McVitty, *Impartial Reporter*, Enniskillen)

Michael Naan killed on 23 October 1972 (along with Andrew Murray).
(Courtesy of John McVitty, *Impartial Reporter*, Enniskillen)

LEFT: Thomas and Emily Bullock on their wedding day. They were both killed on 21 September 1972. (Courtesy of John McVitty, *Impartial Reporter*, Enniskillen)

BELOW: Eviction of Margaret Nolan. (*Fermanagh Herald*, 2 January 1954.)

was found and he was charged with possession in suspicious circumstances. He was remanded in custody at a special court in Enniskillen on the same day.[898] Nonetheless, the charge was withdrawn on 3 December 'in accordance with instructions' that Inspector Norman Walmsley had received from the DPP.[899] It is quite baffling that this charge was dropped, as Bridge was suspected of involvement in the attempted murder of Frank McManus MP.[900]

The gang was also responsible for co-ordinated bomb attacks on 28 December 1972 in Clones, Belturbet and Mulnagoad, near Pettigo. The Belturbet bomb claimed the lives of two teenagers, Geraldine O'Reilly and Patrick Stanley.

LOUIS LEONARD

The first loyalist killing in County Fermanagh was that of Louis Leonard, a 26-year-old IRA member, on 15 December 1972 at his butcher's shop in the village of Derrylin. He was the first IRA member to be killed in Fermanagh, and the only one who was a native of the county. He was deliberately targeted, although it was not generally known that he was an IRA member. The weapons used were two revolvers – a .455 and a .38. They were never recovered and had no history of use prior to, or post, Mr Leonard's death.[901]

After the murder of Robin Bell, a UDR member, on 22 October, and the attack on the home of the Lattimer brothers – also UDR members – there were threats that should another loyalist be murdered or intimidated, immediate retaliatory action would be taken in their respective areas.[902] It was stated that there was a 'strong force of the UDA in Fermanagh' and 'they were keeping a close eye on the enemies of Ulster'. A UDA member said that a 'detailed and complete list along with photographs of IRA members and their supporters in County Fermanagh had been compiled and their every movement noted'.[903]

It was reported shortly after Louis Leonard's death that his movements had clearly been monitored – that the murder was planned with 'fiendish efficiency' and carried out with cold-blooded purpose, suggesting not only 'Belfast gangster expertise' but also considerable local knowledge.[904] It was claimed that a British Army officer, Captain Vernon Rees, had questioned many local men in the area over the previous few weeks. He had threatened nearly all of them and to some had said, 'How would you like to suffer the same fate as Naan at Newtownbutler?'[905] One of those questioned and photographed by Captain Rees was Louis Leonard – just a few days before he was killed.

Captain Rees has already been mentioned in connection with the Naan and Murray deaths, and his role in the loyalist bomb attack that demolished Aghalane Bridge. He is described in the relevant HET Review Summary Report (RSR) as an army intelligence officer based at St Angelo's Camp, Enniskillen. However, there is information that he was, in fact, the Officer Commanding (OC) of A Battery (Chestnut Troop) with responsibility for security in the area around Kinawley.[906] In the Naan-Murray case, he told the investigating RUC officer that there had been no military patrols at or near the scene of the murders on the day, which was later proved to be entirely false. In the aftermath of Louis Leonard's death, Frank McManus MP, aware that Louis had been taken out of his shop and photographed, said it was his belief and 'the unanimous view of the people of Derrylin' that the army was responsible for his murder.[907]

Eyewitnesses provided statements and made phone calls to the RUC (some of them anonymous) regarding possible vehicles and personnel involved in the attack. Several described seeing a large black car on the night in question. The first eyewitness, a woman, was one of the most convincing witnesses.[908] She was sitting in her family car, which was parked facing Louis Leonard's shop in the car park of Lynham's Hotel. She stated that, at 10.40 p.m., on 15 December she saw, parking on the forecourt of the hotel, 'an expensive looking large glittering black car [...] very clean [...] and the rear bumper was elaborate and appeared to have ridges on it'. She told the police that there were two men in the car, and after a few minutes, one of the men, who was well dressed and stoutly built, got out, walked across the road and down the side of the butcher's shop, and looked in the window. He then returned to the car, and after about five minutes, they drove off. A short time later, the same car returned and parked just beyond the butcher's shop. This time, both men got out of the car; the well-dressed man went into the shop followed by the second man, who was of a lighter build, fair-haired and was wearing 'labouring clothes'. Both men remained in the shop for about five minutes before returning to the car and driving off. The woman noticed that as the men left the shop, the light was switched off.[909]

A very similar account was given, with a slight variation in the time and colour of the car, by a 16-year-old girl who was walking past the butcher's shop with her 12-year-old sister at around 11 p.m. As they passed the shop, she noticed that the light was on. On their return journey, about ten minutes later, she saw that the light had been switched off. She noticed what she described as a large green car parked close to the shop. A man was standing at the rear of the car and appeared to be inspecting the wheel. She said he was about 40 years old and six feet tall. At that moment, a second man, wearing blue overalls, emerged from the shop. She recalled that he was 5 feet 7 inches with 'normal length' fair hair. He appeared to be locking the front door and then putting something into his pocket. She was startled by a bang, and her sister grabbed her arm. Both men got into the car and drove away at speed. Her younger sister described the bang as 'like a light bulb going pop'.[910] Another eyewitness stated that he had noticed a black Ford Zephyr parked outside the shop at about 10.40 p.m. Like the first eyewitness, he also described the car as very clean and shining; he also indicated that part of the registration number read 'AOI' ('OI' was a 1970s Belfast registration).

An anonymous phone call to the police on Sunday, 17 December described seeing a black Cortina-like car at 10.40 p.m. at Derrylin; the caller also related what they remembered of the registration number: 'COI'. A second anonymous phone call, on Tuesday, 19 December, described driving behind a 'dark black Cortina' in the area at about 10.45 p.m. This caller read 'DOI' or 'COI' on the registration plate.

Appealing for information, the police issued a description of the car as 'a large expensive looking vehicle with wide bumpers which could be either grooved or corrugated'.[911] Inexplicably, when the investigating officer considered that the car might have been hired, turning his attention to car hire companies, the public police appeal reported that the car might have been an Austin Princess or Daimler – it did not mention a Cortina or a Zephyr.[912] The first eyewitness had described ridges on the rear of the car. Such ridges were part of the design of contemporary Mark III Cortinas and Mark IV Zephyrs; they were not a feature of either Austin Princesses or Daimlers. Nor did the police appeal refer to a possible Belfast registration number.

There seemed to be a reluctance to accept the testimony of the woman and two young girls, which dovetailed substantially. Also, the woman was in the advantageous position of having witnessed the entire events as they unfolded outside the shop. Instead, despite a discrepancy in the date of the alleged sighting, the investigating officer focused on the testimony of a man who claimed to have seen Louis with two others outside his shop at around 1.30 a.m. the following morning, 16 December, as he drove past.

Further corroborating the testimony of the female witnesses, Mr Leonard's wife Betty arrived back at the shop – having made deliveries to various customers – at about 11.05 p.m. to find it in darkness and the door locked. She was unable to enter the shop as she had no key. She clearly expected her husband to be there. She made enquiries with friends and relatives without success. She gave up at about 3.30 a.m. and decided she would wait until morning before contacting the police. Despite this detail, the investigating officer reported to his superior in April 1973 that, as a result of the man's testimony, he had reconsidered the time of the murder – he believed that Mr Leonard was taken from the shop, brought back later and killed there.[913] This scenario is highly unlikely, as the female witness in the car park and the two girls corroborate the fact that only the two men left the shop and drove off in the car.

The HET report into the murder concluded that the main suspects were two men who are referred to throughout as suspects A and B. A third suspect, Suspect C – a serving member of the UDR – had been added later, when intelligence was received (in August 1975) about his alleged involvement. Although the HET declined to name the suspects, the first two are believed to be William McMurray and James Campbell. Their identification has been made possible through cross-referencing with newspaper articles on court appearances from 1973.

It transpired that McMurray had hired a black Ford Cortina Mark III, registration number COI 8037, from Avis Rent-a-car at Aldergrove Airport on 15 December – the day of the murder.[914] When it was returned three days later, on 18 December, with 301 miles on the clock, two .38 calibre bullets and two other bullets (calibre unrecorded) were discovered in an ashtray. This information was passed on to RUC Special Branch and recorded, but it was not passed on to the murder investigation team until late April 1973. McMurray's home was not searched by local police in Belfast until January 1973; when it was, two revolvers and ammunition were found. He was charged with this crime but was not questioned about the ammunition found in the hired car.

McMurray was subsequently convicted, in May 1973, and sentenced to six months' imprisonment. At his conviction hearing, he was described as the 'self-confessed liaison officer for the UDA in Counties Tyrone and Fermanagh'.[915] Membership of the UDA and UVF seems to have been interchangeable at that time. It has to be borne in mind that the UDA was a legal organisation despite its involvement in sectarian murders and subversive activity, and it remained so for two decades. As a result, it was more pragmatic to admit to UDA membership than UVF.

In March 1973, while McMurray was out on bail, both he and Campbell, the other principal suspect, were charged with committing a robbery in Boho, County Fermanagh. Despite strong evidence that they were the culprits, Campbell was acquitted, following defence submissions, after three trials in Enniskillen Crown Court. The charge against McMurray was discontinued and recorded as *nolle prosequi* (to be unwilling to pursue).[916]

According to the HET, all three suspects came from Rathcoole in Belfast and were members of the UDA. In actual fact, Campbell was a local who had worked as a customs officer in Belleek in 1971. McMurray was also familiar with Fermanagh, as he had carried out plumbing work there previously and had reportedly stayed at Bothwell's Hotel, Lisnaskea.[917] In his report of November 2004, Justice Henry Barron states that Garda suspects for the Pettigo bombing in September 1973 included 'a former customs officer from County Fermanagh and a former British soldier then serving as a customs officer in Belleek'.[918]

The HET report highlights serious deficiencies in the RUC investigation, including the failure to formally interview the two main suspects. This was despite the fact that there were numerous intelligence records stretching from 1972 to 1981 which pointed to McMurray and Campbell as being responsible. One piece of intelligence reported that RUC officers had passed information to loyalists specifying that Louis Leonard was an IRA member. The failure to carry out a professional investigation amounts to negligent and collusive behaviour. McMurray and Campbell are unlikely to have acted alone, without local support.[919]

As noted above, both suspects were charged with carrying out an armed robbery at Boho in March 1973. They were also charged with possession of a Walther pistol and magazine that had been stolen from a police officer in Belfast the previous July. Suspect C (who cannot be named for legal reasons) and an unconnected individual were both sentenced to six years' imprisonment for possession of a pistol, two magazines and forty bullets with intent to endanger life on 31 May 1973. Lawyers for the Crown withdrew an attempted murder charge and kidnapping and assault charges against him. He was described in court as an electrician and a part-time member of the UDR.[920]

It is surprising that the most notorious loyalist in the area and a serving member of the UDR, Robert Bridge, does not appear to have been considered as a suspect, because after the triple bombing of Clones, Belturbet and Mulnagoad two weeks later, the RUC quickly put his name forward to Gardaí as the leading suspect.[921] It was claimed that he was the leader of the UVF/UDA gang in Fermanagh. New information links Bridge with William McMurray around that time. Following Bridge's arrest and charge with the possession of a firearm in September 1973, a British Army log records the following:

> Bridge was suspected by the RUC of possible involvement in the assassination attempt on Mr Frank McManus MP on 17 September 73. A search at his home revealed part of a gun and he was duly charged with the illegal possession of a firearm. Bridge is carded as a Lt in the Tyrone/Fermanagh UDA and was believed at one time to be the OC of this unit. He is an associate of William 'Billy' McMurray, OC of a UDA Special 'Commando' Team.[922]

In minutes of a meeting of the Western Security Committee held at Lisanelly Camp, Omagh on 29 March 1973, Major J.H. Bryant noted that reference was made to the two men arrested for the robbery at Derrygonnelly. One of them was described as a leading member of a UDA commando-type gang from Belfast who was responsible for 'various explosions in Eire [*sic*].' This may well be a reference to McMurray.[923]

A few days later, an army intelligence summary noted that there had been 'no militant Protestant activity' during the period under review – 2 to 9 April. Captain David Delius recorded that the likely cause of this absence was the recent arrest of McMurray and Campbell on 14 March.[924]

In a Foreign and Commonwealth Office (FCO) file relating to the Enniskillen bombing of November 1987, a list of 'Terrorist Murders in Fermanagh and south Tyrone from 1971 to date' is included, with columns for the names of victims and 'Responsibility for deaths'. Responsibility for Louis Leonard's death is unexpectedly allocated to the 'Army'. [925] At the end of the list, the number of convictions for these murders is noted. With regard to the 'Regular Army', it is stated that convictions have been secured in two out of three murders. The three murders being referred to are that of Michael Naan, Andrew Murray and Louis Leonard.[926]

There are serious questions as to why the police investigation failed to make any progress. The HET report identifies many missed opportunities by those conducting the investigation, and nobody has ever been charged – let alone convicted – of Louis Leonard's murder.

JAMES (JIM) MURPHY

Mr Murphy was a member of NICRA. He had been interned for about four months during Operation Harvest, from December 1959 to March 1960,[927] and was reported to be closely associated with Frank McManus, the Independent MP for Fermanagh and South Tyrone.[928]

He was killed between 11.05 p.m. on Saturday, 20 April and 12.45 a.m. on Sunday, 21 April 1974. It is likely that his attackers arrived at his garage (where vehicles were repaired and petrol and diesel sold) after 11 p.m., as a farmer who lived about 200 yards away heard shots around that time but couldn't be sure where the shots came from. He didn't see or hear anything else suspicious. The evidence suggests that Jim was abducted from his garage but was killed elsewhere. His car was found on the following day at Derryallen Lough. Two revolvers were used in the attack – a .455 Colt and a .455 Smith & Wesson. The bullets removed from his body were all fired from the Colt, while the bullets found inside the garage were fired from the Smith & Wesson. The Colt revolver was one of the weapons used in the shooting at the Corner Bar in Trillick, County Tyrone, the previous January, which forced the McCourt family out of their home and business.[929] There is no record of them being used after this incident, and they have not been recovered.

The post-mortem examination revealed that Mr Murphy had been struck by four bullets – two of them to the chest. Injuries were also found on the back of his scalp, his right shoulder, left elbow, right loin, left buttock, right thigh and left shin.

The scenes of crime officer (SOCO) had noted the severe gash on Mr Murphy's lower back and later found tyre marks in the area of the petrol pumps, which suggested to him that a vehicle might have entered the forecourt, dropped the dead body and made a sharp turn on the tarmac towards Derrylin.[930] Some of the bullets recovered from the garage were found by Mr Murphy's brother.

It was reported that extra detectives had been brought in to assist with the investigation[931] – a report that seems to be at odds with the findings of the HET, which state:

> The HET considers that having insufficient trained detectives in the area and the appointment of a uniform inspector to investigate the murder was an organisational failure at the time and senior detectives should have provided support and guidance in such serious cases.[932]

Staff Sgt Lewis Edward Bean, an ATO, carried out a series of controlled explosions on Mr Murphy's Peugeot car on Sunday, 21 April at 12.45 p.m. He blew open the doors, bonnet and boot and cut open the seats to ensure there were no explosives in the car.[933]

Local people were reported to have noticed that army plainclothes squads in unmarked vehicles were particularly busy in the area on Saturday – the day of Mr Murphy's death. They wondered why the army had carried out a controlled explosion on his car, because many of the locals had already examined it carefully long before the army arrived. There was intense feeling about the actions of the RUC on Sunday, 21 April after the murder investigation had begun. It was claimed that instead of investigating Mr Murphy's death, police spent the day checking for tax, brakes and faulty tyres. It was reported that the security forces harassed him incessantly.[934]

The HET commented that 'The controlled explosions on Jim's car are likely to have eliminated, or greatly minimised, the opportunity for retrieving suspect trace evidence (fibres/hair/fingerprints/DNA). It is not known if the SOCO made an examination of the car.'[935]

Details of an anonymous letter received by the *Fermanagh Herald* were published in that newspaper on 18 May. The author claimed that the 'South Fermanagh UFF' was responsible for Jim Murphy's death, and that the killing was carried out in retaliation for that of the 'ex-UDR man shot down in cold blood'. This is clearly a reference to Lt Col George Saunderson, who was killed by the IRA on 10 April.

It wasn't until 1982 that intelligence was received by the RUC which indicated that the two main suspects implicated in the murder of Louis Leonard were also responsible for Jim Murphy's death.[936] There is no way of knowing how reliable this intelligence was.

Harry Currie, who had been chief inspector in Enniskillen during the early 1970s, provided information to the HET. He told them he had suspected a local man of involvement in the murder; he said the local had access to a van, which may have been used to abduct Mr Murphy from the garage. This man was a UDR member and 'was always in the company of army personnel'. He believed the man to be responsible for organising and taking part in acts of terrorism in the Fermanagh area. His suspicions were heightened when this man was later imprisoned for the murder of a Catholic man and the killings stopped.[937] The man to whom Mr Currie refers is clearly the notorious loyalist Robert Bridge, already referred to in relation to Louis Leonard's murder. The question arises as to why he was not arrested and questioned at the time.

The only link between the Murphy and Leonard murders is the intelligence received seven years later that the same Belfast suspects were involved in both. In the Leonard case there is the circumstantial evidence of the hired car, which strongly supports that intelligence, but there is no corroborating evidence in the Murphy case.

Nobody has ever been questioned or charged – much less convicted – with Jim Murphy's murder, and HET describes the investigation as 'basic at best'. As previously noted, one of the weapons used to kill him was also used in the attack on the Corner Bar only three months previously. A number of men were questioned in relation to that attack, but no arrests were made. It would appear obvious that these men should have been questioned about the Murphy murder.

A report in the *Irish Times* noted that NICRA had complained that Mr Murphy 'had been continually harassed by troops stationed in Kinawley during the last two years' and that an army officer had threatened to shoot him after he had driven over a cratered road.[938] The organisation is quoted as follows, 'NICRA shares the grave suspicion of local people, both Catholic and Protestant, that plain-clothes members of the British Army had a hand in the death of James Murphy. This suspicion is not lessened by the apparent reluctance to carry out a full investigation into his murder.'[939]

Chapter 13

KILLINGS AT THE HANDS OF LOYALISTS – CASE STUDIES (PART 2)

PATRICK (PATSY) KELLY

Mr Kelly, a councillor on Omagh District Council, was abducted and killed on 24 July 1974, three months after the death of Jim Murphy. He was also an active member of NICRA and had appeared on platforms and at meetings in the area. He and his wife's brother were managing the Corner Bar, Trillick, on the Tyrone–Fermanagh border, after Michael McCourt and his family were intimidated into leaving following the shooting there the previous January.

The alarm was raised when Mr Kelly failed to return home to his wife and four young children in Golan, about 2 miles from Trillick, after he closed the pub. Neighbours reported hearing shots in the Golan area, and police later found traces of blood, hair and fragments torn from a shirt with several buttons attached on a narrow country road. According to a report on RTÉ's *Drivetime* programme almost forty-five years later, a UDR VCP had been operating at that location on the night he was killed.[940] The report also referred to forensic evidence in the form of a footprint found at the scene of the abduction that matched army-issue boots. This was not disclosed at the inquest or to the family.[941]

Two days after Mr Kelly's disappearance, his new Mazda car, less than a fortnight old, was found burnt-out in a laneway leading to a disused quarry on the Brookeborough estate midway between Lisbellaw and Brookeborough. The number plates had been removed. The nearby Colebrooke River was searched but nothing was found. Local involvement was suspected, because the laneway where the car was found was a cattle track used solely by local farmers.[942]

When the search was widened to include a large section of Fermanagh and Tyrone, about 1,200 civilians and 100 policemen joined in to assist.[943] However, they were unsuccessful, and after some days, the search was called off.[944] Eventually, on 10 August, Dr A.R. Small from Brookeborough was fishing in a boat on Lough Eyes, near Lisbellaw, when he saw a body floating in the water between his boat and the shore.[945] A 56 lb iron weight had been attached to the body by a new rope tied around the waist. The body had sustained several gunshots.[946] The location was 15 miles from where Mr Kelly was abducted. It would have been very difficult to have travelled so far in those days without encountering a number of VCPs. The RUC claimed that Lough Eyes had been dredged already but without success.[947] After the body's discovery, the authorities brought navy divers from Derry to search the lake for further clues or weapons.[948]

More than 4,000 people attended the removal of Mr Kelly's remains from Tyrone County Hospital to St MacCartan's Church, Magheralough.[949] A very poignant aspect of the case was that his widow, Teresa, discovered she was pregnant with their fifth child while her husband was still missing.

The inquest heard that he sustained six gunshot wounds to the chest but no further details were given.[950] The RTÉ report many years later stated that the bullets recovered from the body were .45 calibre.[951]

In September 1982, Robert Bridge was interviewed by police after he alleged that three UDR members had been involved in the murder. Two months later, Bridge withdrew his allegations, and the police expressed that they were satisfied that his evidence lacked credibility.[952]

In January 1999, nearly twenty-five years later, the family was told that a former UDR man, David Jordan, had broken down in public and confessed to being involved in the killing.[953] Jordan also alleged that Oliver Gibson and two other UDR soldiers – all members of 8 UDR, County Tyrone – were involved.[954] David Jordan died on 26 October 1999, but he had never been interviewed by the RUC. They maintained, rather unconvincingly, that they were unaware of his identity until after his death. Jordan had previously been knocked down in a hit-and-run incident. It was reported that he had died from alcohol consumption or a heart condition. The doctor who carried out the port-mortem later told the family that he had not been alerted to possible foul play.[955]

On 2 May 1999, an article in *Ireland on Sunday* referred to an anonymous letter, dated 1 August 1974, that was sent to the local NICRA organisation. It was written on the back of an RUC form and purported to come from 'serving officers'. The author(s) alleged that certain named UDR personnel, including Oliver Gibson, were involved. It appears that the police did not undertake any investigation on foot of the article.

At a meeting on 22 August 2001 with the family's solicitor, Pat Fahy (who also represented Michael Leonard's family after his murder), D/Supt McArthur informed him that the murder investigation files – containing statements taken during house-to-house inquiries, police log books and records, and details of UDR personnel interviews at an army camp in 1974 – were all missing.

On 1 April 2002, Assistant Chief Constable (ACC) Samuel Kincaid, on taking up his post, reviewed correspondence between McArthur and Fahy. He searched for all of the investigation papers, and some documents were found. As a result, ACC Kincaid directed that a review of the case be carried out, which was undertaken by D/Inspector Harkness and a team of detectives.[956]

On 17 April 2002, Kincaid and Harkness met with the family and their solicitor, along with Jane Winter of British Irish Rights Watch, an NGO. All aspects of the case were discussed. Harkness told them there was nothing to confirm that Gibson or other UDR members were ever interviewed about the killing.[957]

Gibson's car had been reported stolen on the night of Mr Kelly's death and was later found burnt out. Harkness stated that when Gibson was interviewed about his stolen car, a police officer from Beragh station provided an alibi for him. Kincaid informed the family, solicitor and Ms Winter that they would interview people about why 'they did or did not' provide an alibi for Mr Gibson – including the police officer who dealt with the report of his car being stolen.

Harkness said they would be checking the alibis of the UDR personnel named in the anonymous letter to NICRA dated 1 August 1974. Kincaid said they wanted to interview the two witnesses who had heard Jordan confessing to the murder, and they intended to speak to the Jordan family. He assured Teresa Kelly that his presence at the meeting reflected the fact that significant issues about the death required it to be re-examined. After the meeting, Harkness carried out a review into the case, at the end of which Kincaid decided to establish a complete re-investigation.

As a result, D/Supt Andrew Hunter, on secondment to the PSNI from West Yorkshire Police Force, was appointed on 2 June 2003. Leading a team of detectives at Maydown RUC station, Derry, he reopened the case of Patsy Kelly. The family were sceptical and announced that their preference would be for an independent probe. Mr Kelly's brother Peter, a Sinn Féin councillor, claimed that there was security force collusion in the murder and described the original police investigation as a charade. D/Supt Hunter said he would investigate claims that British military patrols had been present in the area on the night Mr Kelly went missing.[958]

In 2004, Teresa Kelly sought a judicial review of the decision of the PSNI not to appoint an external police force to conduct a fresh investigation into her late husband's death. She claimed this was necessary because there was security force collusion involved. Lord Chief Justice Brian Kerr, who did not accept that there was evidence of collusion, rejected her application. He submitted that the new investigation team was sufficiently independent, as it was headed by a senior police officer seconded from an English police force.[959]

A considerable amount of new information emerged with the publication of the court judgement in November 2004. The gunshots on the night of the murder were heard at around 12.30 a.m. A witness stated he had observed a 'large ball of flame' at 2.30 a.m. on 24 July 1974 – Mr Kelly's car being burned. Witness statements were said to have been taken at the time from Oliver Gibson and eighteen of his colleagues regarding their movements on the evening of 23 July and morning of 24 July. During the post mortem, .455 calibre bullets were retrieved. Mr Kelly had been shot six times and four bullets were recovered from his chest. They had been fired from a revolver with no previous history of use. There were lacerations to his scalp and an abrasion to his left wrist and forearm. A fracture of the larynx such as occurs in strangulation was also found, although this might have occurred after death.

Teresa Kelly highlighted several shortcomings in the original investigation:

- The police failed to recover UDR footwear for forensic matching with a footwear impression made at the murder scene, either by a Wellington boot or boots of a type worn by the security forces.

- Members of the UDR were not interviewed under caution, their duty rosters were not obtained and their lockers were not searched.
- The forensic report on the boot-print was not disclosed to the inquest.
- The existence of a DNA sample from a fingerprint found on Mr Kelly's car was not disclosed to the inquest.
- There was conflicting and misleading information on whether Mr Gibson was interviewed and the nature of any alibi provided by the police.
- The police failed to recover the car rug from Oliver Gibson's car for forensic examination. The car, reported stolen around the time of the murder, was found burnt out 10 miles from the scene. The car rug was no longer available for forensic examination.
- The police failed to have handkerchiefs sent for forensic examination that were found at the scene where Mr Kelly's body was recovered from Lough Eyes.
- The police failed to account for missing documents and photographs, including the police report into the theft and burning of Mr Gibson's car, photographs of the boat used to dispose of Mr Kelly's body and any statement from Gibson's alibi.[960]

As part of Hunter's investigation, four men were arrested and questioned in April 2005[961] but no charges were brought against them. These men were said to be former members of the UDR and included Robert Bridge. Pat Fahy demanded that the police explain publicly why they had not arrested those named by David Jordan in 1999.[962] Before April was out, D/Supt Andrew Hunter had returned to England with nothing to show for his investigation. This confirmed the worst fears of the Kelly family.[963]

The latest information on the case was contained in the RTÉ *Drivetime* report of November 2018. Disturbing new information has been uncovered following a freedom of information request on behalf of the Kelly family by Ciarán MacAirt of the charity Paper Trail. [964] This information is contained in a British Army Operations Log dated 13 August 1974 – three days after the discovery of Mr Kelly's body. It records that ammunition connected to the discovery was found in Lough Eyes, some of which matched the calibre of bullet used in the shooting. This crucial evidence disappeared from subsequent police investigations. The ammunition found was: 58 x 9mm, 33 x .45 long, 5 x .45 short and 1 x .38 action.[965] As has been noted, the bullets recovered from the body were .45 calibre. This information had been withheld from the family, and they are now asking what important evidential opportunities were lost by police when they failed to include this find in investigations. It was also withheld from the original inquest into Mr Kelly's death.[966]

The case is currently the subject of a Police Ombudsman's investigation.

PATRICK O'REILLY

Mr O'Reilly was shot dead as he sat in the cab of his lorry on the Kilskeery–Irvinestown road on 27 May 1975, where he had been working on a road-widening scheme for several weeks. He had stopped his lorry alongside an excavator when a gunman, wearing sunglasses and with an anorak hood over his head and a scarf over his mouth, approached him. The gunman fired a burst of shots from a Sterling SMG, hitting his victim four times in the head and chest. Robert Bridge was arrested on the day of the murder and was taken to Enniskillen, where he was held and questioned over the next four days.[967] He protested his innocence and was released on 30 May, when his alibi was purportedly checked and verified by two witnesses.

After further investigation, he was re-arrested and interviewed at Derrygonnelly RUC station on 24 June, when he was questioned about a Sterling SMG.[968] He led police to where the weapon was hidden, and forensic tests proved it was used in the shooting. He signed a confession stating that he had been ordered by 'a superior officer to go and do a job and make a hit'. He admitted knowing his victim.

On 26 June, Bridge was charged at a special court in Enniskillen with the murder of Patrick O'Reilly and was described as an unemployed labourer from Woaghternerry, a townland near Enniskillen. He was remanded in custody.

At the same court, David Andrew Wills, a labourer from Dublin Road, Enniskillen, was charged with possession of an SLR rifle, two Martini–Henry rifles, a sawn-off shotgun and a quantity of 7.62mm ammunition at Woaghternerry. He was also remanded in custody.[969]

A defence lawyer admitted that Wills was a member of the UVF.[970] It is not known if Wills played any role in the death of Mr O'Reilly.

When Bridge's bail hearing took place, Crown counsel said he had made a statement admitting to the murder and stating that he was the commander of the UVF in Enniskillen. Bridge, who was not legally represented, claimed that he was forced to make the statement.[971]

When the case was heard, Alan Beacom, a digger-driver employed by Drew Thompson of Kilskeery who was a part-time UDR member at the time, said he was transferring soil into O'Reilly's lorry when the murder occurred.[972]

Bridge described how he had hidden himself in undergrowth, and as he watched, he saw Drew Thompson at the digger and then saw him leave. He saw Patrick O'Reilly sitting in the cab and emerged from the undergrowth to shoot him.[973] The court heard from the prosecution counsel that Bridge had claimed, falsely, that Mr O'Reilly was an active republican.[974] Mr O'Reilly's brother had been convicted of possession of weapons the previous year,[975] but he had no involvement – a fact of which Bridge and his associates would have been aware. He received a life sentence for the murder.[976]

In November 2015, author Edward Burke interviewed an RUC officer who had served in Fermanagh in the 1970s. The retired officer expressed his mistrust of 'certain elements of the constabulary' serving in the county. In the immediate aftermath of Patrick O'Reilly's death, when this officer received information about the possible involvement of local loyalist paramilitary leader Robert Bridge, he moved quickly to prevent his RUC colleagues from hearing of this development lest they tip off local loyalists who would dispose of the evidence.[977] A Criminal Investigation Department (CID) officer from outside Fermanagh was sent to conduct the investigation. The apparent outcome of the interrogation of loyalist suspects resulted in a list of police officers and UDR personnel suspected of a series of loyalist plots, including a plan to seize weapons from Enniskillen UDR barracks.[978]

The RUC officer, rather than trusting his report to the normal channels of communication, told Edward Burke that he drove to RUC Headquarters in Belfast to present it by hand.[979]

Several questions arise regarding the murder investigation. Were the two persons who had, at the outset, provided a patently false alibi for Bridge charged with perverting the course of justice? What was Wills' link to the murder and to Bridge? He was found in possession of weapons at Woaghternerry, the townland where Bridge lived. Did some of Mr

O'Reilly's workmates set him up? Bridge could not have acted alone. Very few details emerged at the hearing, as Bridge pleaded guilty and therefore no trial ensued. Did anything happen as a result of the findings of the CID officer's investigation?

Collusion is suspected in all four killings carried out by loyalists in Fermanagh. Serious deficiencies were discovered by the HET in Louis Leonard's murder investigation, and intelligence was received that police officers had provided information regarding his IRA membership to loyalists prior to his death.

In Jim Murphy's case, the HET described the RUC investigation as 'basic at best', and suspicions were harboured about the controlled explosion carried out on his car.

With regard to Patsy Kelly's death, all the available information suggests that members of 8 UDR (Tyrone), with assistance from 4 UDR (Fermanagh), were involved. Recently discovered information shows that evidence was withheld from Mr Kelly's inquest.

In Patrick O'Reilly's case, a former RUC officer expressed mistrust in the local police during this investigation. There are also suspicions of limitation damage in the sole conviction of Robert Bridge when clearly he was not acting alone.

It is interesting to note that both Jim Murphy and Patsy Kelly were members of NICRA – as was Frank McManus, who had an attempt made on his life in September 1973. Michael Naan, killed by members of the British Army in October 1972, was another member of the organisation.

THE TRIPLE BOMBING OF CLONES, BELTURBET AND MULNAGOAD (PETTIGO)

Although this co-ordinated attack occurred in the three adjoining counties of Monaghan, Cavan and Donegal, it is being included in this work because all the available evidence points to the fact that the UVF/UDA unit from Fermanagh and associates were responsible for this triple bombing.[980]

The timing of the three explosions, which all took place on 28 December 1972, meant that this was a co-ordinated and well-planned series of attacks. From the perspective of the perpetrators it was a very successful operation.[981]

Clones

A bomb contained in a blue Austin 1100 – registration number 431 LZ – exploded on Fermanagh Street, Clones at 10.01 p.m.[982]. The car had been stolen between 6.20 p.m. and 7.35 p.m. that evening from the car park on Gas Lane, off Belmore Street, Enniskillen.[983] There were no fatalities, but a number of people were injured, including two young men from Fermanagh.

Belturbet

At 10.28 p.m., a second bomb – 100 lb of explosives in a red 1969 Ford Escort; registration number AIL 2402 – exploded on Main Street, Belturbet, killing two teenagers – Geraldine O'Reilly (15 years old), who was a local girl, and Patrick Stanley (16 years old) from Clara, County Offaly. Geraldine was awaiting an order in a chip shop while her brother Anthony was parked outside waiting for her. Patrick was in a telephone kiosk making a call home to say he would be staying overnight in Belturbet.

Eleven persons were detained in Cavan Surgical Hospital – three of them seriously injured, including Anthony O'Reilly.[984]

The red Ford Escort, the property of William Wilson of Willoughby Place, Enniskillen, was stolen from outside his home after 5 p.m. that evening. Mr Wilson owned the Home Bakery at Townhall Street, Enniskillen.[985]

The Ford Escort was stopped at a Garda checkpoint at Aghalane at about 9.05 p.m. Garda John O'Donnell, who was manning the checkpoint, allowed the car to go through despite the fact that the driver was unable to produce his driving licence. In a subsequent statement, O'Donnell said that there was a female in the front passenger seat and there may have been another person in the rear seat, but he couldn't be sure of that.[986] A photofit was later compiled from the description given by the Garda and an eyewitness who may have seen the same man in Belturbet. When the driver of the Ford Escort was stopped, he, bizarrely, gave the name of the man referred to as Suspect C in the Louis Leonard case, whose killing had been carried out two weeks earlier. He gave his address as 'Derrylin'. Suspect C did not live in Derrylin, which was confirmed to the Gardaí by the RUC. He was described at that time as a known loyalist. The RUC confirmed that the photofits drawn up of the driver did not resemble Suspect C.

It would appear that the gang made their getaway in a lagoon blue Ford Cortina, registration number BIA 477, which was stolen in Belturbet after 9.30 p.m. that night.[987] This car was found, bearing false number plates, in Crumlin, County Antrim in early January 1973. It was initially noticed on 31 December 1972; when it was still there two days later, the RUC called in the British Army, who carried out a controlled explosion on it.[988] The false plates belonged to a Ford Cortina, registration number AIA 9898, which was stolen from outside the home of an RUC officer in Belfast on 27 December 1972 – the day before the bombing. This car was found burnt out in a quarry near Enniskillen on 29 December 1972.

The forensic examination in Belturbet did not yield any evidence. It is likely that in both the Clones and Belturbet bombs, ammonium nitrate and fuel oil (AnFO) was the main ingredient. AnFO was readily available to loyalists in 1972 because there were still stocks of high-content ammonium nitrate on both sides of the border. D/Sgt O'Connor reported that he had found a piece of safety fuse in Clones, which would indicate that the Clones and possibly the Belturbet bomb used this means of initiation. If this was the case, the bombs would have been perfectly safe to transport, and there would have been only a small risk of discovery when the fuse was being lit. The short getaway distances to the border would indicate that only a few feet of safety fuse was necessary to enable the teams to escape across the border before the bombs exploded.[989]

Mulnagoad

At 10.50 p.m. on the same night (28 December), a bomb exploded outside the licensed premises of Hugh Britton of Mulnagoad, a townland near Pettigo, County Donegal.[990] This bomb was left beside the pub and was contained in a beer keg or milk churn. There were no injuries or fatalities, but the bomb caused considerable damage to the pub.

Justice Barron declared himself satisfied that Robert Bridge and his group were responsible for the triple bombings on 28 December 1972.[991] The Gardaí had a number of pieces of intelligence to support this belief:

- A superintendent at Ballyconnell received information from an unidentified source that Robert Bridge and two other named men from the Enniskillen area were involved. This informant claimed that Bridge and one of his associates were seen in a car between Lisnaskea and Enniskillen between 11 p.m.

and midnight on the night of the bombing, and that Bridge was seen near the burnt-out shell of the Ford Cortina with the registration 'AIA 9898'.[992]

- Barron claims that by the time of Bridge's arrest on 27 June 1975, Gardaí had received a number of pieces of intelligence indicating that he had been involved in several bombings in the state.
- Another suspect, George Farrell, supplied more detailed information after his arrest in May 1976. This information suggested that Bridge was in charge of a group of around ten men who planned and carried out a number of attacks in the border area between 1972 and 1975.[993]
- Chief Supt John Paul McMahon of the Cavan-Monaghan Division had written a report in which Robert Bridge was mentioned, forwarding it to the Garda Intelligence Section (C3) on 17 November 1972. The report was entitled 'UDA activities in Co. Fermanagh'.[994]

No person was ever charged or convicted of these bombings or the murders of Geraldine and Paddy.

Bridge's loyalist gang carried out several other attacks in the Republic of Ireland that didn't result in fatalities. One such attack occurred on 10 November 1973 in the townland of Legnakelly, near Clones, about a mile from the border.[995] The security forces had identified a suspected IRA safe house some time previously; it was alleged to be the residence of the OC of the IRA Active Service Unit (ASU) in the Clones area. Shortly before midnight, eight armed and masked men burst into the house, where they found the alleged OC, his wife and three other men. They were forced outside while a bomb was planted with a fuse attached. The men were told they were going to be shot and were directed to a shed. However, all the men except the alleged OC broke free and ran off. Their target was shot in the back and, although badly injured, made it to a neighbour's house. He was taken to Monaghan Hospital and recovered from the attack. The house was completely destroyed in the explosion.[996]

BREVITY OF LOYALIST CAMPAIGN

The first killing carried out in Fermanagh by loyalists was Louis Leonard's on 15 December 1972 and the last was that of Patrick O'Reilly on 27 May 1975. Why was the loyalist campaign in Fermanagh so brief, and why did it fail to follow the pattern that emerged in the adjoining counties of Tyrone and Armagh?

Edward Burke argues that loyalism in rural areas in the early 1970s was different from that found in urban centres, as 'local political and business elites' directed and enabled loyalist paramilitary activity in rural areas, particularly in Fermanagh in the early seventies.[997] Mark McGovern agrees. He observes:

> The social make-up of loyalist paramilitaries in rural areas often differed from urban areas. The UVF in small towns and villages often came from the very same 'respectable' rural social groups, classes and family networks as were members of the UDR and RUC. Such socially embedded networks of family and community could be mobilised in the organisation and conduct of campaigns of violence.'[998]

After Stormont was prorogued in March 1972, its politicians found themselves out of office. The unionist and loyalist community was outraged at its loss. In October, 3,000 loyalists, including the UDA, the UVF, the Loyalist Association of Workers and the USCA, gathered beside the RUC station in Enniskillen to hear accounts of loyalist cross-border raids into the Republic of Ireland.[999] Presumably, this gathering was intended to provide encouragement and show solidarity with those involved in the attacks.

Many Ulster unionists in the border counties were sympathetic to Bill Craig's Vanguard Movement – including John Brooke, the Chairman of Fermanagh County Council, who claimed that all unionists in west Ulster 'were now united with Vanguard'.[1000] His father, Viscount Brookeborough, the former Prime Minister of Northern Ireland, in a speech in Enniskillen in July 1972, advised young Protestants to join the UDR and also praised 'other bodies' which were doing 'good work'. In the autumn, John Taylor, the former Minister for Home Affairs in the Northern Ireland government, said he supported the UDA going across the border and 'rooting out' the IRA, arguing that loyalist cross-border bombings 'have been an advantage to Northern Ireland security'.[1001]

Coinciding with these protests and speeches, the Fermanagh loyalist campaign began when a bomb exploded in Clones at the side of the Creighton Hotel on 16 October 1972 at 11 p.m. Ten minutes later, members of Derry UDA exploded a bomb in Carrigans, County Donegal.[1002] One man was seriously injured in the Clones bombing.[1003] The campaign continued in the southern border counties, as well as in Fermanagh, until 1975. The one loyalist whose name crops up repeatedly is Robert Bridge: after the triple bombing of Belturbet, Clones and Mulnagoad on 28 December, his name appears to have been the only one passed on by the RUC to the Gardaí; during George Farrell's trial for the Pettigo bombing, he named Bridge as the leader of the gang; RUC Chief Inspector Harry Currie suggested to the HET that he suspected Bridge of involvement in Jim Murphy's murder; Bridge was arrested for Cllr Patsy Kelly's murder and was the sole suspect arrested and convicted for Patrick O'Reilly's murder. All of this focus on Bridge gives rise to the suspicion that he was scapegoated.

While Bridge was clearly a major player, there were several other suspects who got away scot-free – who were never charged with any subversive activity. For example, the British Army had intelligence on a UDA 'commando' unit and its leader; the army believed this unit was responsible for bombings in the Republic of Ireland. This information does not appear to have been passed on to the Gardaí investigating the Belturbet bombing and the Dublin bombings of December 1972 and January 1973.

It is, perhaps, easy to scapegoat Bridge. The murder for which he was convicted was the last one committed by loyalists in Fermanagh, suggesting that the killings stopped because he was incarcerated. Nonetheless, that explanation may be too simple. Loyalist murders in the adjoining counties of Armagh and Tyrone dropped significantly after 1976; in Tyrone they stopped completely the following year, resuming in 1991 and continuing up to 1997. In Armagh, it was the mid-1980s before they stopped completely; they resumed in 1990 and continued up to 2001. Throughout Northern Ireland there was a huge upsurge in loyalist killings between 1991 and 1994 inclusive. When the loyalist campaign resumed, it was much more focused on members, or family members, of IRA personnel or elected members of Sinn Féin. As many of the IRA units operating in Fermanagh were based south of the border, it may have been considered too difficult to attack them, or loyalists may have feared their exposure to retaliation.

Edward Burke argues that loyalists may have believed that due to their campaign in the early 1970s, they had succeeded in provoking an increase in the Irish security presence along the border and so their work was effectively done. Therefore, there was no need to resume attacks in the late 1980s and early 1990s.[1004] Nevertheless, IRA attacks from across the border continued – although much reduced – after 1972. It wasn't until 1987, as a result of the Enniskillen bombing, that IRA-caused deaths in Fermanagh reached double figures again. Unionist security concerns, however, remained constant – as will be discussed in the next chapter.

An alternative reason for loyalist inactivity was suggested to the author by a member of the Protestant community in Fermanagh. They contended that local men joined the UDR and RUCR rather than the UVF or UDA and claimed that members of their community, who were very conservative and law-abiding, preferred to rely on the security forces for their defence.[1005]

Chapter 14

SECURITY CONCERNS AND THE ELECTION OF BOBBY SANDS

There had been no conflict-related deaths in the county before the introduction of internment. When it was implemented on 9 August 1971, the nationalist community in general was outraged that only Catholics were being detained. In Fermanagh, a one-day strike in September brought Enniskillen businesses to a standstill when 1,000 people left work to march in protest.[1006] Catholic employees were allegedly sacked and victimised for taking part in the strike.[1007]

The IRA began targeting UDR members (both on- and off-duty) immediately after the introduction of internment, but the targeting of off-duty members in particular shocked and horrified the unionist community.

A former IRA member, Tommy McKearney, told Peter Taylor, a British journalist, author and documentary-maker, of the logic behind targeting off-duty UDR members:

> An off-duty UDR man is a member of the British Army. Now it is very naïve and stretching credulity to the breaking point to suggest that a man delivering the milk, delivering the mail or driving a school bus sets aside his military role while delivering or driving: that he would ignore what he sees through the day, that he ceases to observe, that he ceases to record. Now, by anybody's standards, an intelligence officer for a regular army is carrying out a very necessary function without which the regular forces in uniform cannot and do not operate. It is a key pivotal point.[1008]

Henry Patterson also quotes McKearney as follows, 'Both the UDR and RUCR were recruited locally [...] on or off-duty these men acted as the eyes and ears of the regular army [...] employed as school bus drivers, postmen, refuse collectors, they had a perfect cover for travelling through Republican districts.'[1009]

The idea of UDR members being always on-duty is partly borne out by the fact that sometimes off-duty officers found weapons and explosives.[1010] David Barzilay provides information relating to this fact:

> Not all finds have been accomplished during operational sorties. Two off-duty UDR soldiers, who were out rabbit shooting, surprised some terrorists laying a culvert mine [...] other off-duty soldiers, while picnicking or on country walks, have kept their eyes open and spotted weapons hidden in trees, culverts or on river banks on several occasions.[1011]

But the IRA's decision to target off-duty local forces engendered an increased sense of insecurity among the Protestant and unionist population of Fermanagh, especially those living near the border. It led to distrust and suspicion of their Catholic neighbours and a perception that the IRA had a policy of ethnic cleansing. Thomas Leahy, an academic and author, quotes from an area security review of Fermanagh and west Tyrone carried out in January 1981, '"If a policeman is killed in Belfast he is seen as a policeman, while if a policeman is killed in Fermanagh he is seen as a Protestant."'[1012]

In a county where RUC and UDR recruitment rates have traditionally been very high, the majority of Protestant males were either members or related to members of the local security forces.

Less than a month after internment was introduced, the IRA carried out their first killing in Fermanagh.

SECURITY CONCERNS

As the conflict unfolded, complaints about inadequate security were made to the British authorities by unionist politicians from time to time. As has been noted previously, in November 1972, after the murder of six UDR members that year, John Brooke, MP, the Chairman of Fermanagh County Council and a son of Sir Basil Brooke, led a delegation of UDR family members from Fermanagh to the House of Commons. They met with the Shadow Northern

Ireland Secretary Merlyn Rees, Stanley Orme and Kevin McNamara before meeting with Douglas Hurd, the political secretary to the Prime Minister, Edward Heath. They presented Hurd with a letter that stated:

> Our sons and husbands are members of the UDR [...] that has taken the brunt of IRA attacks across the Frontier. As a consequence, many of us have been forced to leave our homes while some of us have relatives in the struggle to protect lives and property in Fermanagh. Those of us who live near the border have been physically attacked, our homes burnt and our farms destroyed. Many families are evacuating from farmsteads on the border, often with little compensation [...] yet Fermanagh still has the highest membership of the UDR regiment in NI.[1013]

After the meeting, Brooke told reporters that one member of the delegation had been held at gunpoint by men who were seeking to murder her brother; one was the wife of a farmer who had been forced to sell all his dairy stock; and a third was a man who, because of intimidation, had been forced to leave his farm but remained a member of the UDR.[1014]

Seven years later, on 3 August 1979, Michael Alison, the recently appointed Minister of State for Northern Ireland, visited Fermanagh at the invitation of Lord Brookeborough to talk to local Protestant people and reassure them about the security situation. Alison received separate security briefings from the RUC in Enniskillen and the army at St Angelo.

Brookeborough complained about 'propaganda in America' and said it had 'all been started' by John Hume. He expressed the view that a unionist voice was needed there and suggested that Rev. Ian Paisley might be tempted to go. He had arranged for a dozen or so local farmers, tradespeople and professional men to meet Alison at his home. He told the Minister of State that local Protestants believed that 'a serious terrorist cross-border campaign' would take place in the coming winter.[1015]

When Alison expressed surprise that 'the terrorists did not get away with more in Fermanagh', he was told that good community relations and cross-border co-operation between the RUC and Gardaí helped. Brookeborough, however, asserted that it was intolerable that the Garda 'should know all the terrorists but do nothing to capture them'. He remarked, rather chillingly, that 'because Loyalist retaliation had worked so effectively in 1972', the possibility that it would happen again could not be ruled out in the future. He appears to be referring to the cross-border bombings of December 1972 and January 1973 in Dublin and Belturbet.[1016]

The following year, with four security force members dead by mid-February 1980, alarm bells were ringing in the NIO and security circles. It was decided that the Secretary of State, Humphrey Atkins, would visit Fermanagh on 16 February.[1017] In advance of his visit, an internal briefing was prepared which observed that the IRA had the advantage of a long border, 'wild country' and towns close to the border. Nonetheless, it was noted that, unlike south Armagh, the gunmen could not necessarily rely on the support or sympathy of the local population. An exception, it was claimed, was the Donagh area, which had 'a pocket of PIRA supporters' – but there had never been a tradition of inter-sectarian problems in the area. In Fermanagh generally, IRA activity had centred on targeting the security forces, landmine attacks and, occasionally, commercial targets. The assumption made, in a letter to Humphrey Atkins from an army officer following Atkins's visit (the signature is indecipherable), was that a team of IRA activists based in Monaghan had switched its attention from south Armagh to Fermanagh.[1018]

After the visit by the Secretary of State, a report on security in Fermanagh was prepared by a Captain Armstrong. He wrote that the Ulster Unionist members of Fermanagh District Council were 'greatly perturbed' by the deteriorating security situation. He blamed the 'recent outrages' on 'four distinct IRA groups'; two of them were based in west Monaghan, and the two others were in Leitrim and south Donegal – and all four were supported by 'local guides, observers and carriers' in the adjoining parts of Fermanagh.[1019] Most of these men, it was claimed, were known to both the RUC and the Gardaí, and many of them had been taken in for questioning. Nevertheless, these men were 'well-schooled in anti-interrogation techniques' and were soon released for lack of evidence. Amazingly, he stated that security along the border was 'almost non-existent'. [1020]

In the Monaghan sector alone, there were more than fifty road crossings; nearly all of them were open and none of them were manned. Armstrong suggested that the best option would be for the SAS to control them. He recommended two road closures – at Curragunt 'leading to the well-known IRA training and assembly area' of Knockatallon and Lackey Bridge, outside

Clones. He praised the Gardaí, especially in Monaghan, for their readiness to co-operate and to exchange information. The problem was, however, that since they were an unarmed force, they were not really in a position to intercept 'well-armed terrorist groups'.[1021]

Armstrong recommended that, having regard to the size of Fermanagh and the nature of its terrain, the regular army contingent should be increased to full battalion strength and there should be frequent use of SAS detachments, particularly along the frontier. He noted that the part-time strength of 4 UDR was about 400 men at the beginning of 1979 but this had since decreased.[1022] He also indicated that there had been more than 900 UDR members in the county at the time of the IRA truce in June 1972. According to Armstrong, there was a scarcity of part-time soldiers all along the frontier, from Belleek to Roslea. The decline in numbers, he noted, was due to 'assassination, intimidation and lack of confidence in the overall direction of the security battle'.[1023]

With regard to the policing situation, Fermanagh, oddly, did not appear to have substantially more than the 1969 figure – 110 officers – even though the overall strength of the force throughout Northern Ireland had more than doubled during that time. Armstrong believed this to be clearly inadequate for an area of 720 square miles and more than a hundred miles of frontier. Most police stations were undermanned, and some wouldn't have been able to operate at all but for the assistance of the full- and part-time reserve. He remarked that over half of part-timers were 'ex-USC men' of which many current members of the RUC were suspicious. The Special Patrol Group (SPG), now to become the Divisional Mobile Support Unit (DMSU),[1024] had not been properly integrated.[1025]

In the wake of the Secretary of State's visit and the security report, two senior NIO officials, Colin Davenport and Alec Ireland, paid a visit to Fermanagh on 12 March 1980, where they met with senior RUC officers. They reported back that Tom McGowan, the divisional commander, seemed content with the security force efforts despite the recent spate of attacks. RUC morale was good, he said, as were relations with the army. He was pleased, too, with relations between his force and the local population on both sides of the community. He expressed the view that 'the two sides' got on better with each other in Fermanagh than they did in most places.[1026] McGowan was also satisfied with relations with the Gardaí; he thought the border was still the main problem. The commander was looking forward to the arrival of his DMSU, which would augment his capability.[1027]

A Special Branch inspector who was part of the police delegation that met with Davenport and Ireland estimated that the division had to contend with 170 'active terrorists', which struck Davenport as being unexpectedly high. The inspector was, however, confident that there was little support for the IRA within the division. He said that all the activists were well known to both Gardaí and RUC Special Branch but that the usual problem was lack of evidence. He had no fears of a Protestant backlash. In the meeting, it was also mentioned that Kinawley RUC station had been demolished by an IRA bomb and that there were serious difficulties in having it rebuilt. The inability to find a contractor due to intimidation was the main problem.[1028]

On 1 May 1980, a meeting was held at Stormont Castle to discuss security in Fermanagh. Colin Davenport told the meeting that some Protestant families had moved away from the border area but the RUC had confirmed that there was no evidence of an IRA master plan to drive them out.[1029] Nonetheless, the police had pointed out that the IRA would, of course, welcome any evacuation of the area by Protestants, and although there were not, as yet, many instances of families moving, that situation might change in the future.[1030]

Following Richard Latimer's death in June, Rev. Ian Paisley sought a meeting for four widows of the recently deceased security force members with Prime Minister Margaret Thatcher.[1031] At an initial meeting with the Secretary of State, Humphrey Atkins, on 13 June, the widows – Sylvia Kernaghan, Harriet Howe, Martha Morrow and Bonnie Latimer – made several suggestions as to what should be done about the security situation in south Fermanagh. They advocated for road closures with landmines, extradition from the Republic, extra protection in the Newtownbutler area for specific UDR and RUC personnel, and capital punishment or, at least, much stiffer prison sentences.[1032]

Thatcher agreed to meet with them in Downing Street on 7 July 1980 with the caveat that they would not be accompanied by Dr Paisley. Roy Kells, a senior Orangeman and part-time UDR member, travelled with them to London but did not attend the meeting.[1033] On 18 June, prior to the meeting, an internal memo from Mike Hopkins in the NIO to 10 Downing Street noted that 'Unionists of various shades were engaged in a political battle for the favours of isolated Protestant families in south Fermanagh'. Hopkins remarked that the DUP was behaving particularly cynically over these widows and that Paisley's only link with south Fermanagh was as a Member of the European Parliament.[1034]

When the widows met with Thatcher, they informed her that they were representing fifty women whose husbands had been murdered by the IRA, and they presented the Prime Minister with several letters. The widows complained that gunmen were escaping to the Republic; that attacks were planned by locals; that they were disappointed with Thatcher; that there had been no improvement in cross-border co-operation since Haughey had come to power in the Republic; and that members of the Gardaí had been seen drinking in pubs with IRA men. They were assured of the Prime Minister's sympathy and informed that everything possible was being done to ensure maximum security. The widows were subsequently invited to a Trooping the Colour event in June 1981.[1035] It seemed to be a case of 'tea and sympathy' and nothing concrete resulted.

Patterson notes that Fermanagh and South Tyrone had traditionally been 'a bastion' of the Ulster Unionist Party, but he claims that the 'fears and resentments' caused by the IRA campaign encouraged Paisley 'to try and establish a presence for his DUP.'[1036] He observes that Paisley was loud in his protests about 'IRA genocide'.[1037]

Lady Rosamund Langham of Tempo Manor had written to the Prime Minister on 18 June 1980 expressing concern about the security situation in Fermanagh. Alec Ireland, the NIO official who paid a visit to Fermanagh with Colin Davenport, responded that the county posed particular problems for the security forces – more so than in other border areas. He repeated earlier concerns that many of the difficulties stemmed from geographical factors. Most notable was the nature of the county's terrain and the length of the border.[1038]

An organisation called Fermanagh United Protestant Action for the Defence of Family and Home held a 'Protestant Rally' in the overwhelmingly nationalist village of Newtownbutler on 23 June 1980. It was attended by at least 7,000 people with about half of them bussed in from other areas such as Belfast and Kilkeel. Alec Ireland attended as an observer and reported that the contingent from outside Fermanagh were followers of Paisley rather than a party interested in security. The rally began with a lengthy religious service, including hymn singing, bible reading and a sermon. This was followed by the rally proper, which was chaired by a local teacher. On the platform were Rev. Ian Paisley, James Molyneaux MP, Henry Crichton (the Earl of Erne) and Rev. Edwy Kille – the last of these was said to be the chairman of the organisation. Paisley gave a rabble-rousing speech while Molyneaux's was more restrained.[1039] They both condemned the Irish government and spoke of 'genocide' against the Protestant population of the area. A resolution was passed calling for the sealing of border roads.[1040]

In a memo dated 28 July 1980, NIO official, Mike Hopkins, informed 10 Downing Street that an area review of County Fermanagh was to be carried out.[1041] He wrote that cross-border security was good 'at all levels' and had improved since Haughey became Taoiseach. The Garda and RUC continued to consult closely and frequently, exchanging intelligence and CID investigation papers, and they had both increased their capabilities on the border. He explained that the Garda were also operating more effectively in the Republic and had considerably increased their finds of weapons and explosives. They had, since the beginning of the year, recovered 63 weapons, 6,000 lb of explosives, 123 explosive devices and 10,000 rounds of ammunition. He noted that they had just made significant use of the extraterritorial offences legislation.[1042]

The RUC, Hopkins continued, had recently introduced DMSUs, and one of these had been set up in Fermanagh. He noted that the RUC agreed that, in some cases, 'terrorists operating from across the border' received help from local inhabitants – a problem not confined to Fermanagh or even the border areas. On the other hand, he also explained that the security forces received 'some useful anti-terrorist information' from the Catholic population of the county. He noted the Secretary of State's concern that inter-sectarian tension was being inflamed by some unionist politicians.[1043]

Hopkins referred specifically to the arrests in Monaghan of 'three of the most important terrorists operating on the border'. He observed that 'these men are known to have been directly involved in the past in operations into County Fermanagh' and that their arrests 'would be likely to disrupt the activities of the IRA Active Service Unit in question'.[1044] They were Aidan McGurk, Laurence McNally and James Lynagh – they were charged with the murder of Henry Livingstone, a UDR member, at Tynan, County Armagh, on 6 March 1980.[1045]

He also noted that the two police forces – the Gardaí and the RUC – had established arrangements for co-ordination. The Chief Constable and the Garda Commissioner met regularly at 2–3 monthly intervals; the Joint Co-ordinating Committee met monthly, and the Border Superintendents met every six weeks. During operations, full use was made of a direct inter-force radio network.[1046] These arrangements between the Gardaí and the RUC had been in place since late 1974 and had been improved and refined in the intervening years.

Six years later, in February 1986, at the funeral of Constable Derek Breen in Lisbellaw Methodist Church, Rev. Skillen, the President of the Methodist Church, said that sometimes people in Northern Ireland blamed the southern authorities for not appearing to do enough. However, he remarked, the people should not have to depend on them to guard the border. He was firmly of the belief that it was up to the British government 'to secure our borders to keep the violence out of our houses'. 'The Government', he continued, 'has the strength but has it got the will?'[1047]

At the end of 1985, the RUC announced that it was considering withdrawing its training centre from Enniskillen. This caused great unease among unionists, who saw this development as a withdrawal of security from the border and from west of the Bann to safer areas in the east. The IRA had attacked the training centre the previous September; although no lives were lost, considerable damage was done to the main building, which contributed to the decision to close the centre. Ken Maginnis claimed that the closure was part of an 'under the table' agreement between the British and Irish governments.[1048]

It is clear that security on the border was a bone of contention for local Protestants throughout the Troubles, and they were often deeply dissatisfied with the efforts of the British government while always expressing suspicions of the Irish government's intentions.

THE ELECTION OF BOBBY SANDS AS MP FOR FERMANAGH AND SOUTH TYRONE

Ten republican hunger strikers died in 1981. The election of Bobby Sands as MP for Fermanagh and South Tyrone by nationalists during his hunger strike was, according to Henry Patterson, viewed as 'an act of treachery' by their Protestant neighbours.[1049] During the election campaign, the British government expressed concern that Sands might win or even get a 'respectable' vote. David Blatherwick of the Political Affairs Division of the NIO believed it would be 'highly embarrassing for HMG not only in terms of the hunger strike, but in its implication that the Provos were a democratic alternative to the SDLP.'[1050] He hoped there would be sufficient nationalist abstentions to prevent Sands being elected.

NIO officials agonised over what could be done if the unthinkable happened and Sands were to win. They discussed whether he should be disqualified or expelled. They searched their archives for precedents. They found that Cahir Healy was elected for Fermanagh in 1922 while interned but no attempt had been made to expel him; he remained interned for the duration of the parliament and was re-elected in 1924.[1051] Two Dublin republicans, Phil Clarke and Tom Mitchell, had won seats in Fermanagh and mid-Ulster, respectively, in 1955. They were convicted prisoners and were disqualified by the House of Commons. The officials discovered, however, that they could not prevent Bobby Sands from standing because the law had been changed in 1967.[1052]

The only candidate who stood against Bobby Sands was Harry West, Fermanagh native and former leader of the Ulster Unionist Party. Other potential nationalist candidates either withdrew or didn't put their names forward. Nearly all British government contacts predicted that West would win on the basis that not more than fifteen to twenty thousand nationalists would vote for an IRA candidate.[1053] In the event, they were proved wrong and Sands emerged victorious with 30,492 votes against Harry West's 29,046. The turnout was more than 86 per cent. In the post-mortem that followed, various reasons were suggested for the outcome: the sharp divisions in this border constituency around elections (Sands automatically assumed 'the anti-Partition mantle in a straight Orange–Green battle'); West was particularly disliked in local nationalist circles as the 'authentic hard-line Stormont unionist' with links to the UDA and a reputation for 'fiddles over land deals';[1054] West also had the audacity to advertise in local Catholic newspapers, quoting the Pope's sermon about peace in Ireland; Sands's sponsors cleverly put out the idea that the seat was being 'borrowed' – better Sands for two weeks than West for two years.[1055]

All sides were in agreement that the election had polarised the population to a greater degree than at any time over the previous years. Blatherwick noted that moderate unionists felt that 'all their atavistic suspicions' about their Catholic neighbours had been confirmed.[1056] Sands died twenty-six days later, and his election agent, Owen Carron from Enniskillen, won the subsequent by-election.

NIO officials comforted themselves with the view that the result of the election was an anti-unionist rather than a pro-IRA vote. They were also reassured by the fact that Sands had not stood explicitly on behalf of the IRA.[1057]

Chapter 15

INTIMIDATION AND ALLEGATIONS OF ETHNIC CLEANSING

INTIMIDATION

Intimidation was a weapon used by both sides from the earliest days of the conflict. This was a case of history repeating itself and old historical antagonisms recurring. The word conjures up images of the notorious expulsion of Catholics from their homes in Bombay Street, Belfast in August 1969. In 1974, the Northern Ireland Community Relations Commission published a report on intimidation in Belfast between August 1969 and February 1973. It concluded that, although there were about 25 per cent fewer Catholic than Protestant families in Belfast, over 80 per cent of housing movements resulting from intimidation were Catholics. It also stated that the loyalist sympathies of certain members of the RUC coloured their perception, judgment and response in dealing with intimidation and its associated problems.[1058]

There are reports of intimidation of Protestant businesses in Newry – threatening phone calls and the burning of premises.[1059] There was intimidation of Catholic families in Portadown by Tartan gangs. Catholic youths were afraid to leave the Tunnel area there for fear of being beaten up.[1060] Commander Albert Anderson, MP for Derry City, claimed that Protestants in the city were intimidated, especially on the western side of the Foyle, which resulted in people having to leave their homes or wishing to leave their homes.[1061] There are claims of Protestants being intimidated in Craigavon.[1062] The same is the case for Catholics from the Willowfield area of East Belfast,[1063] and along the Shore Road and in the areas of Rathcoole, Whiteabbey,

Mountdown and Carrickfergus.[1064] Thirty Catholic homes were burned by the UDA in Lenadoon, where the Alliance Party and NICRA claimed that the British Army stood by and allowed them to proceed.[1065]

Frank McManus MP claimed that loyalists were making a 'co-ordinated attempt to kill them [Catholics] off or to intimidate them out of this strongly Protestant area'. He was referring to Carnteel, near Aughnacloy, County Tyrone.[1066] As noted previously, Michael McCourt, a Catholic, sold his pub in Trillick, County Tyrone (on the Fermanagh border) and moved from the area with his wife and two small children. He had suffered appalling intimidation, and the last straw came for him on 18 January 1974, when shots were fired into his premises following the murder of Robert Jameson, a local UDR man.[1067] A hail of bullets, twenty-two in all, ripped through the front door and window. Three customers drinking at the bar sustained thigh and back injuries. Mrs Mary McCourt said it was a miracle nobody was killed.[1068] Pistols were used in the attack and police questioned a number of men, but no arrests were made.[1069] As has been noted, when the McCourts moved, the management of the pub was taken over by Cllr Patsy Kelly, who was abducted and killed on his way home from work the following July.

In 1992 it was reported that 60,000 people (11 per cent) of the population of Belfast had been forced to evacuate their homes in the early 1970s. The worst single year for such mass intimidation was 1974.[1070]

It is clear from this sample of reports that intimidation was rife throughout the conflict and throughout many areas of Northern Ireland, both urban and rural. It is also clear that both communities were guilty of these acts.

How did Fermanagh fare? As early as March 1972, it was reported:

> As a fifth member of the UDR moved on Friday from his home in the border area of Co. Fermanagh with his family and belongings, the UDR HQ, Lisburn said that a welfare action group was being set up in the county to help families who had to move because of intimidation.[1071]

Chris Ryder writes that these families decided to leave after the murder of Johnny Fletcher, a UDR soldier, on 1 March. Troops and police stood by as their furniture and other possessions were loaded onto farm trailers and taken to new homes. Their livestock was taken to the market in Enniskillen and auctioned. All said they had left after threats to their lives and families.[1072]

Later that month, two brothers in 4 UDR, George and Richard Latimer, were intimidated from their home but held on to their farm. In July, it was reported that two Protestant farmers in the Roslea area had their houses burned, and one of the two also had his car, tractor and hayshed burned.[1073]

At 10.30 p.m. on 29 November 1972, the home of Private Wigan (of the UDR) was set on fire. He was on patrol at the time, while his family were with neighbours. The fire was quenched by the fire brigade, but at 6 a.m. the following morning, the house was again set alight and this time was completely destroyed. There were no casualties, as Wigan was still on patrol and his family had remained with neighbours.[1074]

Brian Irvine of Kilmacormack, Enniskillen – a Catholic and a full-time sergeant major in the UDR – endured a frightening ordeal in December 1974 when he was stopped on his way home from work and bundled into a car.[1075] He was taken to an isolated house, where he was slashed on the face and body with a sharp instrument and dumped on a grass verge by the roadside in the Ely Lodge area of Enniskillen. He was able to make his way to a nearby house, where he was initially taken care of; he was then moved to the Erne Hospital. Irvine had spent nine years in the British Army – one of the few jobs available to Catholics in his younger days. When the UDR was formed in 1970, he joined up. Before this incident there had been two attempts to set his house on fire.[1076] Some businesses had to endure multiple attacks – Patterson notes that when Johnston's drapery and footwear shop was destroyed by blast incendiaries in April 1979, it was the tenth time it had been attacked.[1077]

Arlene Foster, the DUP leader, witnessed the aftermath of the attempted murder of her father, John Kelly, on their farm at Roslea in 1979, when she was 9 years old. He was a former B-Special and a member of the RUCR. She described the attack to a journalist in 1985, 'They shot him in the head as he was closing in the cattle. He came crawling into the house, blood streaming down his face. We couldn't stay in Roslea. I'd to move house and school – it was traumatic.'[1078] As a teenager, in 1988, she survived a bomb that exploded under her school bus, which was being driven by a UDR man. Nobody was killed in the attack, but the girl sitting next to Arlene was badly injured.[1079]

Intimidation, harassment and violence, however, were experienced by both communities. As early as April 1971 – before any conflict deaths occurred in Fermanagh – St Molaise's GAA Club in Irvinestown had half its pavilion demolished by a bomb that contained 10–15 lb gelignite. Several people had lucky escapes.[1080] This was, most likely, the work of loyalist paramilitaries.

A shop in Kinawley owned by the Catholic Curry family was wrecked in a bomb explosion in October 1972.[1081] A year later, men with revolvers, an SLR and a Thompson planted three large bombs in Derrylin. The UFF (the flag of convenience used by the UDA)[1082] claimed responsibility.[1083]

William Clarke and Mrs Drumm, both residents of Aghalane, were threatened by two men claiming to be from the UVF in January 1974. They told Mrs Drumm that her husband would be shot if further explosions occurred at Protestant-owned properties in the locality.[1084]

On 11 July 1974, Cormac Smyth of Doon Forest was hijacked by the IRA and forced to drive a bomb into Lisnaskea – to a pub that police and soldiers were alleged to frequent. His mother was held hostage during the incident. Cormac gave a warning when he parked at the pub. He was arrested and taken to Lisnaskea barracks, where he was handed over to the army. He was released the following day, but a loyalist terror campaign against the family began immediately afterwards. Four men called at Cormac's home, where he lived with his mother, and warned him to clear out or else.[1085]

Towards the end of July, a police officer called to the home of Cormac's brother Francis and threatened him, telling him he would never 'walk up the lane again'. At the end of his first day back to work after the holidays, Francis found his car had two flat tyres. On his return home, the police officer who had threatened him drove into his private lane in a black saloon car full of men and passed his house. The police officer got out of the car, opening and closing the gate to allow the car access.[1086]

The following morning, while driving to work in Lisnaskea shortly before 6 a.m., Francis was subjected to a dreadful ordeal. He had travelled only a short distance when he found the road blocked outside Ballindarragh Orange Hall by a Fiat 124 car with Derry registration plates. Three masked men grabbed him, overcame him in a struggle. One produced a pistol, but the weapon misfired. The driver of the Fiat inflicted a severe gash to Francis's head with a dagger that was about 6–9 inches long. After giving him a terrible beating and tramping on him in the back of his van, they tied his ankles and his hands behind his back. They then placed a diesel-soaked sack over his head and tied it tightly around his neck. They drove his van to a spot off the road at Tamlaght, near Lisbellaw. There they left him, presumably for dead. Eventually, he located a knife in the van and managed to free himself. He staggered to a nearby house several hours after he was abandoned and the police were informed. He was taken to the Erne Hospital, where he was treated and detained for two days.[1087]

During his hospital stay, Francis was placed in the maternity ward for his own safety. While his wife was travelling to visit him, she was stopped by the RUC and turned back. The RUC advised her that it was unsafe for her and the children to remain in their home, as the keys had been taken from the van by Francis's attackers. The next day, she and her two daughters, aged twenty-eight months and ten months, moved to Monaghan. On his second night in hospital, a British soldier, armed and in uniform, came to Francis's bedside and read his name and medical notes. The nurse on duty told Francis that, in her opinion, it was too dangerous for him to remain in hospital. She contacted the RUC to inform them that there had been a security breach within the hospital. It was arranged for Francis to leave with a police escort and a family member. He was taken by the police to Lisnaskea RUC station, while the family member was sent home. He was interviewed and his fingerprints were taken. Francis was then escorted in a police car to the border near Roslea. He had to hitch a lift to Monaghan to join his family.[1088]

There was unrelenting intimidation of the extended family in the weeks that followed. Their sister Teresa unwittingly allowed two young men with English accents into her home in Lisburn. One of them produced a revolver and searched the house, looking for Cormac and Francis, who had been there a short time previously. Soldiers pointed guns at Cormac through windows of his house. Several other incidents occurred.[1089] All four homes of the Smyth family were vacated due to this intimidation: Francis and his wife, children and mother, Sarah, moved out; Teresa and her husband and children all moved to Monaghan;[1090] and Cormac emigrated to Scotland, where another brother, Joe, had already moved.[1091]

Two young Catholic men, Kevin Clancy and Luke McKiernan, both from Newtownbutler, endured dreadful harassment from the British Army; it began in 1973 and got so bad over the following year that they were forced to move to Clones, County Monaghan.[1092] Luke McKiernan and Brendan Clancy (possibly a brother of Kevin's) were injured in the Clones bomb on 28 December 1972, the same night that the two teenagers were killed in Belturbet, County Cavan. Frank McManus MP held a press conference with Kevin and Luke, during which he accused British troops of beating them and threatening to shoot them if they did not leave Northern Ireland.[1093] They both described the most recent incidents of intimidation. Kevin Clancy said the soldiers had forced their way into his home, pulled him out of bed and dragged him outside. He was beaten and had a hood placed over his head. One of the soldiers clicked his gun and threatened to shoot him. Another produced a knife and threatened to cut his throat. Finally, they lifted him and threw him over a hedge. McKiernan described a similar experience.[1094] Luke's brother Oliver and a County Armagh man had been arrested by Gardaí at the Castle Saunderson demesne, County Cavan on 11 March 1973. They were charged with possession of batteries and 107 ft of wires[1095] and were convicted in Dublin's Special Criminal Court in April 1973.[1096] This may have been the cause of Luke's harassment.

Stories abound of Catholics being intimidated out of their homes, and there are reports of empty so-called 'Protestant houses' being burned when it became known that they had been allocated to Catholic families – the houses were set alight before the allotted family had a chance to move in. Michael and Maureen Swift, who were allocated a house near Irvinestown in early 1975, were the victims of such an act.[1097]

Some two months after the Smyths' ordeal, a young Catholic family suffered intimidation near Lisnaskea.[1098] In October 1974, Gerry Rice and his wife, Marie, and two young children took up residence in an old labourer's cottage at Drumcrin, Ballindarragh. The couple had been living in condemned houses for more than a year. At last, the Housing Executive offered them the old labourer's cottage, which had no electricity, no sanitation and just a single water tap outside the dwelling. They were advised to take up immediate occupancy for fear that the house might be burned down. This they did, and the following morning they found the kitchen window broken and an object on the floor. The object was a stone with a piece of paper and a live bullet attached to it by sellotape. On the paper were written the words, 'GET OUT'.[1099]

Charles and Margaret McElholm suffered severe harassment at a UDR checkpoint – again in the Irvinestown area – in late 1975. Those manning the checkpoint were local UDR men, one of whom was known to the couple. The incident culminated in the letters 'UFF' being scraped onto the rear of their car.[1100]

During the hunger strike, there were many claims of intimidation of Catholics by the UDR and the RUC. Members of the RUC were accused of blowing up the partially built house of a brother of Owen Carron,[1101] the new MP for Fermanagh and South Tyrone. An RUC patrol had been seen in the grounds some hours before the explosion.[1102]

The journalist, Andy Pollak,[1103] wrote in April 1983:

> The majority of Catholics still put the UDR in virtually the same category as the old B Specials it replaced, fearing and distrusting it far more than the RUC or the British Army. Along the Fermanagh border there are Catholic-owned shops, which will take an RUC man's money but will refuse even to acknowledge that a UDR man has entered the premises. The RUC tell tales of UDR men turning out the contents of cars belonging to members of Owen Carron's entourage and then disappearing to the other end of the county and of known Republicans who find they can't restart their cars after a UDR search on an isolated country road because the rotor arm has been removed. A UDR unit on the Fermanagh border is a different animal altogether from one in Antrim or Down officered by schoolteachers and civil servants.[1104]

An arson attack was carried out on the Church of the Immaculate Conception at Monea, Derrygonnelly in February 1986. The parish priest, Fr Patrick Gallagher, said it had 'shocked and horrified people of all creeds' in the area. Intruders forced open a locked door and hurled a petrol bomb at the tabernacle. A number of similar incidents had taken place throughout Northern Ireland; they were believed to be connected with the campaign against the Anglo-Irish Agreement.[1105]

ALLEGATIONS OF 'ETHNIC CLEANSING' AND 'GENOCIDE' ALONG THE BORDER

Ethnic cleansing is generally understood to be the elimination or attempted elimination of a population from the 'homeland' in order to create a more secure, ethnically homogeneous state.[1106] Lewis and McDaid quote the definition given by UN Special Rapporteur on the Situation of Human Rights in the Territory of the Former Yugoslavia as being 'the systematic purge of the civilian population based on ethnic criteria, with the view to forcing it to abandon the territories where it lives.'[1107] They also quote author Andrew Bell-Fialkoff's definition, 'the expulsion of an "undesirable" population from a given territory due to religious or ethnic discrimination, political, strategic or ideological considerations, or a combination of these.'[1108]

With regard to genocide, they turn to the definition of historian and genocide expert Donald Bloxham, 'the physical destruction of a large proportion of a group in a limited or unlimited territory with the intention of destroying that group's collective existence.'[1109] They explain that the purpose of ethnic cleansing is to 'cleanse' a particular group from a specific area while the purpose of genocide is to eliminate a group entirely.[1110]

'Ethnic cleansing' and 'genocide' are emotive, headline-grabbing words and we associate both these terms with what happened in the Balkans in the 1990s. According to Toal and Dahlman, the first recorded mention of the term 'ethnic cleansing' in the western media can be traced back to an article in the *New York Times* dated 15 April 1992 'in a quote by an anonymous western diplomat'.[1111] That same year, James Molyneaux MP claimed that Protestants in border areas 'had been the victims of ethnic cleansing' for over twenty years.[1112] Ken Maginnis, who served as Ulster Unionist MP for Fermanagh and South Tyrone from 1983 to 2001, and who was also a former B-Special and part-time officer in 4 UDR, referred to IRA killings of part-time UDR men along the border as 'ethnic cleansing' in August 1995.[1113] Roy Bradford also used the term,[1114] and in 1996, the Orange Order was asked to assist in compiling a dossier on 'ethnic cleansing' in certain areas.[1115] On the other hand, the UDA threatened the 'ethnic cleansing' of Catholics in a document entitled 'Doomsday' in February 1994.

Patterson also notes that the term 'ethnic cleansing' was imported from the Balkan wars. He claims that 'however sensationalist the term, it had an emotional truth for border Protestants as the continuing attacks and killings struck at their community's morale and sense of security.'[1116]

The term 'genocide' was used in the past to describe the mass murder of Armenians and Rwandans, the Holocaust of the Jewish people in the Second World War and, more recently, the massacre of 8,000 Muslim men and boys over the age of 12 in Srebrenica within a 72-hour period in July 1995. This term was used to describe the killings of Protestants by the IRA; among those who used it were Ken Maginnis and Jeffrey Donaldson in May 1993.[1117]

While the term 'genocide' was used more sparingly by some unionist politicians in the 1980s, Ernest Baird, former deputy leader of Vanguard, had expressed himself in this way as far back as 1976. He was quoted in the *Impartial Reporter* as follows:

> There are more important things like holding on to your reformed Protestant heritage because the IRA are now on a process of genocide as far as Protestants are concerned. Their attacks are not against the army but against Protestant policemen, UDR men and businessmen. Their intention is to drive the Protestants out of Ulster.[118]

The Primate and Archbishop of Armagh, Most Rev. John Armstrong, said in 1980 that there was a disturbing pattern in murders of Protestants in south Armagh and Fermanagh. Sometimes a person killed would be the natural successor to a farm, like an eldest son. He admitted it was difficult to find evidence of an actual plan to eliminate Protestants – the only evidence was, he said, that so many people had been killed. He noted that the majority of Protestants killed were Church of Ireland members. Some in the Presbyterian Church feared that there might be a policy of eliminating or intimidating Protestants who resided near the border, though Dr Victor Lynas, the convenor of the governing committee of the Presbyterian Church in Ireland, agreed that it would be difficult to prove there was a plan to exterminate Protestants in south Armagh and Fermanagh.[119]

Unionists constantly maintained that the IRA deliberately targeted Protestant UDR men who were members of the farming community. While in such a rural community, one would expect to find a preponderance of farmers in the UDR, an analysis of the occupations of the twenty serving and five former UDR members killed in Fermanagh shows the actual breakdown in occupations: seven men (28 per cent) were described as farmers only, and of these, Thomas Bullock's farm was let out; two were full-time members of the regiment; two had unknown occupations; and the rest each had completely different professions – forestry worker, librarian, PO engineer, butcher, milk lorry-driver, bread delivery man, delivery driver, shop owner, coalman, factory worker, building contractor, shop manager, headmaster. Nevertheless, it is possible that some of those with other occupations may also have been part-time farmers and owned a few acres of land, like Johnny Fletcher and Jimmy Graham.

In an interview with author Susan McKay, Alan Henry Brooke[1120] – Viscount Brookeborough and a grandson of Sir Basil Brooke – criticised the business classes for their failure to support the security forces actively. He noted that the local UDR was drawn largely from farming and working-class communities, but 'by and large the business classes, while they supported peace, didn't support the fight against terrorism'. He was scornful of their complaints about the disruption checkpoints caused, observing that 'they jumped in their Jags and headed for tennis and tea parties.'[1121] This view is supported by an observation in a report of Brigadier John Oborne, the defence attaché at the British Embassy in Dublin, after a visit to Northern Ireland in September 1984. He noted a view expressed to him – that the unionist middle-class were ducking out of their responsibilities, believing that, whatever happened, their own lifestyle would survive or, alternatively, they would be able to leave Ireland. He was told that 'the backbone of the UDR was the farmers, mechanics and, indeed, the unemployed'.[1122]

It is also believed by many that the only sons and eldest sons of farmers were targeted. If we take account of the twenty serving and five former UDR members killed in Fermanagh, the average age is 45; if the five former UDR members are excluded, the average age is 38. Three young farmers were killed. There was Francis Veitch, the first UDR soldier to be killed in Fermanagh. He died on 3 September 1971 and was 23 years old; he was an only son whose father had died only a short time earlier. Another was Robin Bell, killed on 22 October 1972; he was 21 years old, though he was not an only son. Lastly, there was Ronald Funston, a former UDR member, killed on 13 March 1984; he was 28 years old and was not an only son. The five other farmers killed were aged 53, 51, 44 and 42.

Cabinet Office official Christopher Mallaby amended an essay on the UDR in February 1986, which was intended to be included in a Defence White Paper. In this particular document, 'Amendments to draft essay on UDR', there is reference to the first twenty-one members of the UDR to be killed by the IRA in Northern Ireland. Of these members, eight of them – or 38 per cent – were Catholics.[1123] There is no reason to believe that this trend would not have continued if a higher percentage of Catholics had remained in the regiment.

An examination of the twenty-eight Protestant civilians killed in Fermanagh yields the following information: eleven were killed in the Enniskillen bomb (including a retired RUC officer); nine civilians (including five former UDR members and one former RUC officer) were directly and deliberately targeted; and seven of the deaths were unintentional, or they were cases of mistaken identity, where the attacks were intended for the security forces.

The twenty-eighth civilian, Emily Bullock, was shot dead along with her husband Thomas, a UDR member. It would appear that she was shot because she tried to thwart the killers, which is evidenced by the bullet lodged in her right hand. This dreadful attack was the only one carried out inside the home of a member of the security forces in Fermanagh.

Of the six Catholics killed by the IRA in Fermanagh, one was an alleged informant brought from Belfast and killed in Fermanagh; the other five were killed in attacks intended for the security forces.

While the IRA campaign was vicious, with victims being shot at point-blank range and soft security force targets selected, it is impossible – based on the facts presented above – to support the claim that there was a deliberate IRA policy of either 'genocide' or 'ethnic cleansing' toward the Protestant farming community of Fermanagh. Lewis and McDaid argue that using such terms is arguably insensitive to the victims of these abhorrent practices elsewhere.[1124] It has to be acknowledged, however, that this was, and is, the perception of many border Protestants. A number of the killings were clearly sectarian – as was the intimidation of Protestant farmers and businesses.

An evaluation of UDR deaths and intimidation in Fermanagh must also take into account:

1. The lack of employment choices in the county, and particularly in the south of the county, which led to a higher percentage of Protestants joining the part-time security forces than elsewhere in the north.
2. Given the rural nature of the county, many of those who joined the UDR were farmers or at least held a few acres of land – this was in contrast to the many professionals who joined in more urban centres.
3. People left their farms for reasons other than intimidation – many holdings of 25 to 30 acres were no longer viable. In these cases, the motive for leaving was purely economic.[1125]

4. Farmers' sons were receiving a better education than before, and they were leaving the farms to take up careers in Belfast and further afield.
5. Many of those who moved did not actually sell their farms. Official Unionist Assemblyman Raymond Ferguson said that, in the 1970s, some UDR men then living on the border, on the advice of their officers, moved into Enniskillen but did not sell their land or property.[1126]
6. According to Rowthorn and Wayne, approaching one in ten of all Protestant men in Northern Ireland worked for the security forces in the 1980s.[1127]

The majority, but certainly not all, of available reports of intimidation of Protestants in Fermanagh were against members, or the homes of members, of the local security forces; this was unlike many other areas, where both Catholics and Protestants were intimidated solely on the basis of their religion. Indeed, Catholics in Fermanagh were, for the most part, intimidated solely on the basis of their religion.

If one reflects on the precise meaning of ethnic cleansing – the attempted elimination of a 'politically unreliable' population in order to create a more secure, ethnically homogeneous state – it can be argued convincingly that what was attempted in Fermanagh during the fifty years of unionist rule from 1922 to 1972 was an effort to reduce, if not eliminate, the 'politically unreliable' population. Assuredly, the Plantation of Ulster was a model form of ethnic cleansing – removing the native Irish and replacing them strategically with colonists. Would unionist politicians consider the plantation to be ethnic cleansing or genocide?

During its fifty years in power, the Stormont parliament tried to force Catholics out through discrimination in housing, jobs and the siting of industries; through gerrymandering (to prevent them gaining power); and through the use of draconian laws against them. They also encouraged Protestants to come into the north from the Free State. All of these policies were designed to increase the homogeneity of the northern state – particularly in Fermanagh and Tyrone, where there was a Catholic majority. This resulted in the forced emigration or migration of Catholics from Fermanagh; it was significantly successful in the 1950s, but less so thereafter. This type of manipulation through the selective encouragement of emigration and immigration is described by Paul Morland as 'demographic engineering'.[1128]

Prominent, influential politicians like Lord Brookeborough endorsed this policy, both publicly and in the Stormont House of Commons, on more than one occasion. Such endorsements sanctioned the treatment of Catholics as second-class citizens as the accepted norm – the dominant narrative of the northern state.

Chapter 16

THE BORDER

By the time the recent conflict began, the border had been in place for almost fifty years. Since it was imposed in 1920 – against the wishes of the vast majority of the Irish people – it has been a contentious issue down through the decades. It was not originally intended to be an international border; it was to be an internal division between two devolved United Kingdom administrations under the Government of Ireland Act.[1129] After the Treaty was signed in December 1921, it was still regarded as a temporary measure (or at least that was how it was viewed by Irish eyes) pending the outcome of the Boundary Commission.[1130] As has been noted, when the Boundary Commission was scrapped, an agreement was reached between the three governments on 3 December 1925 that amended the Treaty of 1921, revoking Article 12. The existing boundary was confirmed, and so it has remained ever since. It has seen customs posts, the cratering and spiking of roads, and military and police checkpoints over its lifetime.[1131]

In December 1956, at the start of the IRA's border campaign, the British Ambassador to Ireland at the time, Sir Alex Clutterbuck, observed:

> Any Irish Government might be expected to argue that, since it is Britain which devised and persists in maintaining the injustice of partition, it is Britain which is ultimately to blame for the continuation of border incidents and for the consequences that flow from them.[1132]

When the recent conflict began, the border soon became a focal point for violence – a compelling target for the IRA, which set about blowing up customs posts and attacking permanent vehicle checkpoints. Preventing the IRA from committing offences in one jurisdiction and crossing into the other to evade the security forces became, for the British, a constant struggle. It was their absolute priority to obtain maximum co-operation from the Irish government on border security. On the other hand, British Army incursions into the Republic and the cratering of cross-border roads were a source of controversy – a principal example was the international incident caused by the incursion of two carloads of SAS men on 5 May 1976.

In July 1974, C.E. Goddart, an NIO official, in a speaking note for Merlyn Rees, the Secretary of State for Northern Ireland – who was preparing to deliver a speech in Oxford – provided a very striking description of the border and its impact on the local inhabitants:

> The Border with the Irish Republic is some 300 miles in length running from Lough Foyle in the north to Carlingford Lough in the south. It is very largely undefined and undefinable, bisecting farmlands, parishes and even, in one or two cases, buildings. In many cases, therefore, it cuts rural communities in half, separating doctors and parish priests from their people and farmers from their herds. The border is crossed by some 287 roads and tracks, 41 of which are either approved or concessionary crossings.[1133]

Goddart highlighted some of the difficulties caused by the border, referencing a particular concessionary road (one without customs checks at either end) that divides Fermanagh from Monaghan, 'It is the small enclave just west of the Monaghan salient where the concessionary road is the only means of access without which [...] [one] would be wading up a short stretch of the river Finn.'[1134]

The reference here is to the Drummully Salient in Monaghan, which is almost completely surrounded by Fermanagh. Writing in the *Irish Times,* journalist Frank McNally suggested that Drummully was 'almost certainly a ballybetagh [an ancient unit of territory, usually comprising sixteen townlands]'. He observed that 'it was clearly never designed to withstand the stresses of international border duty.'[1135] Goddart noted that the Monaghan salient 'is the main base from which terrorists act against the south of the Province'. [1136]

Two months earlier, in May 1974, another NIO official, J.F. Halliday, in a paper on border security, noted that the border was not clearly delineated on the ground and that different maps gave varying information on its location. He recorded that 'terrorist activity thrives on the existence of the border.' [1137]

IRISH GOVERNMENT AND SECURITY FORCES CO-OPERATING WITH BRITISH AUTHORITIES ON BORDER SECURITY

Over the period of the conflict, all of the focus has been on IRA attacks into Northern Ireland from the Republic; forays carried out by loyalists crossing in the opposite direction have received far less attention. The well-established unionist claim is that successive Irish governments failed to deal with the IRA during the conflict, particularly with regard to cross-border attacks. This claim will be explored, but it is clear that such commentators have failed to consider that the border was porous in both directions. Some fifty citizens of the Republic were killed in a total of thirteen loyalist cross-border attacks. Eleven of these attacks occurred in the 1970s, killing forty-eight people; two further attacks in the 1990s account for the remaining two deaths. Nobody has ever been convicted for any of the killings. These figures follow the overall pattern of loyalist killings, which fell off in the mid-1970s and increased again in the late 1980s and early 1990s. Numerous non-fatal attacks were carried out in the border counties of the Republic – several of them by loyalists based in Fermanagh.

Two loyalist paramilitaries , one from Down and one from Derry, were also killed in cross-border attacks into County Donegal – a UVF member electrocuted himself in an abortive attempt to blow up the Cathleen's Falls power station in Ballyshannon in October 1969, and a UDA member lost his life in a premature explosion outside a pub in Cloughfinn in March 1973. After the latter's death, Ivan Cooper, a founding member of the SDLP, claimed that he had given information to the RUC in Derry indicating that the dead man had been responsible for at least three previous explosions in the Republic.[1138]

In Operation Motorman, the British Army proceeded into the 'no-go' areas of Derry and Belfast and removed republican barricades. The operation began at 4 a.m. on 31 July 1972. After this, many IRA members fled south and set up bases in border towns. This led to a reduction in IRA activity in Belfast and Derry, and a corresponding increase in attacks across the border. This activity further heightened British demands for Irish security co-operation.[1139]

This was also the year that British spies were found to be operating in the Republic. The Littlejohn brothers had attached themselves to a renegade unit of the Official IRA and were acting as *agents provocateurs*, carrying out robberies and bombing Garda stations, which at the time, as intended, were blamed on the IRA. These activities were designed to create the conditions for a massive legislative crackdown on republicans. Increasing pressure was brought to bear on the Minister for Justice, Des O'Malley, to introduce draconian legislation. In this they were effective, although their career came to an abrupt end when they were identified after carrying out the largest bank robbery in the history of the state in October 1972. They robbed an Allied Irish Bank in Dublin and fled to Britain, where, to their dismay, they were arrested and charged. The hearing into their case was held in London *in camera* (excluding the press and public) and they were later extradited to Ireland on the understanding that the bank robbery would not be treated as a political crime.

John Wyman, a British agent, was operating in the Republic from at least the date of Operation Motorman. His role was clearly to accumulate as much information as possible about the IRA along the border. He succeeded in suborning Sgt Patrick Crinnion, who was a member of the Garda Síochána and a Special Branch detective.[1140] From the sensitive documents copied to him by Crinnion, Wyman was able to compile a dossier (which the British authorities referred to as the 'border dossier') containing incredibly detailed information on all IRA ASUs in the border region. Each unit is discussed – names and the numbers involved, along with former and contemporary addresses and dates of birth.[1141]

The British made a decision to present Taoiseach Jack Lynch with this dossier after his meeting with Prime Minister Ted Heath on 24 November 1972; Lynch received it from the British Ambassador on 6 December.[1142]

Meanwhile, in late November, the Irish government introduced a bill in the Dáil to strengthen the Offences against the State Act. (The Minister for Justice, Des O'Malley, had already reinstated the non-jury Special Criminal Court in May). The bill was proving very controversial, as it was regarded by many citizens – and not just republicans – as an attack on human rights. The most draconian aspect was that a person could be convicted of membership of an illegal organisation on the word of a senior Garda. It was viewed by many as internment under another name. The British were most anxious that this legislation should be passed.

The debate on the bill continued over a number of days in late November, and the legislation looked set for defeat. As well as the entire opposition, several members of the government were expected to vote against it. On 1 December, however, the intervention of two car bombs – the first in the Republic, killing two men and injuring many more – changed the opposition's minds. Fine Gael abstained from the vote, allowing the bill to be passed.[1143]

After Lynch received Wyman's dossier the following week, alarm bells quickly began ringing. Senior Gardaí were said to be dumbfounded by its detail and realised the information could only have come from secret Special Branch files. The arrest of a minor agent, Alexander Forsey, on ammunition charges led Gardaí to his handler, Wyman, and, in turn, to Crinnion.[1144] Their arrests on 19 and 20 December caused a sensation in the media, with the British Ambassador denying all knowledge.[1145]

Wyman's and Crinnion's trial was held *in camera* in February 1973 and, because the Attorney General refused to make the documents at the heart of the case available to the court, it wasn't possible to convict the two men on the more serious charge of passing secret information prejudicial to the safety or preservation of the state. They were convicted on the lesser charge of communicating information about Garda operations and, because they had spent time in custody, were released immediately and departed for Britain. This unprecedented action by the Attorney General raised suspicions that a deal had been done between the two governments. The Littlejohns were extradited to Ireland the following month.

Throughout 1972, the British government's major focus was on the control of explosives. Several meetings about the issue had taken place between the Gardaí and the RUC, resulting in legislation being enacted by the Fianna Fáil government that was in line with similar legislation in Northern Ireland.[1146] The Dangerous Substances Bill 1970, which dealt with the control of explosives, petroleum and other dangerous substances, was passed by the Oireachtas on 4 May 1972.[1147] Legislation was passed on 9 August that reduced the amount of ammonium nitrate in fertilisers and banned the use of sodium chlorate. This was followed by nitro-benzene being made subject to controls of the Explosives Act 1875 on 7 September.[1148]

The British Ambassador, John Peck, had obtained the consent of the Taoiseach to establish direct contact with 'the appropriate authorities' on security matters. He had discussions with Minister for Justice Des O'Malley and General O'Carroll, the Army Chief of Staff. O'Malley was anxious that the Gardaí should be as co-operative as possible. According to Peck, General O'Carroll was anxious to develop closer working contacts with the British Army but needed the 'green light' from his minister. Peck crowed about 'extracting a promise' from the Taoiseach that these closer links would be sanctioned 'on the basis of an ingenious and completely deniable arrangement about communications that has been worked out with Lisburn'.[1149] Peck was clear that all arrangements should be deniable.[1150] These actions give the lie to the charge that there was little co-operation from the Irish government prior to the Cosgrave Coalition taking office.

A general election in February 1973 resulted in a Fine Gael–Labour coalition government being formed. It is true to say that co-operation between the British and Irish governments reached a whole new level under Cosgrave.[1151] The two governments worked together closely throughout the operation involving the capture of the ship *Claudia* off Helvick Head, County Waterford at the beginning of April; the ship contained a large consignment of arms, ammunition and explosives for the IRA from Colonel Gadhafi's regime in Libya. The captured weapons were passed to the British, whose military attaché at the British Embassy, Brigadier McMullan, transported them to British Army Headquarters in Lisburn.[1152] While the IRA members on board were charged and convicted, the crew of the *Claudia*, at the instigation of the British, was let go without charge – probably to protect an informant.[1153]

On 13 April, the Minister for Defence, Paddy Donegan, met the British Ambassador, Arthur Galsworthy, at his residence in Glencairn, County Dublin, where a 'revised' version of Wyman's dossier was handed over for the Taoiseach's attention. Another clandestine meeting followed hard on its heels, held specifically to discuss border security. It was again held at Glencairn, at Donegan's request, away from 'prying eyes' at the Department of Defence.[1154] This meeting, on 25 April, was attended by Donegan and the secretary of his department, along with the British Ambassador and MI6's Allan Rowley, William Whitelaw's Director and Co-ordinator of Intelligence, who was based in Stormont Castle.[1155]

Donegan explained that he had been requested by the Taoiseach to take the lead in discussions with the British. His colleague, Minister for Justice Paddy Cooney, had been instructed to hold fortnightly meetings to achieve co-ordination between the Irish Army and Garda on security matters, including border security. British Ambassador Galsworthy reported that Donegan had asked 'point blank' what the British would like the Irish to do.[1156] Rowley explained that what they required was 'authorised and entirely clandestine contacts' at specified border points between the British Army and police with their local Irish counterparts. He suggested a meeting with himself and the senior army and police intelligence officers on his staff, and that it should take place in Britain for secrecy reasons.[1157]

Donegan said there was apprehension that if it became apparent that there was close co-operation between the two governments in 'clobbering the IRA', it could lead to a resurgence of sympathy for the organisation.[1158] Successive Irish governments were always anxious to keep co-operation with the British concealed from Irish society.

The outcome of the meeting was that the British Army's Chief Ammunition Technical Officer held meetings with his Irish counterpart, Commandant Denis Boyle – and Commandant Gerard Bates, the Irish Inspector of Explosives, and Col Jack MacDonald, the Director of Ordnance. The Minister for Justice instructed Garda superintendents in border areas to co-operate fully with their RUC counterparts, and shortly afterwards meetings were arranged – both at the top level, between Assistant Garda Commissioner Garvey and Chief Superintendent Wren (Head of Special Branch) and RUC Assistant Chief Constable Johnston and Chief Superintendent Hood; and also at local level, between the two police forces.[1159]

In Fermanagh, Chief Superintendent Cordner and Inspector Currie, both of whom belonged to the RUC's 'L' Division, met with senior Gardaí in Sligo, Letterkenny and Monaghan. They also initiated contact with the superintendents in Clones, Ballyshannon, Cavan and Manorhamilton (County Leitrim).[1160]

It was decided that the Army Director of Intelligence, Col Quinlan, should begin to make regular visits to London to exchange intelligence with 'whoever the British designated', and in between these visits, Col Quinlan should meet with the British military attaché, Brigadier McMullan. He would report directly back to the Minister for Defence, Donegan, but also 'keep in close touch' with Chief Superintendent Wren; Donegan would report to the Taoiseach and Minister for Justice.[1161]

By the beginning of 1974, despite the establishment of all these ad hoc contacts, British ministers and officials were determined to have co-operation placed on a formal footing after the Sunningdale Agreement was implemented, putting structures in place whereby panels were formed and regular meetings would take place. They sought a top-level meeting between the two governments, suggesting a target date of 16 May. The Irish government, however, were unable to comply with that date. The British government was insisting that particular members of the British Army attend meetings on cross-border security and was pressing the Irish government to allow certain members of the Irish Army to attend also. This was being resisted by the Irish government.[1162]

The General Officer Commanding of the British Army in Northern Ireland, General Frank King, told the Prime Minister at a meeting in Army Headquarters, Lisburn on 18 April that there were regular meetings with the Irish Army, but they 'had to accept' that the Irish armed forces were unable to do much, as they had no power to arrest and the Gardaí were unarmed.[1163] At a meeting in the NIO on 3 May, however, it was remarked that the problems needed to be 'forcibly brought home to the Irish to move them from their ivory tower and to bring home to them the importance of proper representation on both sides'.[1164]

On 17 May 1974, Dublin and Monaghan were bombed, ostensibly by the UVF; thirty-four people were killed, the highest death toll in any single day of the conflict. Three days earlier, rather ironically, an NIO official cited the reason for the less-than-desirable co-operation from the Irish government:

> because almost all violence takes places in the North, the demands for assistance are usually one way and it is seldom that the RUC gets an opportunity to reciprocate assistance given by the Gardaí.[1165]

Therefore, the Gardaí should have been pushing an open door in seeking co-operation on identifying and capturing the perpetrators. Nonetheless, there is no indication that any serious demands were made by the Gardaí or co-operation provided by the RUC. Judge Henry Barron stated that the Gardaí had claimed an inability to pursue the bomb suspects because they were based outside the jurisdiction, in Northern Ireland (Armagh and Belfast). He noted that they had contacted the RUC on a number of occasions seeking information on persons of interest but that responses were disappointing.[1166]

In the wake of the bombings, the Minister for Foreign Affairs, Garrett FitzGerald, told the British Ambassador that the government would now find overt co-operation easier, and the ambassador reported back that this reaction was 'healthy and helpful'. Galsworthy also remarked that 'It is only now that the south has experienced violence that they are reacting in the way that has been sought for so long.' He warned against rubbing this point in, saying, 'the Irish have taken the point.'[1167]

The long-sought high-level security meeting took place at Casement Aerodrome, Baldonnel, County Dublin on 18 September. It was attended by Secretary of State for Northern Ireland, Merlyn Rees; the Minister for Justice, Paddy Cooney; the Garda Commissioner; the RUC Chief Constable; and senior officials. The minutes do not provide any reference to the bombings, despite the enormous loss of life, nor is there any allusion to anxiety over possible future forays across the border by loyalists. The discussions had one focus – IRA attacks from the Republic into Northern Ireland.[1168]

At the meeting, a Joint Co-ordinating Committee (JCC) with representatives from both police forces was agreed, and four technical panels (committees which included members of the Gardaí and RUC) were decided upon: communications; exchange of information on ballistics, explosives and methods of control; advance planning; and detection of sources of supplies of arms, ammunition and explosives.[1169] The panels were set up by the Chief Constable and Garda Commissioner in November, and they were co-chaired by RUC Deputy Chief Constable Baillie and Assistant Chief Constable Johnston, along with Garda Assistant Commissioner Garvey and Chief Superintendent Wren. The JCC meetings alternated between Dublin and Enniskillen each month, with Baillie and Garvey communicating by direct telephone link.[1170]

Before the end of 1975, the Irish government was co-operating fully with the British government. They were agreeing, without demur, to the closure of border roads, and they were allowing 'reconnaissance overflights' into the territory of the Republic. Additionally, the two police forces were co-ordinating VCPs and pre-planned incidents, and they had direct telephone and radio links with secure speech up to the highest level.[1171] The radio links had been made available to the Gardaí by the British Army. They were called 'Goliath' and were used for mobile communications, which allowed the Gardaí to respond quickly.[1172]

In the immediate aftermath of the killings of the Reavey and O'Dowd family members and the Kingsmill massacre in County Armagh in early January 1976, the British Prime Minister, Harold Wilson, wrote to Taoiseach Liam Cosgrave. While Wilson stressed the need to step up co-operation on the border, he expressed his gratitude 'for all the help that has been given to us in the past months and for the excellent results that the Gardaí have achieved.'[1173]

When Patrick Cooney, the former Minister for Justice, appeared at the public hearings of the Joint Oireachtas Committee on Justice, Equality, Defence and Women's Rights in 2004,[1174] he confirmed that the panels formed the basis for co-operation between the two police forces from the moment of their foundation; this co-ordination was gradually refined and improved down through the years.[1175] Co-operation became ever closer after the signing of the Anglo-Irish Agreement in 1985.

When Fianna Fáil returned to power in 1977, all existing arrangements for security co-operation continued unchanged. In a telegram to FCO in August, the British Ambassador noted that Seán Donlon (the Secretary General of the Department of Foreign Affairs who later served as Irish Ambassador to the United States of America) had informed him that the new government had made this decision. The most sensitive of these arrangements was the programme of photo reconnaissance overflights, but these, too, had been approved.[1176]

Needless to say, this co-operation did not always run smoothly, and the RUC and British government did not always play a straight hand. The Irish government was often deeply uneasy about actions or inaction by the British at various times. In the mid-1970s, at a time when the IRA was on ceasefire, there was consternation over the lack of action taken by the RUC in the face of the sectarian murder of Catholics by loyalist paramilitaries. Irish government protests regarding the treatment of nationalists in Northern Ireland by some British Army regiments were routinely dismissed out of hand. Tensions also ran high in the wake of the major SAS incursion into County Louth in May 1976.

SDLP members and Catholic clergymen were separately receiving regular reports of collusion between the northern security forces and loyalist paramilitaries. At the end of 1975, the Irish government was clearly concerned about the UDR. At a meeting between Mr Corcoran, the chargé d'affaires at the Irish Embassy in London, and J.D.W. Janes, an NIO official, Corcoran queried the recent decision to temporarily make the UDR active on a full-time basis.

The regular army serving in Northern Ireland had been cut in half – down from 26,000 to 13,000. Janes told Corcoran that the UDR was needed in south Armagh. Corcoran raised concerns about their bias; Janes later reported that he 'bridled at this' and criticised Séamus Mallon for 'spreading malicious and irresponsible stories about the UDR'.[1177] This exchange took place at a time when killings by the infamous Glenanne Gang, comprising members of the UDR, RUC and loyalist paramilitaries, were at their height.[1178]

The 1980s were even more difficult, with the shoot-to kill cases,[1179] the Dowra[1180] and the Stalker affairs,[1181] which all occurred under the stewardship of Chief Constable Sir John Hermon.

Despite these tensions and major concerns, cross-border co-operation continued. In 1983, at the height of the standoff between Chief Constable Hermon and Garda Commissioner Wren over the Dowra affair, the British Prime Minister and Secretary of State for Northern Ireland publicly stated their appreciation of Irish co-operation on security matters.[1182] A memo to a senior NIO official refers to the 'undoubted commitment of the Irish Government to combatting terrorism'.[1183]

In the wake of the Enniskillen bombing in 1987, the Gardaí ordered a huge nationwide search for IRA arms and explosives. Highly sophisticated electronic equipment, capable of detecting explosives and pinpointing underground hideouts, was loaned by the British to help 'step up the war against terrorism'.[1184] One of the discoveries made by Gardaí at that time was an underground bunker on a beach near Arklow, County Wicklow, which although empty, appeared to have been prepared to receive an arms cache. The British regarded this operation as providing 'tangible evidence of the Irish commitment to defeat terrorism'. It was noted that this also illustrated the more effective security co-operation that resulted from the Anglo-Irish Agreement.[1185] Tony Stephens, a senior MoD official, noted that the finding of the bunker 'demonstrated the scale of the challenge presented by terrorism in Ireland'. In a briefing document, there was criticism of some elements of the media – in particular, the *Belfast Newsletter.* It was observed that

> Critics of the Irish security forces cannot have it both ways – they are always ready to accuse them of doing too little. When they mount one of the biggest anti-terrorist operations in the history of their State, they charge them with pulling a stunt and rubbish their achievements.[1186]

During the previous August, there were twenty-two seizures by Gardaí of arms, ammunition and explosives.[1187]

On the other hand, a thorough perusal of contemporary official declassified documents has failed to uncover any evidence of significant co-operation being provided by the British government and security forces in the face of loyalist paramilitary attacks in the Republic. The single exception is the killings of Oliver Boyce and Bríd Porter in Donegal on 1 January 1973, where Detective Inspector John Courtney, the Garda officer leading the investigation, did receive significant co-operation from the RUC. This led to the extradition of one loyalist to the Republic; he was acquitted after a nine-day trial in the Special Criminal Court.[1188]

In early October 1972, the UDA claimed to have carried out a raid on an IRA arms dump in Monaghan.[1189] This incident was reported by FCO official Kelvin White in a memo to Sir Stewart Crawford. White had spoken to a legal adviser about the possibility that the UDA might have committed an offence in Northern Ireland, but he was reassured that this was not the case, as the UDA had 'handed the weapons to the authorities straightaway'. He observed that if the Irish sought to extradite the UDA men, the British would have enough time 'to think how best to cope'. Incredibly, he suggested that they should 'informally warn the UDA not to take such grave risks'.[1190]

On 7 October, Bill Craig of Vanguard and Billy Hull of the Loyalist Association of Workers[1191] publicly congratulated the UDA commando units involved in the Monaghan raid when they addressed a 3,000-strong loyalist rally in Enniskillen.[1192]

In the wake of the Dublin bombings of 1 December 1972, Alec Douglas Home, Home Office, advised the British Embassy in Dublin not to send a congratulatory message to the Taoiseach on the successful passage of the Offences Against the State (Amendment) Act, as had been intended, as it 'wouldn't be appropriate'. Instead he suggested that the ambassador should seek a meeting with Lynch to impress on him that 'continued unpublicised co-operation at all levels offers the best hope of success'; that, so far, they had 'no intelligence that indicates UDA or UVF involvement in the outrages in Dublin', but if they did learn anything, 'it will of course be passed on forthwith.'[1193] It is worth noting that no useful information was ever passed on regarding this bombing or any of the later bombings in the State.

A compelling example of this failure to pass on information occurred in March 1997 when a bomb was placed outside the Sinn Féin office in Monaghan town. The Police Ombudsman for Northern Ireland included this case in her *Statement by the PONI on her investigation into the death of Raymond McCord Junior and related matters*, which was published in January 2007. Her investigation found that several RUC Special Branch officers colluded with North Belfast (Mount Vernon) UVF members, who were involved in more than a dozen murders. A number of Special Branch officers were complicit in protecting agents and informants, even though they were directly involved in murders.[1194] During the course of her work, the Police Ombudsman found a document prepared for the DPP for an informant's arrest. The document noted that the informant had 'thwarted a bombing campaign in the Republic of Ireland in 1996' and that he 'thwarted a bomb attack in Monaghan on 3 March 1997'. The document did not mention that the informant had a role in this attack and that the explosives had been returned to him by the police.[1195]

Dr Nuala O'Loan reported:

> There is no evidence that the [RUC] Special Branch informed the Garda Síochána at any stage of this bombing attempt, or of who was behind it. The Garda Commissioner has confirmed to the Police Ombudsman that Special Branch did not provide them with any intelligence about this incident.[1196]

A major consideration when examining the level of cross-border security is the huge burden that policing the border placed on successive Irish governments in terms of resources and manpower. It was a constant struggle to maintain adequate levels of Garda and army personnel to patrol the border area.

While the British government was sometimes quick to criticise perceived Garda shortcomings, their security forces were not always 'up to scratch' themselves.

In May 1984, Brigadier John Oborne, the serving defence attaché at the British Embassy in Dublin, visited Northern Ireland. He was briefed at Army Headquarters in Lisburn that there were then only 9,000 regular servicemen compared with 22,000 in 1972, and that the army now played a subordinate role to the RUC. He heard criticism of the RUC, whose members, he was told, were 'accustomed to reacting to incidents and not really staffed or trained for longer term operational planning'.[1197]

Oborne paid a second visit in September 1984 when he again heard criticism of retired RUC officers as 'old died-in-the-wool policemen in the border areas whose only way of operating was to react after an incident happened'. He was pleased to note that most of these officers had now been replaced with men who could participate in operational planning with the army.[1198]

While it has already been noted that both RUC and UDR force levels were surprisingly low in the 1980s, it is clear that the British government did little to protect UDR members living or working in vulnerable areas. UDR commanders told Oborne that men living in such areas should not be permitted to join the UDR. They indicated that a very large number lived within range of attack on foot and were 'virtually unprotectable', and they explained that patrolling the areas where UDR and RUC men lived was expensive in terms of manpower. Some commanders believed it should not be done.[1199] In the analysis of deaths presented in previous chapters, it is clear that many UDR members were living very close to the border, making it extremely easy for IRA members to slip across, kill their target and slip back again. In early 1986, it was noted that 'UDR members generally live in areas where terrorists can operate with the greatest confidence.'[1200]

Sometimes, it wasn't even necessary to cross the border at all – aim could be taken across the border, as was the case in Pte Alan Ferguson's killing. However, more than a year after the Oborne visits, in an internal FCO memo about an essay on the UDR for possible inclusion in a Defence White Paper, a senior official asserted that while some would like to disband the UDR, 'the MoD finds this part-time local militia essential for financial and manpower reasons.'[1201]

When soldiers of the Argyll and Sutherland Highlanders were sent to Fermanagh in October 1972, 'because of a serious outbreak of sectarian murder', it would appear, due to its short duration, to have been a mere cosmetic exercise rather than a serious attempt to provide protection in a vulnerable area. It has to be acknowledged, however, that it is possible the Argylls were removed rather hastily after the murders of Michael Naan and Andrew Murray.

When the four widows of border UDR and RUC officers met with Margaret Thatcher in 1980, all they got was tea and sympathy. Even after the Enniskillen bombing, when she met with unionist politicians, Thatcher apparently made no suggestions as to how security could be improved. She listened to their grievances but nothing more.

The dominant narrative of a negligent Irish government failing to co-operate with the British on border security does not stand up to scrutiny, as the evidence of Irish efforts laid out above demonstrates. The often-clandestine nature of this co-operation, which successive Irish governments believed to be necessary, meant that much of the liaison was under the radar and could be used for propaganda purposes by partial observers. Patrick Mulroe provides a revealing example of the fear Irish politicians had of being seen to collaborate with British forces. He recounts a rather trivial incident that occurred when British troops met with an Irish Army patrol at Lackey Bridge on the Monaghan–Fermanagh border on 5 October 1974. He notes that one of the British soldiers sought 'to mark the occasion' by taking a photograph. The Minister for Justice, Patrick Cooney, was informed of the incident and promptly contacted the British Embassy, fearing that the photograph would leak out.[1202]

CONCLUSION

It is evident from the analysis presented that the two communities in Fermanagh were deeply divided and remained so up to, and beyond, the signing of the Good Friday Agreement in 1998. Based on my research, the sole instance of cohesion throughout the 400 years under review occurred during the period of the Land War. This cohesion, sadly, was sustained for less than four years.

The Catholic community had endured so much hurt. There was the Ulster plantation; the Cromwellian Settlement; the Penal Laws; the Government of Ireland Act, which partitioned Ireland; the aftermath of the failed Boundary Commission, which copper-fastened partition; their abandonment by the Free State government; and the structural inequality and discrimination in the new state of Northern Ireland, which was underpinned by the draconian Special Powers Act and the deployment of the B-Specials.

For Fermanagh Protestants, the terror caused by the Rebellion of 1641 resonated down through the centuries. Operation Harvest (the IRA border campaign of 1956–62) caused them to distrust their Catholic neighbours anew; and during the recent conflict, their sense of being surrounded on all sides by the enemy caused tension, fear and suspicion. This resulted in fractured relationships between previously fairly harmonious mixed communities and has left in its wake an enduring legacy of polarisation and enmity. Both communities suffered during the famine years.

Catholic suffering and oppression arose from decisions made by successive governments – firstly, by the British government and, after partition, primarily by the Northern Ireland/Stormont government but also by the Free State government.

Protestant suffering resulted from the violent reactions of some members of the Catholic population to government policies and decisions, which had devastating consequences. Tragically, for both communities, Stormont's attempts to maintain unionist domination succeeded only in alienating the entire Catholic-nationalist population.

While all of these issues were relevant throughout Northern Ireland, nowhere were they more acutely felt than among the rural heartlands of Fermanagh. Events, such as the election of Bobby Sands and the Enniskillen bombing, caused insecurity and uncertainty for Protestants. Due to the Protestant community's close connections with the UDR in particular, the targeting of the local security forces created a sense of a community under siege.

The statistics for conflict deaths in Fermanagh confirm that the IRA was very active there and that the focus of the conflict was primarily between the IRA and the security forces, although civilians from both communities also suffered losses – 48 of the 115 people killed were civilians. Loyalist activity, especially in terms of fatalities, was minimal compared to other counties, such as Tyrone and Armagh.

With regard to the claim that the Irish government failed to stop the IRA from making cross-border forays into Northern Ireland, it is clear from the above analysis that, in terms of structures established and efforts made, successive Irish governments, at least from 1972 onwards, made serious efforts to prevent these occurrences, and their efforts were often acknowledged by the British. Human nature being what it is, communication and co-operation at the coalface may not always have lived up to the desired standard.

On the other hand, it is clear that the British made little attempt to provide information or to act when loyalists carried out attacks in the Republic. The Irish government can be criticised for not being more forceful in their requests for reciprocal co-operation after these attacks. It is also evident that the British failed to take adequate measures to protect vulnerable members of their own local security forces, particularly the UDR, in border areas.

In order to attempt to heal the division and bitterness between the two communities in Fermanagh and Northern Ireland generally, it is essential that comprehensive mechanisms for dealing with the legacy of the past are established. The continuing failure to deal with the past is a constant source of tension in political relationships, and it is undermining efforts to build reconciliation. There is an urgent need for the past to be addressed; the mechanisms of the Stormont House Agreement, which the five Northern Ireland parties and the British and Irish governments signed up to in December 2014, would appear to be the best way forward. Until the past is addressed, barriers to cross-community interaction will continue to exist, particularly in border areas most affected by the conflict.

This book details how both communities experienced past conflicts and how political decisions made in London, Belfast and Dublin have led to varying perspectives, whether right or wrong when compared to the evidence. Reconciliation is vital in terms of starting a process of acknowledging other people's readings of what happened and why they hold that particular view. It is to be hoped that this publication, which attempts to portray the history and politics of Fermanagh as dispassionately as possible, will be received by both communities in the spirit in which it is intended.

ABBREVIATIONS

APL	Anti-Partition League
CID	Criminal Investigation Department
DPP	Director of Public Prosecutions
DUP	Democratic Unionist Party
FCO	Foreign and Commonwealth Office
GAA	Gaelic Athletic Association
HET RSR	Historical Enquiries Team, Review Summary Report
IRA	Irish Republican Army
IRB	Irish Republican Brotherhood
MoD	Ministry of Defence
PSNI	Police Service of Northern Ireland
RMP	Royal Military Police
RUC	Royal Ulster Constabulary
SDLP	Social Democratic and Labour Party
SIB	Special Investigation Branch
SPA	Special Powers Act
UDA	Ulster Defence Association
UDR	Ulster Defence Regiment
UFF	Ulster Freedom Fighters
USC	Ulster Special Constabulary
USCA	Ulster Special Constabulary Association
UVF	Ulster Volunteer Force

TABLES

The tables that follow have been compiled from an analysis of deaths taken from D. McKittrick, S. Kelters, B. Feeney, C. Thornton and D. McVea, *Lost Lives: The Stories of the Men, Women and Children Who Died as a Result of the Northern Ireland Troubles* (Edinburgh: Mainstream Publishing Company, 2007).

TABLE 1: COUNTY FERMANAGH DEATHS

Year	UDR	RUC	British Army	Protestant Civilians	Catholic Civilians	IRA	Garda	Total
1971	1		1					2
1972	7	2	5	2	2	1	1	20
1973	1	1	1		3	1		7
1974			2	1	2			5
1975			1	1	1	1		4
1976		3		1				4
1977		1	2	1				4
1978	1			1				2
1979	1	1	1	1	1	1		6
1980	3	4		2				9
1981	3				1			4
1982		1	1	1				3
1983				1				1
1984			4	1		2		7
1985	1	2			1			4
1986	1	2			1	1		5
1987	1	2	1	10				14
1988	1	1		3	1			6
1989			2					2
1990								0
1991		1		1				2
1992		1				1		2
1993								0
1994					1			1
2000				1				1
Totals	**21**	**22**	**21**	**28**	**14**	**8**	**1**	**115**

TABLE 2: COUNTY TYRONE DEATHS

Year	UDR	RUC	British Army	Protestants Civilians	Catholic Civilians	IRA	INLA	UDA	Total
1970						2			2
1971	3	1	1	6	4				15
1972	2	1	4	2	4	5			18
1973	1	2	10	2	4	7			26
1974	4	2	4	3	11	4		1	29
1975		4		4	10				18
1976	2	4		5	8	2			21
1977	5	5			3				13
1978	2	2	1	1		1			7
1979	5	1	4	2	1	1			14
1980			1	1	2				4
1981	2	6		1					9
1982	1	1		2					4
1983	8	2	1	2	1	2	2		18
1984	7	1		2	2	1			13
1985	1	2			3	3			9
1986	4			3	1				8
1987	3	1		1	1				6
1988	4	1	9		4	4	1		23
1989	1	2	1	4	1	2			11
1990	3			2	3		1		9
1991				5	4	6			15
1992				9	5	4			18
1993		3		3	4	2			12
1994					3				3
1995				1					1
1996				1					1
1997					1				1
1998				12	17				29
1999									0
2000									0
2001				1	1				2
Totals	**58**	**41**	**36**	**75**	**98**	**46**	**4**	**1**	**359**

TABLE 3: COUNTY ARMAGH DEATHS

Year	UDR	RUC	British Army	Protestant Civilians	Catholic Civilians	Republicans	Loyalists	Other	Total
1969					1				1
1970		2							2
1971			5	2	2	1			10
1972	7	2	18	6	12	5			50
1973	2	3	14	7	2	3			31
1974		5	12	1	6		1	1	26
1975	4	2	9	13	19	3	2		52
1976	6	3	6	17	23	1	1		57
1977	1	1		4	3	1			10
1978		2	8	1	3	1			15
1979	3	8	6	3	6	1			27
1980	1	1	5	4	4				15
1981		3	6	4	4				17
1982	4	5		4	4	5			22
1983	1	2	1	6	8				18
1984	1	4	1	2	3	2			13
1985		6			1				7
1986		4	3	1	2	1			11
1987				3	3	13			19
1988	1		2	4	1	2			10
1989	1	3	1	2	1				8
1990	1	8	2	2	6	4			23
1991	6		1	2	7				16
1992	1	1	2		4	3	1		12
1993		2	6	2	3				13
1994	1		1	2	6				10
1995									0
1996					2	1			3
1997		2	1		1				4
1998		1		2	2				5
1999				1	3				4
2000				2			1		3
2001				1	1				2
2002									0
2003					1	1			2
2004									0
2005					1				1
Totals	**41**	**70**	**110**	**98**	**145**	**48**	**6**	1	**519**

TABLE 4: COUNTY FERMANAGH – RESPONSIBILITY FOR DEATHS

Year	IRA	British Army	UDR	RUC	UVF / UDA	Total
1971	2					2
1972	16	3			1	20
1973	6			1		7
1974	3				2	5
1975	2	1			1	4
1976	4					4
1977	4					4
1978	2					2
1979	6					6
1980	9					9
1981	3	1				4
1982	3					3
1983	1					1
1984	5	2				7
1985	3	1				4
1986	4	1				5
1987	14					14
1988	6					6
1989	2					2
1990	0					0
1991	2					2
1992	1		1			2
1993	0					0
1994	1					1
2000	1					1
Totals	**100**	**9**	**1**	**1**	**4**	**115**

TABLE 5: COUNTY FERMANAGH – RESPONSIBILITY FOR DEATHS (PERCENTAGE)

	Republicans	Loyalists	Security Forces
Totals	100	4	11
Percentage	87.00%	3.50%	9.50%

TABLE 6: COUNTY TYRONE – RESPONSIBILITY FOR DEATHS

Year	IRA / INLA	British Army	UDR	RUC	Loyalist	RIRA / Dissidents	Totals
1970	2						2
1971	13	2					15
1972	11	4	1		2		18
1973	20	1	1		3		25
1974	19	3			7		29
1975	7				10		17
1976	15	1			5		21
1977	12				1		13
1978	5	2					7
1979	14						14
1980	2	2					4
1981	9						9
1982	4						4
1983	13	2		3			18
1984	11	1			1		13
1985	6	3					9
1986	8						8
1987	5				1		6
1988	17	5			1		23
1989	9				2		11
1990	5	1			3		9
1991	5	3		1	6		15
1992	10	4			4		18
1993	8				4		12
1994					3		3
1995	1						1
1996					1		1
1997					1		1
1998						29	29
1999							0
2000							0
2001			1			1	2
Totals	**231**	**34**	**3**	**4**	**55**	**30**	**357**

TABLE 7: COUNTY TYRONE – RESPONSIBILITY FOR DEATHS (PERCENTAGE)

	Republicans	Loyalists	Security Forces
Totals	261	55	41
Percentage	73.10%	15.40%	11.50%

TABLE 8: COUNTY ARMAGH – RESPONSIBILITY FOR DEATHS

Year	IRA/INLA	British Army	UDR	RUC / B-Specials	Loyalist	PIRA / Other	Totals
1969				1			1
1970	2						2
1971	9	1					10
1972	40				8	2	50
1973	25	4			2		31
1974	19			2	4	1	26
1975	31	1			20		52
1976	34	5			18		57
1977	7	1			2		10
1978	13				2		15
1979	24				3		27
1980	13	2					15
1981	16				1		17
1982	14		1	6	1		22
1983	13		2	1	2		18
1984	10	1		1	1		13
1985	7						7
1986	10			1			11
1987	10	9					19
1988	9	1					10
1989	8						8
1990	15	4			4		23
1991	9				7		16
1992	7			1	4		12
1993	10				3		13
1994	6				4		10
1995							0
1996	2					1	3
1997	3				1		4
1998	1				4		5
1999	2				2		4
2000					3		3
2001					2		2
2002							0
2003						2	2
2004							0
2005						1	1
Totals	**369**	**29**	**3**	**13**	**98**	**7**	**519**

TABLE 9: COUNTY ARMAGH – RESPONSIBILITY FOR DEATHS (PERCENTAGE)

	IRA / INLA	RIRA/Other	UDR	RUC	British Army	Loyalists
Totals	369	7	3	13	29	98
Percentage	71.10%	1.30%	0.60%	2.50%	5.60%	18.90%

ENDNOTES

1 The Historical Enquiries Team (HET) was a unit established by the Police Service of Northern Ireland (PSNI) in 2005 to review all conflict-related deaths that occurred in Northern Ireland. It was answerable to the chief constable of the PSNI and closed in 2014. Readers will be unable to access these source documents, as HET reports were private reports compiled for individual families. The author is grateful for their permission to use these reports.

2 The Nine Years' War took place in Ulster from 1594 to 1603. It was led mainly by Hugh O'Neill of Tyrone and Hugh Roe O'Donnell of Tirconnaill against English rule in Ireland. Ulster was the last bastion to hold out against the Tudor Conquest of Ireland.

3 Sir Arthur Chichester was involved in the Nine Years' War, and his tactics included a scorched earth policy. He was vehemently anti-Catholic and oversaw the widespread persecution of Catholics, including the execution of Bishop Conor O'Devany in 1612. (O'Devany was beatified by Pope John Paul II in 1992). Two of Chichester's descendants served as prime ministers of Northern Ireland – Terence O'Neill and James Chichester-Clark.

4 https://www.libraryireland.com/HullHistory/Plantation.php [accessed 7 August 2018].

5 Richard Aldous and Niamh Puirséil, *We Declare: Landmark Documents in Ireland's History* (London: Quercus 2008), 36.

6 Peadar Livingstone states that the word 'acre' must be interpreted very liberally in all plantation documents. It meant an acre of arable land. If it is multiplied by five, we get near to the actual size. Peadar Livingstone, *The Fermanagh Story: A Documented History of the County Fermanagh from the Earliest Times to the Present Day* (Monaghan: Clogher Historical Society, 1969), 61.

7 NAUK, summary of a document entitled 'A Project for the Division and Plantation of the escheated lands in six several counties of Ulster, namely, Tirone, Colraine, Donnegall, Fermanagh, Ardmagh, and Cavan, concluded by his Majesty's Commissioners:- The Bishop of Derry, Sir James Ley, Sir Anthony St. Leger, Sir Henry Docwra, Sir Oliver St. John, Sir James Fullerton, Sir John Davyes'. (The record is held by Lambeth Palace Library) http://discovery.nationalarchives.gov.uk/details/r/0300-f57-e1db-472e-892f-a33bcc27f559 [accessed 14 August 2018].

8 https://cunninghamsway.com/2012/05/12/from-the-broads-to-the-lakelands-english-plantation-in-fermangh-in-the-early-17th-century [accessed 10 August 2018].

9 NAUK, 'A Project for the Division and Plantation of the escheated lands' http://discovery.nationalarchives.gov.uk/details/r/0300-f57-e1db-472e-892f-a33bcc27f559 [accessed 10 August 2018].

10 NAUK, 'A Project for the Division and Plantation of the escheated lands' http://discovery.nationalarchives.gov.uk/details/r/0300-f57-e1db-472e-892f-a33bcc27f559 [accessed 10 August 2018].

11 https://cunninghamsway.com/2012/05/12/from-the-broads-to-the-lakelands-english-plantation-in-fermangh-in-the-early-17th-century [accessed 10 August 2018].

12 Border Reivers were raiders who lived along both sides of the Anglo-Scottish border from the thirteenth to seventeenth centuries.

13 http://www.igp-web.com/fermanagh/Ulster_Plantation.htm [accessed 6 July 2018].

14 https://en-gb.facebook.com/ProjectHawick/posts/1716336815102214 [accessed 4 August 2018]. The article was first published in *The Hawick Paper*, 30 March 2018, written by Alastair Redpath.

15 Robert Bell, 'Sheep Stealers from the North of England: the Riding Clans in Ulster' *History Ireland*, 2, 4, (Winter 1994).

16 www.enniskillen.co.uk/media/6534/Plantation-of-Ulster.pdf [accessed 5 August 2018].

17 Timothy William Ferres, Lord Belmont

in Northern Ireland (blog) lordbelmont-northernireland.blogspot.com/2016/06/the-brooke-baronetcy-1764.html [accessed 19 July 2019].

18 https://cunninghamsway.com/2012/05/12/from-the-broads-to-the-lakelands-english-plantation-in-fermangh-in-the-early-17th-century [accessed 10 August 2018].

19 Livingstone, *The Fermanagh Story*, 61.

20 Aldous and Puirséil, *We Declare*, 32.

21 The Book of O'Conor Don contains a large collection of bardic poems dating from the thirteenth to the seventeenth century and is the most important source for this type of Irish literature.

22 Marc Caball, 'Dispossession and reaction: the Gaelic literati and the Plantation of Ulster', *History Ireland*, 17, 6 (Nov/Dec 2009).

23 *Ibid.*

24 Caball, 'Dispossession and reaction'.

25 Livingstone, *The Fermanagh Story*, 77–8.

26 Aldous and Puirséil, *We Declare*, 42.

27 Trevor Royle, *Civil War: The Wars of the Three Kingdoms, 1638–1680* (London: Abacus, 2004), 139.

28 *Ibid.*, 82.

29 David F. Gerder, 'Providence and the 1641 Rebellion' (PhD thesis, University of Iowa, 2015).

30 www.castlebytheerne.co.uk [accessed 6 August 2018].

31 *Ibid.*

32 GENI, Edward Archdale, https://www.geni.com/people/Edward-Archdale/6000000003216046467 [accessed 19 July 2019].

33 The depositions are witness testimonies – mainly by Protestant settlers – concerning their experiences of the 1641 rebellion. The testimonies document loss of goods, military activity and alleged crimes committed by the Irish insurgents.

34 Gerder, 'Providence and the 1641 Rebellion', 79.

35 TCD, 1641 Depositions Project, online transcript January 1970 http://1641.tcd.ie/deposition.php?depID<php [accessed 3 July 2019].

36 Gerder, 155.

37 *Ibid.*, 213.

38 TCD, 1641 Depositions Project.

39 Gerder, 'Providence and the 1641 Rebellion'.

40 *Ibid.*

41 *Ibid.*, 53.

42 Carlo Gebler, *The Siege of Derry: A History* (London: Abacus, 2006), 257.

43 *Ibid.*, 42.

44 TCD, 1641 Depositions Project.

45 *Ibid.*

46 *Ibid.*

47 *Ibid.*

48 *Ibid.*

49 http://nationalarchives.gov.uk/currency/ [accessed 14 January 2019].

50 TCD, 1641 Depositions Project.

51 Gerder, 'Providence and the 1641 Rebellion'.

52 *Ibid.*

53 *Ibid.*, 83.

54 TCD, 1641 Depositions Project.

55 Raymond Gillespie, 'The murder of Arthur Champion and the Rebellion in Fermanagh', *Clogher Record*, 14, 3 (1993).

56 *Ibid.*

57 *Ibid.*

58 Gerder, 'Providence and the 1641 Rebellion', 148.

59 https://www.libraryireland.com/articles/Hull/Wentworth2-1 [accessed 7 January 2019].

60 TCD, 1641 Depositions Project.

61 Aldous and Puirséil, We Declare, 42.

62 Livingstone, *The Fermanagh Story*, 86.

63 James Godkin, *The Land War in Ireland: A History for the Times* (London: Macmillan, 1870).

64 *Ibid.*

65 Aldous and Puirséil, *We Declare*, 42.

66 www.enniskillencastle.co.uk (accessed 10 August 2018)

67 Livingstone, *The Fermanagh Story*, 93.

68 Anthony Malcolmson, 'The Erne Family, Estate and Archive, c.1610–c.1950' in E.M. Murphy and W.J. Roulston (eds), *Fermanagh: History and Society* (Dublin: Geography Publications, 2004), 207.

69 Pádraig Lenihan, *1690: Battle of the Boyne* (Stroud: Tempus, 2003), 257–8.

70 Patrick J. Corish, 'The Cromwellian Regime 1650–1660' in W. Moody, F.X. Martin and F.J. Byrne (eds), *A New History of Ireland: Early Modern Ireland*, 1534–1691 (Oxford: Oxford University Press, 1976), 292.

71 Livingstone, *The Fermanagh Story*, 96.

72 Aldous and Puirséil, *We Declare*, 48.

73 *Ibid.*

74 *Ibid.*, 98.

75 *Ibid.*, 103-4.

76 *Ibid.*, 105; Edward Burke, *An Army of Tribes: British Army Cohesion, Deviancy and Murder in Northern Ireland* (Liverpool: Liverpool University Press, 2018), 242.

77 Livingstone, *The Fermanagh Story*, 97.

78 *Ibid.*, 106.

79 William K. Parke, 'A Short History of the Royal Inniskilling Fusiliers' in E.M. Murphy and W.J.

Roulston (eds), *Fermanagh History and Society* (Dublin: Geography Publications, 2004), 603.
80 Livingstone, *The Fermanagh Story*, 106.
81 Aldous and Puirséil, *We Declare*, 48.
82 As a result of the Treaty of Limerick, many of those who had supported King James were transported to France; this event became known as the Flight of the Wild Geese.
83 Livingstone, *The Fermanagh Story*, 107.
84 *Ibid.*
85 With the passing of the Act of Supremacy, the English monarch replaced the pope as the supreme head of the church.
86 With the passing of the Act of Uniformity, the Book of Common Prayer was declared to be the only legal form of worship.
87 Livingstone, *The Fermanagh Story*, 108.
88 *Ibid.*, 109.
89 *Ibid.*, 111.
90 The diocese of Clogher includes all of County Monaghan, most of County Fermanagh and parts of counties Tyrone, Donegal, Louth and Cavan.
91 Henry A. Jefferies, 'Penal Days in Clogher', *History Ireland*, 17, 3 (May–June 2009).
92 *Ibid.*
93 Livingstone, *The Fermanagh Story*, 112.
94 *Ibid.*, 113–14.
95 *Ibid.*, 109.
96 The Scots in Ulster, http://ancestryireland.com/scotsinulster/pockethistory/7.%20Presbyterianism.html#:~:text=Other%20brands%20of%20Presbyterianism%20originating,congregations%20and%20presbyteries%20in%20Ulster [accessed 25 February 2020].
97 Aldous and Puirséil, *We Declare*, 60.
98 *Ibid.*, 140.
99 Roslea, www.rooneys-of-roslea.com/roslea2.html [accessed 25 February 2020].
100 Aldous and Puirséil, *We Declare*, 140.
101 Livingstone, *The Fermanagh Story*, 141.
102 *Ibid.*
103 Livingstone, *The Fermanagh Story*, 142–3.
104 *Ibid.*, 256.
105 *Ibid.*, 145.
106 *Ibid.*, 147.
107 *Ibid.*
108 Livingstone, *The Fermanagh Story*, 148–9.
109 Catholic emancipation was the removal of restrictions on Catholics that had been introduced by the Acts of Uniformity and Supremacy.
110 Livingstone, *The Fermanagh Story*, 149–50.
111 Kevin Whelan, *The Tree of Liberty: Radicalism, Catholicism and the Construction of Irish Identity 1760–1830* (Cork: Cork University Press, 1997), 124.
112 *Ibid.*
113 Brown, Stewart J., 'Ireland' in Stewart J. Brown, Peter Nockles and James Pereiro (eds), *The Oxford Handbook of the Oxford Movement* (Oxford: Oxford University Press, 2017), 442.
114 *Ibid.*
115 M. McManus, 'The Macken Fight', http://www.mexlist.com/mcmanus/macken.htm [accessed 31 October] 2018].
116 Livingstone, *The Fermanagh Story*, 160.
117 Daragh Curran, *A Society in Transition: The Protestant Community in Ulster 1825–45*, Academia. 4 August 2020. http://www.academia.edu/9059578/The_revival_of_the_Orange_Order_1828?auto=download.
118 Tony Gray, *The Orange Order* (London: Bodley Head, 1972), 114.
119 Burke, *An Army of Tribes*, 228.
120 McManus, 'The Macken Fight'.
121 *Thom's Directory of Ireland for the Year 1932* (London: Alex Thom & Co Ltd, 1933).
122 https://cunninghamsway.com/2012/03/18the-great-silence-the-famine-in-fermanagh-1845-1850 [accessed 4 August 2018].
123 E.M. Crawford, 'Fermanagh: Food, Famine and Fever' in E.M. Murphy and W.J. Roulston (eds), *Fermanagh: History and Society* (Dublin: Geography Publications, 2004), 274.
124 www.workhouses.org.uk/lisnaskea [accessed 21 February 2019].
125 *Ibid.*
126 Fermanagh sources, Enniskillen Workhouse Indoor Registers, 1 December 1845 – 4 July 1847, www.igp-web.com/Femanagh/Donated.htm [accessed 30 March 2020].
127 *Ibid.*
128 Timothy Guinnane, Desmond McCabe and Cormac Ó Gráda, 'Agency and Famine Relief: Enniskillen Workhouse During the Great Irish Famine', Working Paper Series, School of Economics, University College Dublin (2004).
129 *Ibid.*
130 *Ibid.*
131 John B. Cunningham, *The Great Silence: The Famine in Fermanagh, 1845–1850* (Fermanagh: Davog Press, 2012), 72–3.
132 *Ibid.*
133 beef hock bone is a flavourful combination of two bones joined together by tendons and ligaments
134 Brian MacDonald, *A Time of Desolation: Clones Poor Law Union, 1845–50* (Monaghan: Clogher

Historical Society, 2017), 59–60.
135 Cunningham, *The Great Silence*, 25.
136 A seneschal presided over a manor court in which tenants were punished and often forced to pay fines for their offences.
137 Crawford, 'Fermanagh', 282–3.
138 The figures for Enniskillen parish may be misleading due to the location of the workhouse there, which, in 1851, would have been crammed with inmates (Conversation with Brian MacDonald, 25 March 2020).
139 University of Essex, Online Historical Population Reports, www.histpop.org [accessed 24 March 2020].
140 Brian MacDonald notes that Currin (spanning Fermanagh and Monaghan) was very badly hit by the famine, with a total decline of 43 per cent and the loss of almost a third of all occupied households. MacDonald, *A Time of Desolation*, 72.
141 www.enniskillencastle.co.uk/history-heritage/famine-memorials-in-fermanagh [accessed 4 August 2018].
142 *Thom's Directory of Ireland for the Year 1932*.
143 K.J. Rankin, 'The Provenance and Dissolution of the Irish Boundary Commission', Institute for British-Irish Studies, University College Dublin (2006).
144 The Irish National Land League was founded in 1879. Its aim was to abolish landlordism and enable tenant farmers to own the land they worked on.
145 William F. Bailey, 'The Ulster tenant-right custom: its origin, characteristic and position under the Land Acts', *Journal of the Statistical and Social Inquiry Society of Ireland*, 10, 74 (1893/1894), 12–22.
146 *Ibid.* Bailey argues that the Land Act of 1870, in legalising the 'Ulster Custom', refers to it in the plural as 'usages', which changed the interpretation of the statute and undoubtedly weakened the position of the Ulster farmers. Instead of treating it as *one* custom, the statute now legalised a variety of different customs. The immediate result was that the onus was now shifted onto the tenant of proving what the privileges were to which he was entitled.
147 Frank Thompson, 'The Land War in County Fermanagh' in E.M. Murphy and W.J. Roulston (eds), *Fermanagh: History and Society*, (Dublin: Geography Publications, 2004), 287.
148 *Ibid.*
149 *Ibid.*, 288.
150 *Irish Times*, 27 December 1879.
151 *Ibid.*
152 Livingstone, *The Fermanagh Story*, 212.
153 Livingstone, *The Fermanagh Story*, 259.
154 J.R.B. McMinn, 'The Land League in North Antrim 1880–1882', *The Glynns*, 11 (1983); British Prime Minister Gladstone introduced both the Landlord and Tenant (Ireland) Act 1870 and the Land Law (Ireland) Act 1881.
155 *Irish Times*, 27 March 1880.
156 McMinn, 'The Land League in North Antrim 1880–82'.
157 *Irish Times*, 6 November 1880.
158 *Ibid.*, 8 November 1880.
159 *Irish Times*, 8 November 1880.
160 Jeremiah Jordan (1830–1911), a Methodist, was MP for South Fermanagh from 1885 to 1892 and from 1893 to 1910.
161 *Irish Times*, 11 November 1880.
162 *Ibid.*, 25 November 1880.
163 *Ibid.*, 1 December 1880.
164 Livingstone, *The Fermanagh Story*, 256.
165 *Irish Times*, 6 December 1880.
166 *Ibid.*
167 Thompson, 'The Land War in County Fermanagh', 295.
168 *Irish Times*, 8 December 1880.
169 Andrew Kettle (1833–1916) was a leading Irish nationalist politician, progressive farmer, agrarian agitator and founding member of the Land League; he was known as the 'right-hand man' of Charles Stewart Parnell.
170 *Irish Times*, 8 December 1880
171 *Ibid.*
172 *Ibid.*, 9 December 1880.
173 *Ibid.*, 11 December 1880.
174 *Ibid.*, 23 December 1880.
175 Livingstone, *The Fermanagh Story*, 260.
176 *Irish Times*, 23 December 1880.
177 Thompson, 'The Land War in County Fermanagh', 298.
178 *Irish Times*, 28 December 1880.
179 *Ibid.*, 8 January 1881.
180 *Ibid.*, 19 January 1881.
181 Livingstone, *The Fermanagh Story*, 261.
182 Margaret Urwin, *A County Wexford Family in the Land War: The O'Hanlon Walshs of Knocktartan* (Dublin: Four Courts Press, 2002), 26.
183 The Marquess of Ely also owned a large estate at Loftus Hall in Wexford. Trouble was breaking out on that estate at around this time.
184 When an area was proclaimed, it meant that martial law was imposed. If a meeting or other event was proclaimed, it meant that it was

banned.

185 *Irish Times,* 23 March 1881

186 Crichton's father, the 3rd Earl, also John Crichton, had appointed the notorious Charles Cunningham Boycott, a former British Army officer, as the land agent on one of his small Mayo estates of approximately 1,500 acres. At that time, 1872, the Earl of Erne owned 40,386 acres, of which 31,389 were in Fermanagh, 4,826 were in Donegal, 1,986 were in Sligo and 2,184 were in Mayo. He also owned properties in Dublin. Liam Ó Raghalaigh, 'Captain Boycott: Man and Myth', *History Ireland,* 19, 1, (Jan–Feb 2001).

187 Burke, *An Army of Tribes,* 248.

188 Livingstone, *The Fermanagh Story,* 261.

189 *Irish Times,* 26 July 1881.

190 *Ibid.,* 12 May 1881.

191 Thompson, 'The Land War in County Fermanagh', 296.

192 *Ibid.,* 297.

193 *Ibid.*

194 Aldous and Puirséil, *We Declare,* 90.

195 Urwin, *A County Wexford Family in the Land War,* 24.

196 Aldous and Puirséil, *We Declare,* 90.

197 Thompson, 'The Land War in County Fermanagh', 299.

198 *Irish Times,* 14 August 1882.

199 Urwin, *A County Wexford Family in the Land War,* 42.

200 *Freeman's Journal,* 17 October 1883; *Irish Times,* 20 October 1883.

201 *Irish Times,* 20 October 1883.

202 The leader of the Ulster Unionist Council.

203 Livingstone, *The Fermanagh Story,* 271.

204 The Ulster Covenant pledged to use 'all means which may be necessary to defeat the present conspiracy to set up a Home Rule Parliament in Ireland'. Within weeks, a total of 471,414 men and women had signed.

205 B.E. Barton, 'The Origins and Development of Unionism in Fermanagh, 1885–1914' in E.M. Murphy and W.J. Roulston (eds), *Fermanagh: History and Society* (Dublin: Geography Publications, 2004), 326.

206 Andrew Scholes, '"Neither Whigs, Tories, nor Party Politicians?" The Church of Ireland and the Ulster Crisis 1910–14' in *The Home Rule Crisis, 1912–14: Cork Studies in the Irish Revolution* (Cork: Mercier Press, 2014)

207 *Ibid.*

208 Barton, 'The Origins and Development of Unionism in Fermanagh', 328.

209 Livingstone, *The Fermanagh Story,* 272.

210 *Ibid.,* 274.

211 Barton, 'The Origins and Development of Unionism in Fermanagh', 329.

212 *Ibid.,* 331.

213 *Ibid.*

214 *New York Times,* 18 August 1973, Sir Basil Brooke, obituary.

215 Myers, Jason, 'Reconsidering Irish Fatalities in the First World War', The Irish Story. https://www.theirishstory.com/2015/03/25/reconsidering-irish-fatalities-in-the-first-world-war/#.XqqTJ6hKjIU [accessed 9 January 2019].

216 *Ibid.*

217 *Ibid.*

218 www.judecollins.com/2016/02/that-extremely-rare-thing-george-irvine-the-fermanagh-protestant-and-easter-rebel-by-ciaran-mc/ [accessed 9 January 2019].

219 www.judecollins.com/2016/02/that-extremely-rare-thing-george-irvine-the-fermanagh-protestant-and-easter-rebel-by-ciaran-mc/ [accessed 9 January 2019].

220 Livingstone, *The Fermanagh Story,* 279.

221 www.judecollins.com/2016/02/that-extremely-rare-thing-george-irvine-the-fermanagh-protestant-and-easter-rebel-by-ciaran-mc/ [accessed 9 January 2019].

222 *Irish Times,* 1 July 1954.

223 http://www.rte.i/centuryireland/index.php/articles/material-culture-and-1916 [accessed 9 January 2019].

224 *Fearless but Few: Fermanagh and the Easter Rising* (2016), Fermanagh 1916 Centenary Association, http://www.1916fermanagh.blogspot.com [accessed 16 November 2018].

225 *Ibid.*

226 https://www.cunninghamsway.com/category/1950 [accessed 9 January 2019].

227 *Fearless but Few.*

228 Livingstone, *The Fermanagh Story,* 280.

229 *Fearless but Few.*

230 *Ibid.*

231 https://www.cunninghamsway.com/category/1950 [accessed 9 January 2019].

232 *Ibid.*

233 Livingstone, *The Fermanagh Story,* 281.

234 Edward Mervyn Archdale was first elected for the constituency of Fermanagh North in 1898. He resigned his seat in 1903, citing a lack of time and money to attend to his parliamentary duties. However, circumstances seemed to have changed for him, as he was elected unopposed in a by-election in 1916 and retained the seat in the general election of 1918. He remained an MP for

the following twenty years, until his retirement in 1938. During part of that time, he served as Minister for Agriculture. Royal Irish Academy, Dictionary of Biography, Archdale, Sir Edward Mervyn, https://dib.cambridge.org/viewReadPage.do;jsessionid=3C62CDC3FFFC732F-475B71E4211BDE44?articleld=a0190 [accessed 24 July 2019].

235 Livingstone, *The Fermanagh Story*, 283.

236 Rankin, 'The Provenance and Dissolution of the Irish Boundary Commission', 5–6.

237 Walter Long was rabidly anti-Sinn Féin. It was he who proposed the hiring of ex-servicemen to assist the RIC – a measure that would be adopted in 1920 with the recruitment of the Black and Tans and Auxiliaries to serve in Ireland.

238 House of Commons debate, 11 November 1920.

239 Rankin, 'The Provenance and Dissolution of the Irish Boundary Commission', 5–6.

240 Rankin, 'The Provenance and Dissolution of the Irish Boundary Commission', 6.

241 *Irish Times,* 15 October 2019.

242 'The Border as a social problem', www.trademarkbelfast.com>wp-content>uploads>2015/03 [accessed 7 October 2019].

243 Donnacha Ó Beacháin, 'The Dog that didn't bark: Southern unionism in pre and post-revolutionary Ireland', *History Ireland*, 23, 4 (July/August 2015).

244 *Ibid.*

245 *Ibid.*

246 *Irish Times,* 15 October 2019.

247 *Ibid.*

248 After the general election of 1918, the term Nationalist Party was taken on by the remnants of the Irish Parliamentary Party in the new creation of Northern Ireland. It declined in the late 1960s and was eventually subsumed into the short-lived Irish Independence Party in 1977.

249 *Ibid.*, 4 April 1921.

250 *Ibid.*, 30 May 1921.

251 *Ibid.*

252 *Ibid.*

253 *Irish Times*, 30 May 1921

254 The Ulster Special Constabulary, https://www.revolvy.com/page/Ulster-Special-Constabulary [accessed 16 November 2018].

255 *Ibid.*

256 *Irish Times*, 14 July 1921.

257 Donnacha Ó Beacháin, *From Partition to Brexit* (Manchester: Manchester University Press, 2019), 14.

258 *Ibid.*

259 *Ibid.*

260 Livingstone, *The Fermanagh Story*, 290.

261 Pearse Lawlor, 'Tit-for-Tat: the War of Independence in the Northern Counties' *History Ireland*, 20, 1 (Jan/Feb 2012).

262 *Irish Times,* 23 February 1921.

263 Burke, *An Army of Tribes*, 249.

264 *Irish Times,* 23 March 1921.

265 The Hogan Stand in Croke Park, Dublin is named in his memory.

266 Livingstone, *The Fermanagh Story*, 303.

267 *Irish Times,* 13 February 1922.

268 *Irish Times,* 13 February 1922.

269 *Ibid.*

270 Liam Ó Duibhir, *Donegal and the Civil War: The Untold Story* (Cork: Mercier Press, 2011), 119–31.

271 *Irish Independent,* 2 June 2012.

272 *Ibid.*

273 Ó Duibhir, *Donegal and the Civil War*, 119–31.

274 *Ibid.*

275 *Ibid.*

276 *Irish Independent,* 2 June 2012.

277 George Lunt, December 2015, www.borderroadmemories.com/search-border-crossings/memories/family-life-on-the-fermanagh-monaghan-border [accessed 24 October 2018].

278 Arthur Griffith founded Sinn Féin in 1905, which became an umbrella organisation for all types of Irish nationalism, apart from the Home Rule movement. He joined the Irish Volunteers in 1912. In 1917, he stood down as President of Sinn Féin, allowing Éamon de Valera to take his place. He was part of the first Dáil in 1919 and was elected Vice-President of the Republic. He was acting head during de Valera's time in the US, from June 1919 to the end of 1920. He led the Irish delegation to London to negotiate the Treaty. After the split with those who opposed the Treaty, he replaced de Valera as President of the Dáil. He died of a brain haemorrhage on 12 August 1922, at the height of the civil war. He was 52 years old.

279 Rankin, 'The Provenance and Dissolution of the Irish Boundary Commission', 5–6.

280 *Ibid.*, 7.

281 *Ibid.*, 9.

282 *Ibid.*, 9.
283 Ó Beacháin, *From Partition to Brexit*, 22.
284 Rankin, 'The Provenance and Dissolution of the Irish Boundary Commission', 13.
285 Aldous and Puirséil, *We Declare*, 132.
286 T.P. Coogan, *Michael Collins* (London: Hutchinson, 1990), 240.
287 Rankin, 'The Provenance and Dissolution of the Irish Boundary Commission', 11.
288 House of Commons, speech of Sir Winston Churchill, 16 February 1922, www.ukpol.co.uk/winston-churchill-1922-speech-on-the-ireland-situation/ [accessed 3 April 2020].
289 *Ibid.*
290 *Ibid.*
291 *Ibid.*
292 Ó Beacháin, *From Partition to Brexit*, 18.
293 Ó Beacháin, *From Partition to Brexit*, 18.
294 Rankin, 'The Provenance and Dissolution of the Irish Boundary Commission', 6.
295 Thomas Leahy and Niall Ó Dochartaigh, 'Citizenship on the Ethnic Frontier: Nationality, Migration and Rights in Northern Ireland since 1920' in Steven G. Ellis, *Enfranchising Ireland?: Identity, Citizenship and State* (Dublin: Royal Irish Academy, 2018).
296 *Ibid.*
297 Ó Beacháin, *From Partition to Brexit*, 23.
298 Lee, Joseph, *Ireland, 1912–1985: Politics and Society* (Cambridge: Cambridge University Press, 1989), 147.
299 Rankin, 'The Provenance and Dissolution of the Irish Boundary Commission', 16.
300 NAUK, CAB61/162, The Boundary Commission Report.
301 *Ibid.*
302 Terence Dooley is associate professor and director for the Study of Historic Irish Houses and Estates, NUI, Maynooth.
303 Dooley, Terence A.M., 'Protestant Migration from the Free State to Northern Ireland, 1920–25', *Clogher Record*, 15, 3 (1996).
304 *Belfast Newsletter*, 16 January 1925.
305 NAUK, CAB61/162, The Boundary Commission Report.
306 *Ibid.*
307 Jed Martin, 'The Origins of Partition' in Malcolm Anderson and Bort Eberhard (eds), *History, Politics, Culture* (Liverpool: Liverpool University Press, 1989), 96.
308 Ó Beacháin, *From Partition to Brexit*, 25.
309 Dáil Debates, 7 December 1925, https://www.oireachtas.ie/en/debates/debate/dail/1925-12-07 [accessed 5 August 2020].
310 Enda Staunton, 'The Boundary Commission Debacle 1925, aftermath and implications', *History Ireland*, 4, 2, (Summer 1996).
311 Dáil Debates, 19 November 1925, https://www.oireachtas.ie/en/debates/debate/dail/1925-11-19/13/ [accessed 30 March 2020].
312 House of Lords debate, 9 December 1925, www.api.parliament.uk/historic-hansard/lords/1925/dec/09/ireland-confirmation-of-agreement-bill [accessed 3 April 2020].
313 Dáil Debates, 19 November 1925.
314 *Belfast Newsletter*, 21 November 1925.
315 Ó Beacháin, *From Partition to Brexit*, 24.
316 Dáil Debates, 24 November 1925, https://www.oireachtas.ie/en/debates/debate/dail/1925-11-24/13/ [accessed 5 August 2020].
317 NAUK, CAB61/162 Boundary Commission Report, Draft Conclusions, Section V, p.66, December 1925.
318 Dáil Debates, 24 November 1925.
319 Ó Beacháin, *From Partition to Brexit*, 27.
320 Staunton, 'The Boundary Commission Debacle 1925'.
321 Dáil Debates, 10 December 1925, https://www.oireachtas.ie/en/debates/debate/dail/1925-12-10 [accessed 3 April 2020].
322 Dáil Debates, 9 December 1925.
323 Dáil Debates, 10 December 1925.
324 Brendan O'Leary, *A Treatise on Northern Ireland*, Volume 2 (Oxford: Oxford University Press, 2019).
325 Staunton, 'The Boundary Commission Debacle 1925'.
326 *Ibid.*
327 *Fermanagh Herald*, 23 January 1926.
328 John Crowley, Donal Ó Drisceoil, Mike Murphy and John Borgonovo (eds), *Atlas of the Irish Revolution* (Cork: Cork University Press, 2018), 22.
329 Lord Cameron, September 1969, 'Summary of Conclusions on Causes of Disorders', (Belfast: Her Majesty's Stationery Office, 1969).
330 Laura K. Donohue, 'Regulating Northern Ireland: The Special Powers Acts, 1922–1972', *The Historical Journal*, 41, 4 (December 1998).

331 Lord Cameron, 'Summary of Conclusions on Causes of Disorders'.
332 John Whyte, 'How much discrimination was there under the unionist regime, 1921–68?', *Contemporary Irish Studies* (1983).
333 Donohue, 'Regulating Northern Ireland'.
334 Crowley et al. (eds), *Atlas of the Irish Revolution,* 22.
335 *Ibid.*
336 *Ibid.*
337 *Ibid.*
338 *Ibid.*
339 *Donegal Democrat,* 20 June 1936.
340 *Irish Times,* 26 June 1997.
341 David C. Rapoport, *Terrorism: The Second or Anti-Colonial Wave* (Abingdon: Taylor & Francis Group, 2006), 305–6.
342 NLI, Ms 49, 747/4, catalogue/nli.ie/Record/vtls000082661 [accessed 26 February 2019].
343 The Campaign for Social Justice in Northern Ireland, *Northern Ireland: The Plain Truth* (Dungannon: The Campaign for Social Justice in Northern Ireland, 1964).
344 *Irish Independent,* 12 February 1925.
345 *Fermanagh Herald,* 7 February 1925.
346 *Belfast Newsletter,* 7 February 1925.
347 *Belfast Newsletter,* 7 February 1925.
348 *Irish Independent,* 12 February 1925.
349 *Irish Independent,* 12 February 1925.
350 *Fermanagh Herald,* 21 February 1925.
351 *Donegal News,* 14 February 1925.
352 *Sunday Independent,* 22 February 1925.
353 *Irish Independent,* 29 April 1925.
354 *Irish Independent,* 29 April 1925.
355 *Fermanagh Herald,* 8 May 1926.
356 The IRA campaign of 1956–62.
357 www.theirishstory.com/2018/12/03/revisiting-the-northern-ireland-civil-rights-movement-1968-69#.XzZ6TuhKjIU [accessed 26 February 2019].
358 *Ibid.*
359 Leahy and Ó Dochartaigh, 'Citizenship on the Ethnic Frontier'.
360 *Fermanagh Times,* 13 July 1933.
361 Susan McKay, *Northern Protestants: An Unsettled People* (Down: Blackstaff Press, 2000), 220.
362 Parliamentary Debates, Northern Ireland House of Commons, Vol. XVI, Cols. 617–618.
363 *Ibid.*
364 Thomas Hennessy, 'Ulster Unionism and Loyalty to the Crown of the United Kingdom 1912–74' in R. English and G. Walker (eds), *Unionism in Modern Ireland: New Perspectives on Politics and Culture* (London: Palgrave MacMillan Press, 1996), 119–20.
365 *Ibid.*
366 Fermanagh Civil Rights Association, *Fermanagh Facts* (undated).
367 www.cain.ulst.ac.uk/issues/discrimination/quotes.htm [accessed 14 December 2018].
368 Eric P. Kaufmann, 'Demographic change and conflict in Northern Ireland: reconciling qualitative and quantitative evidence', *Ethnopolitics,* 10 (2011), 369–89.
369 *Ibid.*
370 Paul Morland, *Demographic Engineering: Population Strategies in Ethnic Conflict* (Abingdon: Taylor & Francis Group, 2014).
371 Kaufmann, 'Demographic change and conflict in Northern Ireland'.
372 BBC News, 15 February 2015, Declan Lawn: 'Orange Order says it uses Land Funds to "Counter Republicans Illegal Proceeds"'.
373 Fermanagh Civil Rights Association, *Fermanagh Facts,* 21.
374 NAUK, CJ4/4249, John A. Costello's address in the Mansion House, 6 February 1957.
375 Leahy and Ó Dochartaigh, 'Citizenship on the Ethnic Frontier'.
376 *Ibid.*
377 *Ibid.*
378 *Fermanagh Herald,* 7 March 1953.
379 *Fermanagh Herald,* 30 May 1953.
380 *Ibid.*
381 *Ibid.*
382 *Ibid.*
383 *Ibid.*
384 *Ibid.*
385 *Ibid.*, 2 January 1954
386 *Fermanagh Herald,* 2 January 1954.
387 *Ibid.*, 13 November 1954.
388 *Ibid.*
389 Eamon Phoenix, 'Cahir Healy and Nationalist Politics in County Fermanagh 1885–1970' in E.M. Murphy and W.J. Roulston (eds), *Fermanagh: History and Society* (Dublin: Geography Publications, 2004), 376.
390 *Ibid.*
391 *Ibid.*
392 *Ibid.*, 377.
393 *Irish Times,* 20 April 2019.
394 *Irish Times,* 20 April 2019.
395 Ó Beacháin, *From Partition to Brexit,* 71.
396 CAIN Website, 'Why the Border Must Be': The Northern Ireland case in brief (Northern Ireland Government, 1956) https://cain.ulster.

ac.uk/othelem/docs/nigov56.htm [accessed 24 October 2019].

397 *Irish Examiner*, 11 February 1956.

398 *Ibid.*

399 Many years later, Brookeborough flatly contradicted this statement. At a unionist-loyalist rally held in Belfast on 30 September 1972 to protest the prorogation of Stormont, he told his audience that 'if it had not been for the Special Constabulary, Northern Ireland would not have existed and continued to exist.' He continued with fulsome praise for the militia, 'They were the finest and most self-disciplined force that has even been recruited anywhere in the world.' *Irish Times*, 2 October 1972.

400 CAIN Website, 'Why the Border Must Be'.

401 *Ibid.*

402 *Irish Independent*, 22 February 1956.

403 Phoenix, 'Cahir Healy and Nationalist Politics in County Fermanagh', 378.

404 M.L.R. Smith, *Fighting for Ireland* (New York: Routledge, 1995), 67.

405 Interview with IRA survivor of Operation Harvest, 21 June 2019.

406 NAUK, DO35/4991, Roslea Incident, 26 November 1955.

407 *Ibid.*

408 Interview with IRA survivor.

409 NAUK, CJ4/4249, Memo from Stormont Castle to Home Office, London, 12 December 1956.

410 Brian Hanley and Scott Millar, *The Lost Revolution: The Story of the Official IRA and the Workers' Party* (Dublin: Penguin Ireland, 2010), 3.

411 NAUK, CJ4/4249, Memo from R.F. Dunbar, Ministry of Home Affairs, Stormont to TC Green, Home Office, London, 14 December 1956.

412 Interview with IRA survivor.

413 Hanley and Millar, *The Lost Revolution*, 3.

414 NAUK, CJ4/4249, Memo from Dunbar to Green, 14 December 1956.

415 *Ibid.*

416 NAUK, CJ4/4249, Memo from Dunbar to Green, 18 December 1956.

417 Hanley and Millar, *The Lost Revolution*, 15.

418 NAUK, CJ4/4249, Telegram from Dunbar to Green, 2 January 1957.

419 *Ibid.*

420 Interview with IRA survivor.

421 *Ibid.*

422 BBC Radio Ulster, *The Brookeborough Raid*, 24 February 2019.

423 Interview with IRA survivor.

424 BBC Radio Ulster, *The Brookeborough Raid*, 24 February 2019.

425 *Ibid.*

426 Interview with IRA survivor.

427 BBC Radio Ulster, *The Brookeborough Raid*, 24 February 2019.

428 Interview with IRA survivor.

429 *Ibid.*

430 NAUK, CJ4/4249, Report on incident.

431 Interview with IRA survivor.

432 *Ibid.*

433 Patrick Bishop and Eamon Mallie, *The Provisional IRA* (London: Corgi Books, 1988), 43.

434 NAUK, CJ4/4249, letter to G.W. St John Chadwick, CRO from G. Kimber, British Embassy, 7 January 1957.

435 *Ibid.*

436 BBC Radio Ulster, *The Brookeborough Raid*, 24 February 2019.

437 Interview with IRA survivor.

438 It became publicly available only when the Dominion Office file was declassified on 2 December 2009. The file was originally closed until 2033, but possibly as a result of an FOI, was opened earlier. It had remained closed for more than fifty years.

439 NAUK, DO35/4987, IRA attacks on 12 and 14 December 1956 and subsequent developments (1956–7), Note of British Ambassador to Commonwealth Relations Office (CRO), 27 January 1957.

440 *Ibid.*

441 Seán Cronin was IRA Chief of Staff 1957–8 and 1959–60. He had served in the Irish Army during the Second World War as an officer in Southern Command. After the war, he emigrated to New York, returning to Ireland in 1955 when he became sub-editor of the *Irish Press*. He was the inspiration and strategist for Operation Harvest, the IRA border campaign of 1956–62.

442 NAUK, DO35/4987, Note of British Ambassador to CRO, 27 January 1957.

443 *Ibid.*

444 Ó Beacháin, *From Partition to Brexit*, 77.

445 *Ibid.*

446 *Ibid.*

447 Robert W. White, 'Provisional IRA Attacks on the UDR in Fermanagh and South Tyrone: Implications for the Study of Political Violence and Terrorism', *Terrorism and Political Violence*, 23, 3 (2011), DOI:

10.1080/09546553.2011.561674.
448 *Ibid.*
449 Michael Watters was the owner of the cottage; the four IRA volunteers were Oliver Craven, Newry; Paul Smith, Bessbrook; George Keegan, Enniscorthy; and Patrick Parle, Wexford.
450 'On this day', *History Ireland*, 20, 1 (Jan/Feb 2012).
451 www.revolvy.com/page/Border-campaign-%28Irish-Republican-Army%29?cr=1
452 Phoenix, 'Cahir Healy and Nationalist Politics in County Fermanagh', 382.
453 Phoenix, 'Cahir Healy and Nationalist Politics in County Fermanagh', 383.
454 Graham Walker, 'The 1947 Education Act – A Landmark in Northern Ireland's History' (2017), www.qpol.qub.ac.uk/1947-education-act [accessed 8 November 2019].
455 Fermanagh Civil Rights Association, *Fermanagh Facts.*
456 The Cameron Inquiry was established to investigate the causes and circumstances of the violence and civil disturbances since 5 October 1968; it reported in 1969.
457 Cameron Report, *Disturbances in Northern Ireland: Report of the Commission appointed by the Governor of Northern Ireland,* (Belfast: Her Majesty's Stationery Office, 1969).
458 Fermanagh Civil Rights Association, *Fermanagh Facts*, 17–18.
459 *Ibid.*, 25–8.
460 *Ibid.*, 15.
461 *Ibid.*, 25–8.
462 *Ibid.*, 15–16.
463 *Ibid.*, 31–2.
464 The Campaign for Social Justice in Northern Ireland, *Northern Ireland.*
465 Fermanagh Civil Rights Association, *Fermanagh Facts*, 32–3.
466 The Ulster Special Constabulary http://www.yourirish.com/history/20th-century/ulster-special-constabulary [accessed 24 October 2019].
467 Graham Ellison and Jim Smyth, *The Crowned Harp: Policing Northern Ireland* (London: Pluto Press, 2000), 30.
468 Seamus Heaney, 'The Ministry of Fear', *Opened Ground* (London: Faber and Faber, 1998), 136.
469 Henry Patterson, *Ireland's Violent Frontier: The Border and Anglo-Irish Relations during the Troubles* (London: Palgrave Macmillan, 2013), 15.
470 Kaufmann, 'Demographic change and conflict in Northern Ireland'.
471 *Ibid.*
472 *Fermanagh Herald*, 24 July 2017.
473 Northern Ireland Census 1971, https://www.nisra.gov.uk/statistics/2001-and-earlier-censuses/1971-census [accessed 14 July 2018].
474 D. McKittrick, S. Kelters, B. Feeney, C. Thornton and D. McVea, *Lost Lives: The Stories of the Men, Women and Children Who Died as a Result of the Northern Ireland Troubles* (Edinburgh: Mainstream Publishing Company, 2007), 1556–7.
475 *Ibid.*
476 South-East Fermanagh Foundation, Facebook.com/SEFF.Victims [accessed 5 August 2020].
477 McKittrick et al., *Lost Lives*, 96.
478 *Ibid.*, 111.
479 *Ibid.*, 153.
480 NAUK, WO305/4251, Commander's Diary, 1972.
481 NAUK, FCO87/119, Incidents on the Border.
482 *Ibid.*
483 NAUK, WO305/4251, Commander's Diary, 1972.
484 *Fermanagh Herald,* 11 March 1972.
485 NAUK, WO305/4251, Commander's Diary 1972.
486 *Impartial Reporter*, 27 July 1972.
487 Facebook.com/SEFF.Victims.
488 *Ibid.*
489 Edward Burke, 'Loyalist Mobilisation and Cross-Border Violence in Rural Ulster, 1972–1974', *Terrorism and Political Violence* (2020), DOI: 10.1080/09546553.2020.1745777, 1.
490 *Irish Independent*, 24 February 2010.
491 Duncan Munro McLuckie was convicted of the murder of a woman in 1989. His victim was strangled to death and then stabbed seven times with a meat skewer.
492 *Belfast Telegraph*, 8 October 2009.
493 BBC Northern Ireland News, 20 October 2011.
494 *Ibid.*
495 McKittrick et al., *Lost Lives*, 195.
496 McKittrick et al., *Lost Lives*, 196–7.
497 Facebook.com/SEFF.Victims.
498 McKittrick et al., *Lost Lives*, 244.
499 NAUK, WO305/4251, Commander's Diary (1972).
500 Facebook.com/SEFF.Victims.
501 *Ibid.*
502 NAUK, FCO87/122, Reports on Border Incidents, August 1972.
503 McKittrick et al., *Lost Lives*, 255.

504 Facebook.com/SEFF.Victims.
505 *Belfast Telegraph*, 11 October 2019.
506 NAUK, WO305/4251, Commander's Diary (1972).
507 Facebook.com/SEFF.Victims.
508 NAUK, FCO87/122, Report on the Bullock murders by 2nd/Lt J. Bartholomew.
509 *Ibid.*, WO305/4251, Commander's Diary (1972).
510 *Impartial Reporter*, 28 September 1972.
511 Burke, *An Army of Tribes*, 265.
512 NAUK, WO305/4251, Commander's Diary (1972).
513 NAUK, FCO87/122, Report on the Bullock murders by 2nd/Lt J. Bartholomew.
514 Facebook.com/SEFF.Victims.
515 *Ibid.*
516 *Ibid.*
517 *Irish Press*, 18 November 1972.
518 McKittrick et al., *Lost Lives*, 292–3.
519 *Fermanagh Herald*, 25 November 1972.
520 *Donegal Democrat*, 1 December 1972.
521 McKittrick et al., *Lost Lives*, 355.
522 *Southern Star*, 19 May 1973.
523 *Fermanagh Herald*, 9 June 1973.
524 McKittrick et al., *Lost Lives*, 365.
525 *Fermanagh Herald*, 9 June 1973.
526 McKittrick et al., *Lost Lives*, 388–9.
527 McKittrick et al., *Lost Lives*, 391.
528 NAUK, WO305/4218, Commander's Diary, 7 September 1973.
529 McKittrick et al., *Lost Lives*, 390–1.
530 NAUK, WO305/4218, Commander's Diary, 7 September 1973.
531 On 16 March 1974, three Enniskillen men – former RUC member Norman Kennedy; former soldier John Taylor; and Derek Davis – carried out an arson attack on this house, the property of Michael McTeggart, who lived there with his sister and niece. As the arsonists made their way from the farmhouse, they were apprehended at an army checkpoint and found to be in possession of a Sten machine gun, a Colt pistol and assorted ammunition. They were each sentenced to four years' imprisonment in October 1974. A detective told the court that the attackers believed that the occupants of the house had 'something to do with' the murder of Matthew Lilly. In Justice Barron's report on the Dublin-Monaghan bombings, it is mentioned as an example of co-operation by the British with the Irish Army two months before the bombings occurred. It had been presented by the British Army in two telegrams to the Irish Army, before and after the attack, as a success in preventing an attack on four Cavan villages. This claim does not stand up to scrutiny – if the security forces were aware that an arson attack was planned, why did they allow it to go ahead? It was confirmed that all three occupants were in the house at the time and could have burned to death. (Joint Oireachtas Committee on Justice, Equality, Defence and Women's Rights, *Interim Report on the Report of the Independent Commission of Inquiry into the Dublin and Monaghan Bombings 1974* (2003), Appendix E)
532 McKittrick et al., *Lost Lives*, 395; *Irish Times*, 13 October 1973.
533 *Ibid.*
534 *Ibid.*
535 NAUK, FCO87/2571, Enniskillen Bombing, November 1987.
536 *Ibid.*, WO305/4218, log of 12 October 1973, 3rd Inf. Brigade; *Ibid.*, WO305/4219, Intelligence Summary 44/73, 29 October – 2 November 1973.
537 *Impartial Reporter*, 18 April 1974.
538 *Fermanagh Herald*, 20 April 1974.
539 *Impartial Reporter*, 18 April 1974.
540 Burke, 'Loyalist Mobilisation and Cross-Border Violence in Rural Ulster', 6.
541 *Impartial Reporter*, 18 April 1974.
542 Facebook.com/SEFF.Victims.
543 *Fermanagh Herald*, 11 April 1974.
544 *Ibid.*
545 *Ibid.*, 20 April 1974.
546 McKittrick et al., *Lost Lives*, 438.
547 *Irish Press*, 12 April 1974.
548 *Irish Press*, 467.
549 *Fermanagh Herald*, 7 December 1974.
550 Patrick Mulroe, *Bombs, Bullets and the Border – Policing Ireland's Frontier: Irish Security Policy, 1969–1978* (Dublin: Irish Academic Press, 2017), 157.
551 NAI, Department of Foreign Affairs, 2005/145/2401, UVF assessment by David Donoghue, October 1975.
552 Public Library of US Diplomacy, Cable from American Ambassador to Washington, 31 January 1974 https://www.wikileaks.org/plusd/cables/1974LONDON01455_b.html [accessed 2 January 2017].
553 *Irish Times*, 22 January 1975.
554 *Sligo Champion*, 31 January 1975.
555 *Ibid.*
556 *Ibid.*
557 McKittrick et al., *Lost Lives*, 287.
558 *Fermanagh Herald*, 25 January 1975.
559 *Leitrim Observer*, 4 September 1976.
560 *Fermanagh Herald*, 10 February 1975.
561 McKittrick et al., *Lost Lives*, 515.

562 *Fermanagh Herald*, 10 February 1975.
563 *Ibid.*, 543–4.
564 *Donegal Democrat*, 6 June 1975.
565 *Donegal Democrat*, 6 June 1975; McKittrick et al., *Lost Lives*, 544.
566 *Fermanagh Herald*, 7 June 1975.
567 Facebook.com/SEFF.Victims.
568 *Ibid.*, 22 May 1976.
569 *Strabane Chronicle*, 22 May 1976.
570 McKittrick et al., *Lost Lives*, 663.
571 *Anglo-Celt*, 23 July 1976.
572 *Fermanagh Herald*, 15 January 1977.
573 Facebook.com/SEFF.Victims.
574 *Ibid.*, 708.
575 *Ulster Herald*, 19 March 1977.
576 *Ibid.*, 713; *Donegal Democrat*, 8 April 1977.
577 McKittrick et al., *Lost Lives*, 762.
578 Patterson, *Ireland's Violent Frontier*, 130.
579 *Evening Herald*, 27 June 1978.
580 Facebook.com/SEFF.Victims.
581 Mulroe, *Bombs, Bullets and the Border*, 214.
582 McKittrick et al., *Lost Lives*, 765–6.
583 NAUK, CJ4/3084, Report on shooting of 21 August 1978, 22 August 1978.
584 McKittrick et al., *Lost Lives*, 784; NAUK, CJ4/3084, briefing in advance of PM Thatcher's meeting with Fermanagh widows, July 1980.
585 Facebook.com/SEFF.Victims.
586 McKittrick et al., *Lost Lives*, 784.
587 *Irish Independent*, 7 May 1979.
588 *Fermanagh Herald*, 26 May 1979.
589 *Ibid.*, 28 July 1979.
590 Facebook.com/SEFF.Victims.
591 McKittrick et al., *Lost Lives*, 791.
592 NAUK, CJ4/3084, briefing in advance of PM Thatcher's meeting with Fermanagh widows, July 1980.
593 *Fermanagh Herald*, 20 October 1979.
594 Facebook.com/SEFF.victims.
595 *Fermanagh Herald*, 12 January 1980.
596 *Ibid.*
597 *Ibid.*
598 *Impartial Reporter*, 4 January 1973.
599 Facebook.com/SEFF.Victims.
600 *Anglo-Celt*, 8 February 1980.
601 McKittrick et al., *Lost Lives*, 820.
602 *Fermanagh Herald*, 22 May 1982.
603 NAUK, CJ4/3084, briefing prepared in advance of PM Thatcher's meeting with Fermanagh widows, July 1980.
604 *Irish Press*, 12 February 1980; *Fermanagh Herald*, 23 February 1980.
605 *Fermanagh Herald*, 26 April 1980.
606 Facebook.com/SEFF.Victims.
607 *Anglo-Celt*, 25 April 1980.
608 Paddy Agnew, 'Fear and Loathing in Fermanagh', *Magill* (March 1981).
609 *Fermanagh Herald*, 26 April 1980.
610 *Irish Press*, 18 April 1980.
611 *Irish Independent*, 21 April 1980.
612 NAUK, CJ4/3084, briefing in advance of PM Thatcher's meeting with Fermanagh widows, July 1980.
613 *Anglo-Celt*, 27 August 1971.
614 Facebook.com/SEFF.Victims.
615 RTÉ religious programme, broadcast 28 July 2019, organised by Glencree Centre, testimony of George Latimer.
616 *Irish Examiner*, 25 September 1980.
617 Facebook.com/SEFF.Victims.
618 Republican tribute pamphlet to Séamus McElwain.
619 *Irish Independent*, 27 November 1980.
620 McKittrick et al., *Lost Lives*, 843.
621 *Ibid.*
622 *Irish Examiner*, 6 June 1981.
623 *Irish Independent*, 6 June 1981.
624 *Fermanagh Herald*, 13 June 1981; Facebook.com/SEFF.Victims.
625 McKittrick et al., *Lost Lives*, 867.
626 *Ibid.*, 887.
627 *Evening Herald*, 11 November 1981. The Apprentice Boys of Derry is a Protestant fraternal society with a worldwide membership of over 10,000. It was founded in 1814. Its aim is to commemorate the 1689 siege of Derry, when Catholic King James ll laid siege to the walled city, which was a Protestant stronghold. At the beginning of the siege, the city's apprentice boys shut the gates.
628 *Fermanagh Herald*, 21 November 1981.
629 *Fermanagh Herald*, 28 November 1981.
630 McKittrick et al., *Lost Lives*, 888; *Fermanagh Herald*, 28 November 1981.
631 *Fermanagh Herald*, 30 October 1982.
632 *Ibid.*, 902.
633 *Ibid.*, 13 November 1982.
634 *Ibid.*
635 *Ulster Herald*, 13 November 1982.
636 McKittrick et al., *Lost Lives*, 919.
637 *Ulster Herald*, 26 February 1983.
638 McKittrick et al., *Lost Lives*, 936–7.
639 *Ibid.*, 986.
640 *Fermanagh Herald*, 26 May 1984.
641 *Ibid.*, 998.
642 Facebook.com/SEFF.Victims.

643 McKittrick et al., *Lost Lives*, 1001–2.
644 Palace Barracks Memorial Garden, https://www.palacebarracksmemorialgarden.co.uk/sgt-alistair-slater-mm/ [accessed 10 September 2019].
645 McKittrick et al., *Lost Lives*, 1007.
646 *Fermanagh Herald*, 9 February 1985.
647 *Ibid.*, 9 March 1985.
648 McKittrick et al., *Lost Lives*, 1013.
649 *Fermanagh Herald*, 9 March 1985.
650 *Irish Times*, 4 March 1985; The UFF was a flag of convenience used by the UDA. It was a fictitious organisation and was recognised as such by the British authorities; it ensured that the UDA could remain legal for two decades while sectarian murders were claimed by the UFF. Margaret Urwin, *A State in Denial: British Collaboration with Loyalist Paramilitaries* (Cork: Mercier Press, 2016), 80–5.
651 McKittrick et al., *Lost Lives*, 1015.
652 *Irish Examiner*, 27 September 1986.
653 *An Phoblacht*, 14th March 2002, extracts from a booklet, 'The Untold Truth', published by Fírinne, Lisnaskea, Co. Fermanagh.
654 McKittrick et al., *Lost Lives*, 1015–6; Facebook.com/SEFF.Victims.
655 *Irish Examiner*, 19 June 1975.
656 McKittrick et al., *Lost Lives*, 1020.
657 *Irish Examiner*, 19 June 1985.
658 *Fermanagh Herald*, 22 May 1982.
659 *Irish Press*, 4 February 1986.
660 *Ibid.*
661 *Irish Independent*, 6 February 1986.
662 NAUK, FCO87/2353, memo from G.E. Clarke to Private Secretary, 6 February 1986.
663 McKittrick et al., *Lost Lives*, 1032.
664 *Irish Examiner*, 12 February 1986; *Anglo-Celt*, 13 February 1986.
665 *Fermanagh Herald*, 22 February 1986.
666 McKittrick et al., *Lost Lives*, 1041.
667 *Fermanagh Herald*, 12 July 1986; *Irish Independent*, 10 July 1986.
668 Facebook.com/SEFF.Victims.
669 McKittrick et al., *Lost Lives*, 1059.
670 *Irish Times*, 13 January 1987.
671 *Evening Herald*, 3 April 1987; *Fermanagh Herald*, 11 April 1987.
672 McKittrick et al., *Lost Lives*, 1070.
673 NAUK, CJ4/6872, Note on cross-border security, Enniskillen bombing, 9 November 1987.
674 *Donegal Democrat*, 24 July 1987.
675 NAUK, CJ4/6872, Note on cross-border security, Enniskillen bombing, 9 November 1987.
676 McKittrick et al., *Lost Lives*, 1087.
677 Denzil McDaniel, *Enniskillen: The Remembrance Sunday Bombing* (Dublin: Wolfhound Press, 1997), 55–6.
678 *Ibid.*, 51–2.
679 *Ibid.*, 52–4.
680 *Ibid.*, 49–51.
681 *Ibid.*, 56–8.
682 *Ibid.*, 59–60.
683 *Ibid.*, 58–9.
684 *Ibid.*, 47–9.
685 *Ibid.*, 159–61.
686 McKittrick et al., *Lost Lives*, 1120–1.
687 *Ibid.*, 1124–5.
688 *Ulster Herald*, 16 April 1988.
689 *Irish Examiner*, 6 August 1988.
690 McKittrick et al., *Lost Lives*, 1137–8.
691 McKittrick et al., *Lost Lives*, 1152.
692 *Irish Examiner*, 29 October 1988.
693 *Ibid.*, 31 October 1988.
694 *Ibid.*
695 Interview with former British soldier who served in Fermanagh, 19 March 2019.
696 McKittrick et al., *Lost Lives*, 1187.
697 *Fermanagh Herald*, 23 December 1989.
698 Interview with former British soldier who served in Fermanagh, 19 March 2019.
699 *Fermanagh Herald*, 30 December 1989.
700 *Irish Examiner*, 14 December 1989.
701 *Irish Independent*, 23 January 1991.
702 McKittrick et al., *Lost Lives*, 1225.
703 *Ibid.*
704 *Fermanagh Herald*, 25 May 1991.
705 Facebook.com/SEFF.Victims.
706 McKittrick et al., *Lost Lives*, 1236.
707 *Ibid.*, 1280.
708 McKittrick et al., *Lost Lives*, 1302; *Fermanagh Herald*, 21 November 1992.
709 Facebook.com/SEFF.Victims.
710 *Fermanagh Herald*, 21 May 1977.
711 *Evening Herald*, 13 May 1977.
712 *Ibid.*, 13 May 1977.
713 *Fermanagh Herald*, 21 May 1977.
714 *Evening Herald*, 13 May 1977.
715 Patterson, *Ireland's Violent* Frontier, 129.
716 Facebook.com/SEFF.Victims.
717 Patterson, *Ireland's Violent Frontier*, 130.
718 *Donegal Democrat*, 25 May 1979.
719 McKittrick et al., *Lost Lives*, 785.
720 *Fermanagh Herald*, 26 May 1979.
721 Facebook.com/SEFF.Victims.
722 *Irish Press*, 14 March 1984.
723 McKittrick et al., *Lost Lives*, 979–80.

724 *Ibid.*
725 Facebook.com/SEFF.Victims.
726 Michael Harding, *Staring at Lakes* (Dublin: Hachette Books Ireland, 2013), 59–60.
727 Patterns of Evidence VII: Lessons in Murder – IRA School murders www.onthisdaypira.blogspot.com/2018/10/patterns-of-evidence-vii-lessons-in.html.
728 *Irish Times*, 16 October 1985.
729 Conversations with nationalists, 14 September 2018.
730 Harding, *Staring at Lakes*, 60.
731 Harding, *Staring at Lakes*, 61.
732 *Ibid.*, 60–4.
733 BBC News, 27 June 2019.
734 *Irish Press*, 13 July 1979.
735 Ciarán De Baróid, *Ballymurphy and the Irish War* (London: Pluto Press, 1990), 216–17.
736 *Ibid.*, 217.
737 McKittrick et al., *Lost Lives*, 790.
738 Chris Ryder, *The Ulster Defence Regiment: An Instrument of Peace?* (London: Methuen Publishing Ltd, 1991), 119.
739 *Sunday Tribune*, 28 October 2007.
740 McDaniel, *Enniskillen*, 9–10.
741 *Ibid.*
742 *Ibid.*
743 *Ibid.*, 17.
744 McKittrick et al., *Lost Lives*, 1097.
745 *Ibid.*
746 McDaniel, *Enniskillen*, 27.
747 *Ibid.*
748 McKittrick et al., *Lost Lives*, 1097.
749 McDaniel, *Enniskillen*, 39.
750 *Ibid.*, 63–4.
751 *Ibid.*, 51.
752 *Ibid.*, 104–7.
753 *Ibid.*
754 *Ibid.*, 104–6.
755 McDaniel, *Enniskillen*, 106–7.
756 *Ibid.*, 107.
757 *Impartial Reporter*, 30 November 2017.
758 NAUK, CJ4/6872, Enniskillen bombing, 9 November 1987.
759 Associated Press news archive, 11 November 1987, https://apnews.com/61973ff-2d09ef7925a981f7ee2ea991f [accessed 12 December 2018].
760 NAUK, FCO87/2572, Bombing at Enniskillen, notes of a meeting between PM Thatcher with James Molyneaux and Ken Maginnis, 9 November 1987.
761 *Ibid.*
762 *Irish Times*, 2 November 1987.
763 NAUK, CJ4/6872, Enniskillen bombing, 9 November 1987.
764 An Sionnach Fionn https://ansionnachfionn.com/2017/11/12the-remembrance-day-or-enniskillen-bombing [accessed 12 December 2018].
765 *Irish Times*, 3 November 1987.
766 *Ibid.*
767 An Sionnach Fionn
768 BBC www.bbc.co.uk/history/events/enniskillen_bombing [accessed 12 December 2018]
769 Ó Beacháin, *From Partition to Brexit*, 206–7.
770 *Ibid.*, 207.
771 Thomas Leahy, *The Intelligence War against the IRA* (Cambridge: Cambridge University Press, 2020).
772 Facebook.com/SEFF.Victims.
773 *Donegal Democrat*, 1 April 1988.
774 Facebook.com/SEFF.Victims.
775 Facebook.com/SEFF.Victims.
776 *Donegal Democrat*, 28 October 1988.
777 *Irish Times*, 17 January 1989.
778 *Ibid.*, 18 January 1989.
779 *Irish Times*, 20 January 1989.
780 *Irish Times*, 25 January 1989.
781 *Ibid.*, 3 August 2019.
782 *Ibid.*, 25 January 1989.
783 *Ibid.*, 6 August 1988.
784 *Ibid.*, January 1989.
785 *Sunday Independent*, 24 July 1994.
786 *Ibid.*
787 *Irish Press*, 21 July 1994.
788 *Irish Times*, 9 February 2004. Freddy Scappaticci was a senior republican and alleged British agent known as 'Stakeknife'.
789 *Irish Times*, 11 June 2015.
790 PRONI, CRCT/3/2/2/159A, Hathaway, Byrne, Chestnut and Snowball, Statement of Mrs Mary Ann Murray.
791 MacDonald, Brian, *The Pitchfork Murders: Uncovering the Cover-up* (Derry: Louis Leonard Sinn Féin Cumann, 2012), 13.
792 PRONI, CRCT/3/2/159A, Hathaway, Byrne, Chestnut and Snowball, Inquest report.
793 PRONI, CRCT/3/2/159A, Hathaway, Byrne, Chestnut and Snowball, Inquest report.
794 PRONI, Statement of Oliver Melarkey.
795 PRONI, Statement of Dympna Sheridan (Brady).
796 Just a month after the murders of

Michael Naan and Andrew Murray, Captain Rees colluded with a local leading UDA member and Fermanagh District Councillor, Jack Leahy, in blowing up Aghalane Bridge. Rees was introduced to Leahy by a local RUC chief inspector shortly after the Bullocks were killed. Rees met with Leahy in his pub, the Wyvern Inn, Lisnaskea; Leahy requested him to ensure his soldiers were kept outside the area of the bridge on 21 November. The request was complied with, and the bridge was blown up. However, as it was not badly damaged, Rees ordered an ATO to carry out a further explosion on the pretext that there were unstable explosives on the bridge. The ATO reluctantly obeyed his order and the central arch of the bridge collapsed. Burke, 'Loyalist Mobilisation and Cross-Border Violence in Rural Ulster', 11.

797 Draft HET RSR into the murders of Michael Naan and Andrew Murray.

798 *Ibid.*

799 Martin Dillon, *The Dirty War* (New York: Routledge, 1990), 120.

800 *Ibid.*

801 *Irish Times*, 18 December 1978.

802 Draft HET RSR into the murders of Michael Naan and Andrew Murray.

803 The HET report is contradictory as to whether or not the whistle-blower made a statement. At one point it is noted that he made a statement but refused to sign it, and at another point it is noted that he refused to make a statement.

804 Burke, *An Army of Tribes*, 233.

805 The 6th Earl of Erne served as Lord Lieutenant of Fermanagh from 1987 to 2012.

806 Burke, *An Army of Tribes*, 233.

807 PRONI, CRCT/3/2/2159A, Hathaway, Byrne, Chestnut and Snowball, statement of Major John Jeremy Mackenzie.

808 Brooke's son, Alan, was a British officer who had attended Harrow public school with Andrew Snowball.

809 *Irish Times*, 9 November 1972.

810 Burke, *An Army of Tribes*, 252–3.

811 NAUK, WO305/4251 16th/5th Royal Lancers Commander's Diary, 1972.

812 MacDonald, *The Pitchfork Murders*, 24.

813 Burke, *An Army of Tribes*, 294.

814 *Ibid.*, 294–5.

815 *Ibid.*, 294.

816 *Ibid.*, 312.

817 *Ibid.*, 87.

818 *Ibid.*, 310.

819 Burke, *An Army of Tribes*, 294; 232.

820 The Argyll and Sutherland Highlanders had served in Aden in the 1960s, and this was how they treated the locals.

821 Burke, *An Army of Tribes*, 308.

822 PRONI, CRCT/3/2/2159A, statement of Private John Mcguire.

823 *Ibid.*

824 *Ibid.*

825 Burke, *An Army of Tribes*, 307.

826 A shooting brake was designed to take gentlemen on a hunt with their firearms and dogs – a vehicle generally used by the aristocracy. It was an unusual term for an ordinary soldier to use and would be more likely to be used by officers.

827 Draft HET RSR into the murders of Michael Naan and Andrew Murray.

828 Burke, *An Army of Tribes*, 307.

829 *Ibid.*, 298.

830 PRONI, CRCT/3/2/2159A, Hathaway, Byrne, Chestnut and Snowball, statement of Sergeant Hathaway.

831 Burke, *An Army of Tribes*, 296.

832 *Ibid.*, 299.

833 Major Albert Liddle was the intelligence officer of the UDR in Fermanagh and a member of Clones Masonic Lodge.

834 Draft HET RSR into the murders of Michael Naan and Andrew Murray.

835 *Ibid.*

836 O Group meeting was an intelligence meeting at which army officers, the UDR and police were present.

837 NAUK, FCO87/121, Incidents on the border, copy of a Garda report, 23 October 1972.

838 *Ibid.*

839 *Ibid.*

840 *Ibid.*

841 Burke, *An Army of Tribes*, 297.

842 *The Glasgow Herald*, 16 January 1981; Burke, *An Army of Tribes*, 231.

843 *Ibid.*

844 McKittrick et al., *Lost Lives*, 287.

845 *Glasgow Herald*, 16 January 1981.

846 Fr Joe McVeigh, *The Murder of Michael Leonard* (2019).

847 St Angelo was at least 20 miles from where the killing of Michael Leonard took place. It was situated about 5 miles from Enniskillen and was the base for the British Army and the UDR in Fermanagh.

848 NAUK, WO305/4213, log of 17 May 1973.

849 Reliability of providers of information

were graded alphabetically and numerically.
850 *Ibid.*
851 *Ibid.*
852 NAUK, FCO/248, Telegram from Sir Arthur Galsworthy to FCO, 27 July 1973.
853 NAUK, FCO/248, Telegram from Sir Arthur Galsworthy to FCO, 27 July 1973.
854 *Ibid.*, memo and report from Wendy Clements, NIO to Adrian Hill, FCO, RID, 6 August 1973.
855 *Ibid.*
856 *Ibid.*
Ibid.
857 *Ibid.*
858 McVeigh, *The Murder of Michael Leonard.*
859 *Ibid.*; *Fermanagh Herald*, 3 November 1973.
860 *Fermanagh Herald*, 3 November 1973; McVeigh, *The Murder of Michael* Leonard.
861 *Fermanagh Herald*, 3 November 1973; McVeigh, *The Murder of Michael* Leonard.
862 *Fermanagh Herald*, 3 November 1973; McVeigh, *The Murder of Michael Leonard.*
863 McVeigh, *The Murder of Michael Leonard.*
864 NAUK, CJ4/970, Letter to CJ MacMahon, Royal Courts of Justice from P Coulson, NIO, 21 April 1975.
865 *Ibid.*
866 *Ibid.*
867 Fr Denis Faul and Fr Raymond Murray, *Angela D'Arcy: Irish Catholic Girl Shot Dead by a British Soldier in Enniskillen, 25 November 1981* (1983).
868 *Ibid.*
869 *Ibid.*
870 *Irish Times*, 27 November 1981.
871 Faul and Murray, *Angela D'Arcy.*
872 *Irish Times*, 25, 26 June 1982.
873 *Ibid.*
874 Faul and Murray, *Angela D'Arcy.*
875 *Irish Times*, 14 June 1984.
876 Raymond Murray, *The SAS in Ireland* (Cork: Mercier Press, 2004), 320–8.
877 *Fermanagh Herald*, 29 March 1986
878 *Ibid.*
879 *Ibid.*
880 *Ibid.*
881 *Fermanagh Herald*, 29 March 1986.
882 Murray, *The SAS in Ireland*, 327.
883 *Fermanagh Herald*, 29 March 1986.
884 Murray, *The SAS in Ireland*, 320–8.
885 *Ibid.*, 365.
886 *Ibid.*, 368–9.
887 Mark Urban, *Big Boys' Rules: The Secret Struggle against the IRA* (London: Faber and Faber, 1992), 218–19.
888 *Amnesty International Report 1994* (London: Amnesty International Publications, 1994).
889 *Irish Press*, 13 January 1993.
890 *Fermanagh Herald*, 23 January 1993.
891 *Irish Press*, 13 January 1993.
892 Urban, *Big Boys' Rules*, 219.
893 Burke, 'Loyalist Mobilisation and Cross-Border Violence in Rural Ulster', 5.
894 NAUK, CJ4/1069, memo from T.C. Barker to Under-secretary of State for Northern Ireland, 18 May 1976.
895 *Irish Times*, 4 November 1973.
896 *Ibid.*
897 Joint Oireachtas Committee on Justice, Equality, Defence and Women's Rights, *Interim Report on the Report of the Independent Commission of Inquiry into the Dublin Bombings of December 1972 and January 1973* (2004), 140.
898 *Impartial Reporter*, 4 October 1973.
899 *Ibid.*, 6 December 1973.
900 NAUK, WO305/4218, report on subversives.
901 HET RSR into the murder of Louis Leonard.
902 *Impartial Reporter*, 16 December 1972.
903 *Ibid.*
904 *Fermanagh Herald*, 23 December 1972.
905 *Ibid.*
906 Burke, 'Loyalist Mobilisation and Cross-Border Violence in Rural Ulster', 17.
907 *Impartial Reporter*, 21 December 1972.
908 HET RSR into the murder of Louis Leonard.
909 *Ibid.*
910 *Ibid.*
911 *Impartial Reporter*, 4 January 1973.
912 HET RSR into the murder of Louis Leonard.
913 *Ibid.*
914 It is interesting to note that the cars used in the Dublin bombings of 1 December 1972 were hired in Belfast – the Hillman Avenger that exploded outside Liberty Hall, like the Ford Cortina used in the murder of Louis Leonard, was also hired from Avis at Aldergrove Airport; the Ford Escort that exploded in Sackville Place, killing two bus employees, was hired from Moley's Car Hire; and a Ford Cortina, which was never found, was hired from Hertz at Aldergrove

Airport.
915 *Impartial Reporter*, 24 May 1973.
916 HET RSR into the murder of Louis Leonard.
917 *Ibid.*
918 *Ibid.*
919 *Fermanagh Herald*, 23 December 1972.
920 *Irish News*, 1 June 1973.
921 Joint Oireachtas Committee on Justice, Equality, Defence and Women's Rights, *Interim Report on the Report of the Independent Commission of Inquiry into the Dublin Bombings of December 1972 and January 1973* (2004), 117.
922 NAUK, WO305/ 4218, October 1973.
923 Burke, 'Loyalist Mobilisation and Cross-Border Violence in Rural Ulster'; NAUK, WO305/4212, April 1973, Minutes of meeting of the Western Security Committee, 29 March 1973.
924 NAUK, WO305/4212, HQ 3 Infantry Brigade Int. Summary No. 14/73.
925 NAUK, FCO87/2571, list of deaths Fermanagh/south Tyrone 1971–1987, November 1987.
926 *Ibid.*
927 HET RSR concerning the murder of James Edward Murphy.
928 *Fermanagh* Herald, 27 April 1974.
929 Notes of meeting with HET, 5 April 2011.
930 HET RSR concerning the murder of James Edward Murphy.
931 *Fermanagh Herald*, 25 April 1974.
932 HET RSR concerning the murder of James Edward Murphy.
933 *Ibid.*
934 *Fermanagh Herald*, 4 May 1974.
935 HET RSR concerning the murder of James Edward Murphy.
936 *Ibid.*
937 *Ibid.*
938 *Irish Times*, 30 April 1974.
939 *Ibid.*
940 www.papertrail.pro/patsy-kelly-new-information-uncovered [accessed 14 January 2019]
941 *Ibid.*
942 *Fermanagh Herald*, 3 August 1974.
943 *Irish Times*, 31 July 1974.
944 *Fermanagh Herald*, 8 August 1974.
945 *Ulster Herald*, 17 August 1974.
946 *Fermanagh Herald*, 17 August 1974.
947 *Ibid.*
948 *Ulster Herald*, 17 August 1974.
949 *Ibid.*
950 *Ibid.*, 22 February 1975.
951 *Ibid.*
952 Judgment in The High Court of Justice in Northern Ireland, Queen's Bench Division (Judicial Review), In the matter of an application by Teresa Kelly for Judicial Review, Ref. KERC5130 (November 2004).
953 *Irish Independent*, 30 July 2003.
954 Conversation with Pat Fahy, Kelly family solicitor, 5 September 2012.
955 www.papertrail.pro/patsy-kelly-new-information-uncovered
956 In the matter of an application by Teresa Kelly for Judicial Review, Ref. KERC5130.
957 *Ibid.*
958 *Irish Times*, 30 July 2003.
959 In the matter of an application by Teresa Kelly for Judicial Review, Ref. KERC5130.
960 *Ibid.*
961 *Irish Times*, 7 April 2005.
962 *Irish Republican News*, 11 April 2005.
963 *An Phoblacht*, 28 April 2005.
964 www.papertrail.pro/patsy-kelly-new-information-uncovered
965 *Ibid.*
966 *Ibid.*
967 *Fermanagh Herald*, 6 December 1975.
968 *Fermanagh Herald*, 31 January 1976; *Fermanagh News*, 29 January 1976.
969 *Impartial Reporter*, 3 July 1975.
970 *Fermanagh Herald*, 5 July 1975.
971 *Impartial Reporter*, 21 August 1975.
972 *Fermanagh Herald*, 29 November 1975.
973 *Ibid.*, 6 December 1975.
974 McKittrick et al., *Lost Lives*, 544.
975 *Fermanagh Herald*, 11 May 1974.
976 *Impartial Reporter*, 15 June 1976.
977 Burke, *An Army of Tribes*, 271.
978 *Ibid.*
979 *Ibid.*
980 Joint Oireachtas Committee on Justice, Equality, Defence and Women's Rights, *Interim Report on the Report of the Independent Commission of Inquiry into the Dublin Bombings of December 1972 and January 1973* (2004), 136.
981 Report of Lt. Col Nigel Wylde, British Army (retired), 'Bombings in Republic of Ireland 1972–76' (May 2002);
982 Joint Oireachtas Committee on Justice, Equality, Defence and Women's Rights, *Interim Report on the Report of the Independent Commission of Inquiry into the Dublin Bombings of December 1972 and January 1973* (2004), 116.
983 *Fermanagh Herald*, 6 January 1973.

984 *The Anglo-Celt*, 5 January 1973.
985 *Fermanagh Herald*, 6 January 1973.
986 Joint Oireachtas Committee on Justice, Equality, Defence and Women's Rights, *Interim Report on the Report of the Independent Commission of Inquiry into the Dublin Bombings of December 1972 and January 1973* (2004), 119.
987 *Ibid.*, 120.
988 *Irish Press*, 10 January 1973.
989 Report of Lt. Col Nigel Wylde.
990 Joint Oireachtas Committee on Justice, Equality, Defence and Women's Rights, *Interim Report on the Report of the Independent Commission of Inquiry into the Dublin Bombings of December 1972 and January 1973* (2004), 116.
991 *Ibid.*, 125.
992 *Ibid.*, 122.
993 *Ibid.*, 125.
994 Joint Oireachtas Committee on Justice, Equality, Defence and Women's Rights, *Interim Report on the Report of the Independent Commission of Inquiry into the Dublin Bombings of December 1972 and January 1973* (2004), 116.
995 Burke, 'Loyalist Mobilisation and Cross-Border Violence in Rural Ulster', 8.
996 *Ibid.*
997 *Ibid.*, 4.
998 Mark McGovern, *Counterinsurgency and Collusion in Northern Ireland* (London: Pluto Press, 2019), 130–1.
999 Burke, 'Loyalist Mobilisation and Cross-Border Violence in Rural Ulster', 4.
1000 *Ibid.*, 5.
1001 *Ibid.*
1002 Joint Oireachtas Committee on Justice, Equality, Defence and Women's Rights, *Interim Report on the Report of the Independent Commission of Inquiry into the Dublin Bombings of December 1972 and January 1973* (2004).
1003 *Ibid.*
1004 Burke, 'Loyalist Mobilisation and Cross-Border Violence in Rural Ulster', 14.
1005 Conversation with a member of the Fermanagh Protestant community, 8 April 2019.
1006 Burke, *An Army of Tribes*, 258.
1007 *Ibid.*
1008 White, 'Provisional IRA Attacks on the UDR in Fermanagh and South Tyrone', 333.
1009 Patterson, *Ireland's Violent Frontier*, 41.
1010 Barzilay, David, *British Army in Ulster*, Vol 4 (Belfast: Century Books, 1981), 154.
1011 *Ibid.*
1012 Leahy, *The Intelligence War against the IRA*, 176.
1013 *Irish Times*, 9 November 1972. It was probably an exaggeration to state that 'many families' were evacuating from farmsteads on the border. It is believed, at that time, that only about half-a-dozen families had moved – from around Garrison, Newtownbutler and Roslea.
1014 *Ibid.*
1015 NAUK, CJ4/3084, Notes of a meeting between Michael Alison, Minister of State with Lord Brookeborough, 3 August 1979.
1016 NAUK, CJ4/3084, Notes of a meeting between Michael Alison, Minister of State with Lord Brookeborough, 3 August 1979.
1017 NAUK, CJ4/3084, Internal briefing in advance of Humphrey Atkins' visit to Fermanagh, February 1980.
1018 *Ibid.*
1019 NAUK, CJ4/3084, Report on security in County Fermanagh by Captain Armstrong, February 1980
1020 *Ibid.*
1021 *Ibid.*
1022 *Ibid.*
1023 *Ibid.*
1024 The Special Patrol Group (SPG) was re-named the Divisional Mobile Support Unit (DMSU) in 1980 after two of its members were charged with murder.
1025 NAUK, CJ4/3084, Report of a meeting between NIO officials and senior RUC officers on 12 March 1980.
1026 *Ibid.*
1027 *Ibid.*
1028 *Ibid.*
1029 *Ibid.*, notes of a meeting at Stormont Castle on 1 May 1980.
1030 *Ibid.*
1031 NAUK, PREM 19/501, telegram from Rev. Ian Paisley to Prime Minister Margaret Thatcher, 10 June 1980.
1032 NAUK, PREM 19/501, Minutes of meeting between Secretary of State, Humphrey Atkins with four south Fermanagh widows at Stormont Castle, 13 June 1980.
1033 The IRA made two attempts on Roy Kells's life and his shop was bombed 10 times during the conflict. Patterson, *Ireland's Violent Frontier*, 175.
1034 NAUK, CJ4/3084, Memo from Mike Hopkins to Nick Sanders, 20 June 1980.
1035 NAUK, PREM19/501, Memo from Mike Hopkins, NIO to Nick Sanders, 10 Downing Street, 18 June 1980. Trooping the Colour is a ceremony performed by regiments

of the British and Commonwealth armies. Since 1748, it has marked the official birthday of the British sovereign.

1036 Patterson, *Ireland's Violent Frontier*, 133.

1037 *Ibid.*, 133–4.

1038 NAUK, CJ4/3084, Reply to Lady Langham from Alec Ireland, NIO, June 1980.

1039 *Ibid.*, report on Protestant rally at Newtownbutler, 23 June 1980.

1040 *Irish Times*, 24 June 1980.

1041 NAUK, PREM19/501, Memo from Mike Hopkins, NIO to Michael Alexander, 10 Downing Street, 28 July 1980.

1042 *Ibid.*

1043 *Ibid.*

1044 *Ibid.*

1045 *Irish Times*, 8 July 1980.

1046 NAUK, PREM19/501, memo on cross-border security from M.V. Hopkins to Michael Alexander, 28 July 1980.

1047 *Fermanagh Herald*, 22 February 1986.

1048 *Irish Times*, 10 December 1985.

1049 Patterson, *Ireland's Violent Frontier*, 176.

1050 NAUK, CJ4/3309, internal memo from D.E.S. Blatherwick, 1 April 1981.

1051 *Ibid.*

1052 NAUK, CJ4/3309, Fermanagh and south Tyrone by-election 1981.

1053 NAUK, CJ4/3309, Memo from D.E.S. Blatherwick, 17 April 1981

1054 In April 1967, Prime Minister Terence O'Neill fired Harry West, the Minister for Agriculture and MP for Enniskillen, over a land deal that O'Neill claimed broke the ministerial code he had introduced to govern ministers' business interests. Henry Patterson, 'Unionism 1921–72' in Alvin Jackson (ed.) *The Oxford Handbook of Modern Irish History* (Oxford: Oxford University Press, 2014), 692–710.

1055 NAUK, CJ4/3309, report on by-election.

1056 *Ibid.*, report on by-election.

1057 *Ibid.*

1058 *Irish Times*, 23 February 1974.

1059 *Ibid.*, 12 January 1972.

1060 *Ibid.*, 8 June 1972.

1061 *Ibid.*, 21 June 1972.

1062 *Ibid.*

1063 *Ibid.*, 20 October 1972.

1064 *Ibid.*, 3 November 1972.

1065 *Ibid.*, 8 November 1972.

1066 *Ibid.*, 31 October 1973.

1067 *Ibid.*, February 1974.

1068 *Impartial Reporter*, 23 January 1974.

1069 *Ibid.*, 30 January 1974.

1070 *Ibid.*, 28 August 1992.

1071 *Impartial Reporter*, 13 March 1972.

1072 Ryder, *The Ulster Defence Regiment*, 55.

1073 *Impartial Reporter*, 27 July 1972.

1074 *Ibid.*

1075 *Fermanagh Herald*, 28 December 1974

1076 *Ibid.*

1077 Patterson, *Ireland's Violent Frontier*, 130.

1078 BBC News, 11 January 2010.

1079 *Ibid.*

1080 *Fermanagh Herald*, 8 April 1971.

1081 *Ibid.*

1082 Urwin, *A State in Denial*, 80–5.

1083 *Fermanagh Herald*, 27 October 1973.

1084 *Ibid.*, 19 January 1974.

1085 *Fermanagh Herald*, 27 July 1974.

1086 Interview: Francis Smyth with PFC, 19 January 2012.

1087 *Ibid.*

1088 Conversation with Francis Smyth, 1 June 2020.

1089 *Ibid.*

1090 *Fermanagh Herald*, 10 August 1974.

1091 Conversation with Francis Smyth, 1 June 2020.

1092 *Irish Times*, 17 August 1974.

1093 *Ibid.*, 15 August 1974.

1094 *Irish Times*, 9 and 12 August 1974.

1095 *Irish Examiner*, 14 March 1973.

1096 *Irish Independent*, 14 April 1973.

1097 *Ibid.*, 15 February 1975.

1098 *Fermanagh Herald*, 28 October 1974.

1099 *Ibid.*

1100 *Ibid.*, 29 November 1975.

1101 Owen Carron was elected MP for Fermanagh and South Tyrone in the wake of death of Bobby Sands.

1102 *Irish Times*, 26 August 1981.

1103 Andy Pollak is the founding director of the Centre for Cross Border Studies, with offices in Armagh and Dublin. Before that, he was religious affairs correspondent, education correspondent and assistant news editor with the *Irish Times* from 1986 to 1999.

1104 *Irish Times*, 9 April 1983.

1105 *Ulster Herald*, 15 February 1986.

1106 Andrew Bell-Fialkoff, 'A Brief History of Ethnic Cleansing', *Foreign Affairs* (Summer 1993).

1107 Matthew Lewis and Shaun McDaid,

'Bosnia on the Border? Republican Violence in Northern Ireland during the 1920s and 1970s', *Terrorism and Political Violence*, 29, 4 (2017), 635–55, DOI: 10.1080/0946553.2015.1043429.

1108 *Ibid.*

1109 *Ibid.*

1110 *Ibid.*

1111 Gerard Toal and Carl T. Dahlman, *Bosnia Remade: Ethnic Cleansing and Its Reversal* (New York: Oxford University Press, 2011), 3.

1112 Patterson, *Ireland's Violent Frontier*, 197.

1113 *Irish Times*, 29 August 1995.

1114 *Ibid.*, 2 September 1995.

1115 *Ibid.*, 15 November 1996.

1116 Patterson, *Ireland's Violent Frontier*, 194.

1117 *Irish Times*, 6 May 1995.

1118 *Impartial Reporter*, 5 August 1976.

1119 *Irish Times*, 19 June 1980.

1120 Alan Henry Brooke, 3rd Viscount Brookeborough, was commissioned into the 17th/21st Lancers in 1970 and later served in the UDR and Royal Irish Regiment. Since 2012, he has been the serving Lord Lieutenant of Fermanagh.

1121 McKay, *Northern Protestants*, 224.

1122 NAUK, FCO87/1741, report on a visit to Northern Ireland by Brigadier John Oborne, Defence Attaché at the British Embassy, Dublin, 18–20 September 1984.

1123 NAUK, FCO87/2353, Amendments to draft essay on UDR, February 1986

1124 Lewis and McDaid, 'Bosnia on the Border?'

1125 *Irish Times*, 15 October 1985.

1126 *Ibid.*, 16 October 1985.

1127 Bob Rowthorn and Naomi Wayne, *Northern Ireland: The Political Economy of Conflict* (Cambridge: Polity Press, 1988).

1128 Morland, *Demographic Engineering*.

1129 K.J. Rankin, 'The Creation and Consolidation of the Irish Border', Institute for British-Irish Studies, University College Dublin (2005).

1130 *Ibid.*

1131 *Irish Times*, 11 February 2019.

1132 NAUK, CJ4/4249, Telegram from British Ambassador to Commonwealth Relations Office (CRO), December 1956.

1133 NAUK, CJ4/810, Speaking note prepared by C.E. Goddart for Secretary of State, Merlyn Rees, 4 July 1974.

1134 *Ibid.*

1135 *Irish Times*, 1 September 2018.

1136 NAUK, CJ4/810, Speaking note prepared by C.E. Goddart for Secretary of State, Merlyn Rees, 4 July 1974.

1137 NAUK, FCO87/371, Paper on Border security, J.F. Halliday, 16 May 1974.

1138 *Evening Herald*, 13–19 March 1973.

1139 NAUK, FCO87/28, Paper on cross-border activities in the aftermath of Operation Motorman, August 1972.

1140 NAUK, FCO87/48 Arrests of Wyman & Crinnion, Telegram from British Ambassador to FCO, 21 December 1972; NAI 2006/161/85 Crinnion & Wyman.

1141 NAUK, FCO87/247, Wyman Dossier, 31 July – 2 November 1972.

1142 NAUK, FCO87/121, Telegram from Douglas-Home to British Ambassador, 5 December 1972.

1143 Joint Oireachtas Committee on Justice, Equality, Defence and Women's Rights, *Interim Report on the Report of the Independent Commission of Inquiry into the Dublin Bombings of December 1972 and January 1973* (2004).

1144 Margaret Urwin and Niall Meehan, 'The 1972–3 Dublin bombings: The "third man" in the case of British agent John Wyman and Garda Sergeant Patrick Crinnion', *History Ireland*, 26, 3 (May–June 2018).

1145 NAUK, FCO87/48, Telegram to FCO from British Ambassador, 21 December 1972.

1146 NAUK, FCO87/130, Co-operation between the Governments of Republic of Ireland and Northern Ireland on the control of explosives and weapons, 1972.

1147 *Ibid.*

1148 *Ibid.*

1149 NAUK, FCO87/130, Telegram from British Ambassador John Peck to FCO, 30 May 1972.

1150 *Ibid.*

1151 *Ibid.*, FCO87/248, Letter from W.K.K. White, FCO to Allan Rowley, Stormont Castle, 3 May 1973.

1152 *Ibid.*, FCO87/247, Telegram from Arthur Galsworthy to FCO and UK Rep, Belfast, 14 April 1973.

1153 *Ibid.*

1154 NAUK, FCO87/248, Report from Arthur Galsworthy, British Ambassador to WKK White, 26 April 1973.

1155 *Ibid.*

1156 *Ibid.*

1157 NAUK, FCO87/248, Report from

Arthur Galsworthy, British Ambassador to W.K.K. White, 26 April 1973.

1158 *Ibid.*

1159 *Ibid.*

1160 *Ibid.*

1161 *Ibid.*

1162 NAUK, FCO87/293, Record of meeting of officials at Iveagh House, 2 May 1974.

1163 NAUK, CJ4/826, Notes of a meeting at Army Headquarters Northern Ireland, 18 April 1974.

1164 NAUK, FCO87/293, Notes of a meeting in NIO on 3 May 1974, 6 May 1974.

1165 NAUK, FCO87/293 Paper on co-operation between RUC and Gardaí prepared by S.S. Bampton, 13 May 1974.

1166 Joint Oireachtas Committee on Justice, Equality, Defence and Women's Rights, *Interim Report on the Report of the Independent Commission of Inquiry into the Dublin and Monaghan Bombings 1974* (2003).

1167 NAUK, FCO87/350, Telegram to FCO from Sir Arthur Galsworthy, 20 May 1974.

1168 NAUK, FCO87/294, Notes of meeting held at Baldonnel Aerodrome, 18 September 1974.

1169 NAUK, FCO87/295, Memo from J.B. Bourn, NIO to G.W. Harding, RID, FCO, 6 December 1974.

1170 NAUK, FCO87/484, Note on conversations at RUC HQ by G.W. Harding, 9 April 1975.

1171 NAUK, CJ4/833, Memo to Douglas Janes from Bill Webster, 4 September 1975.

1172 NAUK, CJ4/833, Staff Paper, 27 November 1975.

1173 NAUK, PREM16/959, Letter from Prime Minister Harold Wilson to Taoiseach Liam Cosgrave, 6 January 1976.

1174 The Joint Oireachtas Committee hearings were held in the aftermath of the publication of each of four reports of Justice Henry Barron in the early 2000s. The hearings referred to here were held in the wake of the publication of the report of the Dublin/Monaghan bombings.

1175 Joint Oireachtas Committee hearings on the Barron report, 28 January 2004.

1176 NAUK, CJ4/1753, telegram to FCO from British Ambassador, 11 August 1977.

1177 NAUK, FCO87/423, Memo from J.D.W. Janes, NIO to G.W. Harding, FCO, 29 December 1975 re meeting between Janes and Mr Corcoran, Chargé d'Affaires at the Irish Embassy on 23 December 1975.

1178 Anne Cadwallader, *Lethal Allies: British Collusion in Ireland* (Cork: Mercier Press, 2013).

1179 The shoot-to-kill cases include: the three unarmed IRA members at an RUC checkpoint in Lurgan, Co. Armagh on 11 November 1982; the killing of Michael Tighe and the wounding of Martin McAuley at an IRA arms cache on a farm near Lurgan on 24 November 1982; and the killing of two INLA members at a checkpoint on 12 December 1982. When a police constable was acquitted despite admitting that he had been instructed to lie about the circumstances of the INLA shootings, there was a public outcry. This outcry led Chief Constable Sir John Hermon to appoint John Stalker, the Deputy Chief Constable of Greater Manchester Police, to investigate the cases.

1180 This refers to the arrest of Jimmy McGovern by RUC Special Branch in the early hours of 27 September 1982 at his cousin's house in Belcoo, County Fermanagh – allegedly on the basis of intelligence passed to them by the Gardaí that he was involved in terrorism. He was arrested on the day he was due to testify in court against Thomas Nangle, who was accused of assaulting him. Nangle was the brother-in-law of Seán Doherty, the Minister for Justice. The arrest was authorised by the Head of RUC Special Branch despite serious objections from Detective Inspector Ian Carter, Enniskillen Special Branch. The whole affair caused a major rift between the two forces, which resulted in Sir John Hermon and the Garda Commissioner, Larry Wren, declining to meet for two years, right up to the signing of the Anglo-Irish Agreement.

1181 As noted above, John Stalker was appointed to investigate allegations of shoot-to-kill by the RUC in 1984. He was removed from the investigation amid false allegations of his involvement in criminality in 1986.

1182 NAUK, CJ4/6609, Anglo-Irish Joint Studies Review of activity since November 1981, 29 November 1983.

1183 NAUK, CJ4/6609, Memo to Stephen Boys-Smith, NIO.

1184 NAUK, CJ4/7194, Anglo-Irish security co-operation, *Irish Press* article, 21 December 1987.

1185 *Ibid.*, Memo to Mr Elliot from Tony Stephens, MoD, 29 November 1987.

1186 *Ibid.*, Briefing document on 'Irish search operations,' 30 November 1987.

1187 *Ibid.*
1188 *Irish Times*, 11–21 September 1973.
1189 NAUK, FCO87/121, 6 October 1972.
1190 NAUK, FCO87/121, 6 October 1972.
1191 The Loyalist Association of Workers was a militant unionist organisation that sought to mobilise trade union members to the loyalist cause.
1192 NAI, 2003/17/34, Department of Foreign Affairs, Border patrolling and security of the border.
1193 *Ibid.*, Telegram to British Ambassador from Douglas-Home, 5 December 1972.
1194 *Irish Times*, 20 January 2007.
1195 Statement by the Police Ombudsman for Northern Ireland on her investigation into the circumstances surrounding the death of Raymond McCord Junior and related matters, para 24.10, 102.
1196 Statement by the Police Ombudsman for Northern Ireland on her investigation into the circumstances surrounding the death of Raymond McCord Junior and related matters, para 24.11, 103.
1197 NAUK, FCO87/1741, Report on visit to Northern Ireland by John Oborne, Defence Attaché, 10–11 May 1984.
1198 NAUK, FCO87/1741, Report on visit to Northern Ireland by John Oborne, Defence Attaché, 18-20 September 1984.
1199 *Ibid.*
1200 NAUK, FCO87/2353, Memo to A.D.E. Goodall, FCO from G.E. Clarke, FCO RID, 2 January 1986.
1201 *Ibid.*
1202 Mulroe, *Bombs, Bullets and the Border*, 109.

SELECT BIBLIOGRAPHY

Agnew, Paddy, 'Fear and Loathing in Fermanagh', *Magill* (March 1981).

Aldous, Richard and Niamh Puirséil, *We Declare: Landmark Documents in Ireland's History* (London: Quercus, 2008)

Bailey, William F., 'The Ulster tenant-right custom: its origin, characteristic and position under the Land Acts', *Journal of the Statistical and Social Inquiry Society of Ireland*, 10, 74 (1893/1894), 12–22.

Barton, B.E., 'The Origins and Development of Unionism in Fermanagh, 1885–1914' in E.M. Murphy and W.J. Roulston (eds), *Fermanagh: History and Society* (Dublin: Geography Publications, 2004).

Barzilay, David, *British Army in Ulster,* Vol 4 (Belfast: Century Books, 1981).

Bell, Robert, 'Sheep Stealers from the North of England: the Riding Clans in Ulster', *History Ireland*, 2, 4, (Winter 1994).

Bell-Fialkoff, Andrew, 'A Brief History of Ethnic Cleansing', *Foreign Affairs* (Summer 1993).

Bishop, Patrick and Eamon Mallie, *The Provisional IRA* (London: Corgi Books, 1988).

Brown, Stewart J., 'Ireland' in Stewart J. Brown, Peter Nockles and James Pereiro (eds), *The Oxford Handbook of the Oxford Movement* (Oxford: Oxford University Press, 2017).

Burke, Edward, 'Loyalist Mobilisation and Cross-Border Violence in Rural Ulster, 1972–1974', *Terrorism and Political Violence* (2020), DOI: 10.1080/09546553.2020.1745777.

Burke, Edward, *An Army of Tribes: British Army Cohesion, Deviancy and Murder in Northern Ireland* (Liverpool: Liverpool University Press, 2018).

Caball, Marc, 'Dispossession and reaction: the Gaelic literati and the Plantation of Ulster', *History Ireland*, 17, 6 (Nov/Dec 2009).

Cadwallader, Anne, *Lethal Allies: British Collusion in Ireland* (Cork: Mercier Press, 2013).

Coogan, T.P., *Michael Collins: A Biography* (London: Hutchinson, 1990)

Corish, Patrick J., 'The Cromwellian Regime 1650–1660' in W. Moody, F.X. Martin and F.J. Byrne (eds), *A New History of Ireland: Early Modern Ireland, 1534–1691* (Oxford: Oxford University Press, 1976).

Crawford, E.M., 'Fermanagh: Food, Famine and Fever' in E.M. Murphy and W.J. Roulston (eds), *Fermanagh: History and Society* (Dublin: Geography Publications, 2004).

Crowley, John, Donal Ó Drisceoil, Mike Murphy and John Borgonovo (eds), *Atlas of the Irish Revolution* (Cork: Cork University Press, 2018).

Cunningham, John B., *The Great Silence: The Famine in Fermanagh 1845–1850* (Fermanagh: Davog Press, 2012).

Curran, Daragh, *A Society in Transition: The Protestant Community in Ulster 1825–45*, Academia. 4 August 2020. http://www.academia.edu/9059578/The_revival_of_the_Orange_Order_1828?auto=download

De Baróid, Ciarán, *Ballymurphy and the Irish War* (London: Pluto Press, 1990).

Dillon, Martin, *The Dirty War* (New York: Routledge, 1990).

Donohue, Laura K., 'Regulating Northern Ireland: The Special Powers Acts, 1922–1972', *The Historical Journal*, 41, 4 (December 1998).

Dooley, Terence A.M., 'Protestant Migration from the Free State to Northern Ireland, 1920–25', *Clogher Record*, 15, 3 (1996).

Ellison, Graham and Jim Smyth, *The Crowned Harp: Policing Northern Ireland* (London: Pluto Press, 2000).

Gebler, Carlo, *The Siege of Derry: A History* (London: Abacus 2006).

Gerder, David F., 'Providence and the 1641 Rebellion' (PhD thesis, University of Iowa, 2015).

Gillespie, Raymond, 'The murder of Arthur Champion and the Rebellion in Fermanagh', *Clogher Record*, 14, 3 (1993), 52–65.

Godkin, James, *The Land War in Ireland: A History for the Times* (London: Macmillan, 1870).

Gray, Tony, *The Orange Order* (London: Bodley Head, 1972).

Guinnane, Timothy, Desmond McCabe and Cormac Ó Gráda, 'Agency and Famine Relief: Enniskillen Workhouse During the Great Irish Famine', Working Paper Series, School of Economics, University College Dublin (2004).

Hanley, Brian and Scott Millar, *The Lost Revolution: The Story of the Official IRA and the Workers' Party* (Dublin: Penguin Ireland, 2010).

Harding, Michael, *Staring at Lakes* (Dublin: Hachette Books Ireland, 2013).

Heaney, Seamus, *Opened Ground* (London: Faber and Faber, 1998).

Hennessy, Thomas, 'Ulster Unionism and Loyalty to the Crown of the United Kingdom 1912–74' in R. English and G. Walker (eds), *Unionism in Modern Ireland: New Perspectives on Politics and Culture* (London: Palgrave MacMillan Press, 1996).

Jefferies, Henry A., 'Penal Days in Clogher', *History Ireland,* 17, 3 (May–June 2009).

Kaufmann, Eric P., 'Demographic change and conflict in Northern Ireland: reconciling qualitative and quantitative evidence', *Ethnopolitics*, 10 (2011), 369–89.

Lawlor, Pearse, 'Tit-for-Tat: the War of Independence in the Northern Counties' *History Ireland,* 20, 1 (Jan/Feb 2012).

Leahy, Thomas and Niall Ó Dochartaigh, 'Citizenship on the Ethnic Frontier: Nationality, Migration and Rights in Northern Ireland since 1920' in Steven G. Ellis, *Enfranchising Ireland?: Identity, Citizenship and State* (Dublin: Royal Irish Academy, 2018).

Leahy, Thomas, *The Intelligence War against the IRA* (Cambridge: Cambridge University Press, 2020).

Lee, Joseph, *Ireland, 1912–1985: Politics and Society* (Cambridge: Cambridge University Press, 1989).

Lenihan, Pádraig, *1690: Battle of the Boyne* (Stroud: Tempus, 2003).

Lewis, Matthew and Shaun McDaid, 'Bosnia on the Border? Republican Violence in Northern Ireland during the 1920s and 1970s', *Terrorism and Political Violence*, 29, 4 (2017), 635–55, DOI: 10.1080/0946553.2015.1043429.

Livingstone, Peadar, *The Fermanagh Story: A Documented History of the County Fermanagh from the Earliest Times to the Present Day* (Monaghan: Clogher Historical Society, 1969).

Malcolmson, Anthony, 'The Erne Family, Estate and Archive, c.1610–c.1950' in E.M. Murphy and W.J. Roulston (eds), *Fermanagh: History and Society* (Dublin: Geography Publications, 2004).

Martin, Jed, 'The Origins of Partition' in Malcolm Anderson and Bort Eberhard (eds), *History, Politics, Culture* (Liverpool: Liverpool University Press, 1989).

McDaniel, Denzil, *Enniskillen: The Remembrance Sunday Bombing* (Dublin: Wolfhound Press, 1997).

MacDonald, Brian, *A Time of Desolation: Clones Poor Law Union, 1845–50* (Monaghan: Clogher Historical Society, 2017).

McGovern, Mark, *Counterinsurgency and Collusion in Northern Ireland* (London: Pluto Press, 2019).

McKay, Susan, *Northern Protestants: An Unsettled People* (Down: Blackstaff Press, 2000).

McKittrick, D., S. Kelters, B. Feeney, C. Thornton and D. McVea, *Lost Lives: The Stories of the Men, Women and Children Who Died as a Result of the Northern Ireland Troubles* (Edinburgh: Mainstream Publishing Company, 2007).

McMinn, J.R.B., 'The Land League in North Antrim 1880–1882', *The Glynns*, 11 (1983).

Morland, Paul, *Demographic Engineering: Population Strategies in Ethnic Conflict* (Abingdon: Taylor & Francis Group, 2014).

Mulroe, Patrick, *Bombs, Bullets and the Border – Policing Ireland's Frontier: Irish Security Policy, 1969–1978* (Dublin: Irish Academic Press, 2017).

Murray, Raymond, *The SAS in Ireland* (Cork: Mercier Press, 2004).

Myers, Jason, 'Reconsidering Irish Fatalities in the First World War', The Irish Story. https://www.theirishstory.com/2015/03/25/reconsidering-irish-fatalities-in-the-first-world-war/#.XqqTJ6hKjIU

Ó Beacháin, Donnacha, 'The Dog that didn't bark: Southern unionism in pre and post-revolutionary Ireland', *History Ireland*, 23, 4 (July/August 2015).

Ó Beacháin, Donnacha, *From Partition to Brexit* (Manchester: Manchester University Press, 2019).

Ó Duibhir, Liam, *Donegal and the Civil War: The Untold Story* (Cork: Mercier Press, 2011).

Ó Raghalaigh, Liam, 'Captain Boycott: Man and Myth', *History Ireland*, 19, 1, (Jan–Feb 2001).

O'Leary, Brendan, *A Treatise on Northern Ireland*, Volume 2 (Oxford: Oxford University Press, 2019).

Parke, W.K., 'A Short History of the Royal Inniskilling Fusiliers' in E.M. Murphy and W.J. Roulston (eds), *Fermanagh: History and Society* (Dublin: Geography Publications, 2004).

Patterson, Henry, '1974 – Year of Liberty? The Provisional IRA and Sunningdale' in David McCann, Cillian McGrattan (eds), *Sunningdale, the Ulster Workers' Council Strike and the Struggle for Democracy in Northern Ireland* (Manchester: Manchester University Press, 2017).

Patterson, Henry, 'Unionism 1921–72' in Alvin Jackson (ed.) *The Oxford Handbook of Modern Irish History* (Oxford: Oxford University Press, 2014), 692–710.

Patterson, Henry, *Ireland's Violent Frontier: The Border and Anglo-Irish Relations during the Troubles* (London: Palgrave Macmillan, 2013).

Phoenix, Eamon, 'Cahir Healy and Nationalist Politics in County Fermanagh 1885–1970' in E.M. Murphy and W.J. Roulston (eds), *Fermanagh: History and Society* (Dublin: Geography Publications, 2004).

Rankin, K.J., 'The Creation and Consolidation of the Irish Border', Institute for British-Irish Studies, University College Dublin (2005).

Rankin, K.J., 'The Provenance and Dissolution of the Irish Boundary Commission', Institute for British-Irish Studies, University College Dublin (2006).

Rapoport, David C., *Terrorism: The Second or Anti-Colonial Wave* (Abingdon: Taylor & Francis Group, 2006).

Rowthorn, Bob and Naomi Wayne, *Northern Ireland: The Political Economy of Conflict* (Cambridge: Polity Press, 1988).

Royle, Trevor, *Civil War: The Wars of the Three Kingdoms, 1638–1680* (London: Abacus, 2004).

Ryder, Chris, *The Ulster Defence Regiment: An Instrument of Peace?* (London: Methuen Publishing Ltd, 1991).

Scholes, Andrew, '"Neither Whigs, Tories, nor Party Politicians?" The Church of Ireland and the Ulster Crisis 1910–14' in *The Home Rule Crisis, 1912–14: Cork Studies in the Irish Revolution* (Cork: Mercier Press, 2014).

Smith, M.L.R., *Fighting for Ireland* (New York: Routledge, 1995).

Staunton, Enda, 'The Boundary Commission Debacle 1925, aftermath and implications', *History Ireland*, 4, 2, (Summer 1996).

Thompson, Frank, 'The Land War in County Fermanagh' in E.M. Murphy and W.J. Roulston (eds), *Fermanagh: History and Society,* (Dublin: Geography Publications, 2004).

Toal, Gerard and Carl T. Dahlman, *Bosnia ReMade: Ethnic Cleansing and its Reversal* (Oxford: Oxford University Press, 2011).

Urban, Mark, *Big Boys' Rules: The Secret Struggle against the IRA* (London: Faber and Faber, 1992).

Urwin, Margaret and Niall Meehan, 'The 1972–3 Dublin bombings: The "third man" in the case of British agent John Wyman and Garda Sergeant Patrick Crinnion', *History Ireland*, 26, 3 (May–June 2018).

Urwin, Margaret, *A County Wexford Family in the Land War: The O'Hanlon Walshs of Knocktartan* (Dublin: Four Courts Press, 2002).

Urwin, Margaret, *A State in Denial: British Collaboration with Loyalist Paramilitaries* (Cork: Mercier Press, 2016).

Walker, Graham, 'The 1947 Education Act – A Landmark in Northern Ireland's History' (2017).

Whelan, Kevin, *The Tree of Liberty: Radicalism, Catholicism and the Construction of Irish Identity 1760–1830* (Cork: Cork University Press, 1997).

White, Robert W., 'Provisional IRA Attacks on the UDR in Fermanagh and South Tyrone: Implications for the Study of Political Violence and Terrorism', *Terrorism and Political Violence*, 23, 3 (2011), DOI: 10.1080/09546553.2011.561674.

Whyte, John, 'How much discrimination was there under the unionist regime, 1921–68?', *Contemporary Irish Studies* (1983).

ARCHIVES

National Archives of Ireland (NAI)
National Archives of UK (NAUK)
National Library of Ireland (NLI)
TCD, 1641 Depositions Project
Dáil Debates
Parliamentary Debates: House of Commons
Parliamentary Debates: House of Lords Debates
Parliamentary Debates: Northern Ireland House of Commons

NEWSPAPERS AND PERIODICALS

An Phoblacht
Anglo-Celt
Belfast Newsletter
Belfast Telegraph
Donegal Democrat
Donegal News
Evening Herald
Fermanagh Herald
Fermanagh News
Fermanagh Times
Freeman's Journal
Glasgow Herald
Impartial Reporter
Irish Examiner (Cork)
Irish Independent
Irish News
Irish Press
Irish Republican News
Irish Times
Leitrim Observer
Magill
New York Times
Sligo Champion
Southern Star
Strabane Chronicle
Sunday Independent
Sunday Tribune
Ulster Herald

INDEX